A Pirate Captain's Guide to Leadership

Contents

Shiver Me Timbers

YOU ARE A BOSS. Maybe not THE boss, but you directly supervise or manage other people.

Because you're a boss, you may have one or more employees who seemingly expect you to compensate them for doing whatever they want, whenever and however they choose. For now, let's refer to those employees as "workplace pirates."

The symptoms of workplace piracy can include an unwarranted sense of entitlement, chronic absenteeism, rule violations, insubordinate behavior, lackluster effort, and substandard output.

Having pirates in your workplace today doesn't necessarily make you a "bad" boss. Your pirates may have come aboard (or been converted) as a result of several factors beyond your control.

For example, a tight labor market may have forced your organization to fill vacancies with less-than-ideal employment candidates.

Your industry or geographic location may have limited your ability to attract qualified individuals in specific fields.

A lack of trust between management and labor may have created a collective bargaining situation that continues to deter long-term cooperation, achievement, and performance.

A continuing array of technological, economic, and social changes may have dramatically redefined your business – as well as the jobs of your workers. Economic or social conditions outside the workplace may also have affected the lifestyles of employees – and therefore, the attitudes they bring to work.

The purpose of this book is to help you recognize workplace piracy, understand the employees who practice it, and bring out the very best in these people who, up until now, have been either unwilling or unable to give even a fraction of that.

This book is not an academic study of leadership and management theory. It emphasizes a unique set of practical skills and proven techniques that you can learn quickly and apply immediately. It just so happens that these skills and techniques are remarkably similar to those utilized by some of history's most successful pirate captains.

Of course, effective leadership works with *all* employees, not just workplace pirates – so this is not a mere "problem solving" guide. It's a complete how-to manual for today's managers and supervisors.

Again, having pirates in your workplace doesn't necessarily make you a bad boss. That is, so long as you begin to transform those workplace pirates into competent, motivated, and productive team members – or failing that, get them off of your ship (without a mutiny, and without litigation).

This book explains how.

A Pirate Captain Approach

EVERY LEADER HAS A MISSION (or should have). When you accept a *leadership* role in an organization (a private company, a government agency, a non-profit entity, or a volunteer group), the mission of that organization instantly becomes *your* mission.

For a pirate captain, the mission was to plunder enemy vessels. He may have undertaken that mission for God and country, for his own personal wealth, or both.

To accomplish his mission, the captain needed the same four basic elements that are required for a modern business objective. In the Golden Age of Piracy, these elements were referred to as the Four M's: Men, Machines, Materials, and Methodologies.

To effectively sail a ship or engage in battle, the captain needed men – a crew. Pirate captains didn't have a lot of people to choose from. They often had to take whoever they could find. *Does that sound like the hiring challenges you face?*

Obviously, the captain also needed machines – a ship with suitable rigging and armament. He couldn't be too picky in that area, either. Unlike naval warships that were custom built for a specific purpose, the typical pirate ship was an older craft that had been damaged and captured in battle. *Is your workplace a state-of-the-art facility with modern equipment – or a bit less impressive?*

The materials a captain needed to support his mission, from gunpowder to provisions, had to be covertly sought out and procured. There were no logistical networks or naval bases to supply pirate ships. *Are all the resources you need for your operation readily available – or do you sometimes have to "scrounge" for supplies and materials?*

Finally, the pirate captain needed methodologies. He needed a process for turning a collection of misfits into a crew that could out-sail professional seamen and out-fight trained soldiers. He needed methodologies for the repair and upkeep of a second-hand ship. He needed methods for locating and securing critical supplies.

He also needed methodologies for each of the key tasks we generally associate with piracy – for instance, navigating toward a potential target, engaging in battle, avoiding capture, dividing treasure, and maintaining discipline. These methods absolutely had to work. It was a matter of life and death.

As a business leader, you also need a set of proven methodologies for managing your people and resources, and for accomplishing the key tasks associated with the products and services you offer.

Does your workplace have more than a few things in common with a pirate ship? Can you see yourself as something of a modern day pirate captain in that environment? If so, then you are ready to learn and apply the essential skills and techniques for successfully leading your crew, and for bringing out the best in your workplace pirates.

We'll begin by examining a common myth about the legendary Pirates of the Realm, and a corresponding myth about today's "pirates" of the workplace...

The Truth about Pirates of the Realm

Piracy may be defined as any illegal act committed in international waters by the crew of one ship against the property or crew of another ship for private ends.

Why did the pirates who sailed the Atlantic and Caribbean in the 16th, 17th, and 18th centuries engage in these acts? A predominant myth is that they chose a life of piracy because they were wicked and violent men with no moral standards – or because they were too lazy to undertake a legitimate occupation. That's simply not the case.

Indeed, a few were convicted criminals who signed aboard a pirate ship to escape the hangman, and some were idle misfits. The majority of pirates, however, were not much different in their beliefs and values than any other sailor of the era.

So how and why did these men (and even a few women) become pirates? The Order of the Brethren gained its members from three primary sources.

Privateers

When the colonization of the Americas began, European countries lacked the warships necessary to cover the vast territory they sought to control. To protect their interests in the New World, government officials issued Letters of Marque to private individuals with seafaring skills. These letters gave such an individual – known as a "privateer" – the legal authority to capture wealth from an enemy ship on the high seas in the name of the king or queen. Privateers were typically authorized to keep a percentage of the treasure as payment.

When such attacks occurred, the king or queen in power was often compelled (for political reasons) to deny that the action was officially sanctioned by his or her government – which meant the privateer was labeled a "pirate" by international law.

During the so-called "Golden Age of Piracy," about a third of all buccaneers were at some point "privateers" who carried genuine Letters of Marque. These men saw themselves as patriots, not pirates. They believed that by targeting enemy vessels, they were strengthening their country's economic position and helping to defeat a hostile aggressor. (And they were, in fact – which is why the practice continued for years.)

Conscripted Sailors

Another third of the pirate population began their seafaring careers as conscripted sailors. In addition to employing privateers, European nations were building and launching new warships and merchant ships as rapidly as possible. These expanding fleets created a shortage of professional seaman. To deal with the problem, men from port cities were frequently rounded up by gangs and pressed into service aboard naval ships against their will.

Some of these men eventually became pirates when they escaped (or deserted, depending on your perspective) – while others freely joined a pirate crew when their ships were captured by privateers (the alternative: being put ashore on the nearest uninhabited island).

African Captives

Most of the remaining third of the pirates during that era also spent their first days at sea involuntarily. They were captives from Africa who were being transported to the

Americas aboard slave trading vessels when their ships fell under attack.

Pirate captains were generally "colorblind" when it came to crew members. If a man was able-bodied and willing, he was assigned to learn a specific job. If he did so within a reasonable time, and then swore an oath to follow the code, he was welcomed aboard as an equal.

A Pirate's Life?

These men, especially the latter two groups, had little education and no marketable skill or trade. Many could not read, nor speak English. Separated from their homeland by an ocean, they were fighting for survival in an untamed world of extreme poverty. For most, there was no opportunity other than piracy.

Successful pirate captains recognized these circumstances, and applied a unique set of skills to lead and manage their crews. They realized that for a crew to be motivated, the "pirate life" had to offer a chance at something better. After all, food, water, and the security of an armed vessel were already being provided when these men became pirates. A smart captain worked hard to give the crew something they didn't have previously – self-respect, camaraderie, and a sense of "belonging." Even more important, he gave them hope.

A pirate's life offered the one and only chance these men had to fulfill their dreams. Some wanted great wealth, while others sought freedom and independence. Many wanted a passage back home, but many more imagined a fresh start in a New World. Some longed for a simple life ashore surrounded by a family, while a few looked no farther forward than a pint of ale at their next port of call. A wise captain helped each crew member realize that his unique hopes and desires were not only valid, but within reach – and that the ship's mission was a direct path to total fulfillment.

It should be noted here that the most successful pirate captains were not always the best-known. Many legendary captains achieved their fame as a result of outrageous tactics and brutal methods – but their treasure was meager, and their careers were brief.

The truly great pirates amassed fortunes over several years. They seldom if ever took an innocent life, and were ultimately viewed as heroes by their countrymen. They were respected by their adversaries, peers, and followers. The great pirate captains didn't bury their treasure – they used it to build better lives for themselves and those around them. A few even lived to a ripe old age.

The Truth about Workplace Pirates

WORKPLACE PIRATES are prevalent in today's organizations for reasons similar to those that brought about the Golden Age of Piracy on the high seas.

Like the privateers of yesteryear, many of today's workplace pirates were betrayed by the "powers that be." They saw firsthand (or in the careers of their parents) greedy business owners and self-serving executives who knowingly defrauded investors, cheated customers, and misled employees.

Some of these workers feel completely justified in "sticking it to" the business establishment to avenge those misdeeds when possible. Their actions range from "slacking" on the job to stealing supplies and materials. The resulting cost to the U.S. economy is enormous. Winning the trust, cooperation, and contribution of these employees may not be easy, but it can be done – and the financial gain alone makes it worthwhile to try.

Other workplace pirates – especially those who hold low paying jobs – are very often limited in terms of the employment options and economic opportunities available to them (much like the conscripted sailors and captives from Africa who joined the Brethren of the Coast).

When we consider the freedom we enjoy in the United States, it may be hard to agree that anyone within our borders has limited opportunities. When we further examine the self-defeating habits, destructive behaviors, and negative attitudes exhibited by some of our more "difficult" employees, it would be much easier to conclude that any limitations they have experienced in life are their own fault.

In a small percentage of cases, that's exactly right. However, for most workers "trapped" in low wage or dead end jobs, the *real* limitation is the fact that they reached adulthood without the knowledge, skill, discipline, and sense of responsibility to be anything *other* than workplace pirates.

For instance, many such workers were raised by parents or guardians who were workplace pirates themselves. These adult "role models" may have resented achievement, undermined education, disregarded authority, and showed very little courtesy or respect for the world around them. They may have lied, cheated, and stole – and then explained to their children why the actions were justified and acceptable.

Of course, underachievement and lack of motivation are not just confined to minimum wage positions or to employees with a "grudge" against authority. Workplace pirates come from every background and demographic group, and may be found in almost every type of job.

The point is, as leaders, we need to get past the myth that all of our "less-than-ideal" employees are in some way lesser human beings. That's just not true.

What is true is that most of these employees have simply not yet developed the skills and behaviors that are necessary to be successful in a climate of high achievement. They are not on a path to reach full potential in their lives. As leaders, one of our most important obligations is to *develop* these people. It is our job to help them become the best they can be.

Great leaders provide their followers with something that followers can't provide for themselves. In the case of workplace pirates, that "something" is the opportunity to acquire not only the knowledge and skills to be successful, but also the confidence, motivation, enthusiasm, and self-discipline needed.

Granted, there are a few employees who already have all of that going for them, and seem to be pirates "by nature" – almost as if they are trying to be defiant, selfish, and indolent in their approach to work.

While we, as leaders, cannot change a person's nature, we can – and must – make every effort to influence the way these people perform and behave on the job. Failure to do so allows workplace pirates to operate on their own terms, and that can slowly destroy an organization.

Pirates can drive away our best employees – and eventually, our best customers. They lower our workplace standards. They increase our costs and reduce the value of our products and services. They get us in trouble. They steal from us – if not property, at least our time, and the money we are paying them for the jobs they're not doing.

To address this in your workplace, you must take the same leadership approach as a successful pirate captain. You must make the commitment to *develop* your crew members, help them understand the performance and behavior you expect, and be certain that they recognize the opportunities you are offering.

Once you develop a few "winners," they will begin to bring others up to their standards, rather than allowing the lowest common denominator to dictate group behavior. The resulting output will not be merely "average" or "above average." It will be astounding. With each success, more employees will sign on.

Will every employee respond? Probably not. Just as some Pirates of the Realm were beyond redemption, a few of your workplace pirates may continue to cause problems in spite of your best leadership efforts. What will you do about them?

The great pirate captains knew that a "toxic" crew member could poison an entire ship. They also knew that free of such toxins, a loyal group of well-trained and highly motivated individuals could outperform an "average" crew that was two or three times the size.

In the pirate's realm, if someone violated "the code," there were consequences. If you define a legitimate set of rules, and then do your best to help an employee succeed – only to have the code violated and your guidance rejected – you, too, can have the person "walk the plank."

On a pirate ship, unfair or poorly-handled discipline was a cause for mutiny. In today's world, the equivalent could be just as costly in terms of employee turnover, grievances, work slowdowns, sabotage, and litigation.

Fortunately, there are a few very simple, yet effective ways for you to develop and lead workplace pirates (and, in fact, *all* of your employees). These proven techniques will increase productivity, improve morale, and make your life as a boss a whole lot easier. The first stage of this leadership process begins when you truly "take command" of your ship. If you want to know exactly how to do that, read on.

Welcome aboard, Captain!

Part II.
"I'm Your Captain"

Taking Command

Know Your Purpose

PEOPLE ACCEPT LEADERSHIP positions for a variety of reasons – for example, more money, more freedom, more power, and more prestige. Far too many of these people have no idea of what the *role* of a leader really involves. They may have a title, but they are in no way leaders.

Your first step in taking command is to know your purpose. The purpose of any person in a leadership role, whether it's a pirate captain or a modern day supervisor, is essentially the same.

A leader's purpose is to consistently produce desired results through other people working with competence, commitment, and collaboration. What does that mean, exactly? Let's break the definition into four parts.

Results

Good leaders "consistently produce desired results." They get the job done.

For the pirate captain, that may have meant capturing a galleon loaded with treasure without losing a single crew member. Likewise, today's leader must have his or her eyes on a prize, and keep the crew focused on attaining it.

If you are an executive or senior manager, part of your job is to *choose* the prize you'll pursue. Continuous improvement (better, cheaper, faster), while noble, is not a prize. The prize must be a concrete achievement (for example, delivering each order on time and perfect, or attaining a coveted industry certification).

Another part of a senior manager's job is to *follow through*. When a prize is almost within reach, an organization can't suddenly change direction to pursue a new or bigger target on the distant horizon. The crew will eventually become frustrated and skeptical, and begin to put forth no more than a half-hearted effort.

For a middle manager or supervisor, the role is slightly different. The commodore of a pirate fleet may have selected a particular target, but a captain was still the captain of his ship when it came to pursuing that prize. Likewise, once the executive team defines the mission, it's your job to figure out the best way to achieve it. You plan the work, mobilize the resources, and stay on task. You apply knowledge, skill, experience, and judgment to adapt to changes, and to adjust your "plan of attack" as the situation evolves.

Perhaps most important of all, you talk about the prize. You want your crew to not only see it, but to feel it, smell it, and taste it – and then grab it!

Other People

Once the leaders decide where a ship is going and determine the best course to take, it is up to the crew to get it there. Leaders ensure that the people they've hired to do the work *do the work*.

Supervisors often continue to perform non-supervisory tasks long after they're promoted. Sure, at times it may be necessary to work alongside an employee to help the person learn a new job or to cover an unforeseen demand. If it's a daily routine, however, something is wrong.

As a leader, you already have a full time job of your own – clarifying the results to be achieved, developing the competence and commitment of your staff, and building teamwork.

If employees fail to complete an assigned task, it's not your job to complete the work for them. It's your job to develop their proficiency, confidence, and motivation – so *they* can complete it.

If workplace pirates figure out that you'll do the job yourself or give it to someone else – rather than holding them accountable for learning and performing it effectively – they'll let you. And it will become almost impossible to grab the prize.

Competence and Commitment

Leaders produce results through people working "with competence and commitment." Competence is knowledge, skill, experience, and judgment. Commitment is the confidence and motivation to do a job right.

Leaders have two options here. They can either *hire* people who are already highly competent and committed (and therefore, very hard to find), or they can *develop* them.

Good leaders teach, coach, and support their people. They offer praise and encouragement, as well as corrective feedback and assistance – each in the appropriate way at the appropriate time.

Collaboration

Leaders consistently produce desired results through other people working together. Whether it's a pirate ship, a sports team, a business enterprise, or a group of volunteers – when everyone is working together toward the same goal, the outcome is almost always achieved.

True leaders build collaboration and teamwork. It's the only way a small pirate vessel with a handful of men could defeat a heavily armed warship. It's also the only way an undersized and under-funded business unit can outperform the competition – with *everyone* working together.

In your working experience, which have you seen more often -- dysfunctional teams or highly effective ones? Most leaders recognize that building teamwork is a key part of their job – but actually getting people to work together toward a common goal is not that easy a task (on a pirate ship, on a playing field, or in a modern workplace).

In Summary

Your purpose, as a leader, is to consistently produce desired results through other people working with competence, commitment, and collaboration. The obvious question now is *how* you do that.

This book will provide the answers. You'll learn a step-by-step process for defining goals and outcomes. You'll gain a new understanding of people – why they do the things they do, and how you can influence their behaviors to produce amazing results. You'll adopt a practical set of tools to develop the competence and commitment of your followers. You'll master the essential skills and techniques for getting people to work together.

It's all here, and it all begins with the cardinal rule for any pirate captain – "keep to the code."

Keep to the Code

PIRATES KNEW THAT DISCIPLINE was essential to their success and survival. While most had a general disdain for the rigid structure and demanding regulations found on a Royal Navy vessel (and in society at-large), they nevertheless agreed to impose strict codes of conduct upon themselves.

Contrary to popular belief, there was never a single, universal "Pirate Code." The Code was specific to a particular ship (yet, most codes were similar). When a captain assumed command, the crew voted on each article of the code, and then all crew members signed the document and swore an oath to uphold its tenets. As new crew members were added, they were required to do the same.

Many of these documents can be found in museums. The following example illustrates the components that appeared in most.

A Sample Pirate Code of Conduct

Article 1. Every man shall obey the Captain's orders, and he who fails to do so shall suffer punishment as the Captain and Company think fit.

Article 2. No man shall leave the Company until he and all who were in the Company before him have each accumulated prizes of not less than 1,000 pounds.

Article 3. Every man shall have an equal voice in affairs affecting the Company.

Article 4. Every man shall have equal title to the fresh provisions seized. Other prizes shall be divided as follows: 2 shares to the Captain; 1½ shares to the Quartermaster. 1¼ shares to other officers; 1 share to each ordinary seaman or private gentleman of fortune.

Article 5. Any man to first see and declare an enemy sail shall have title to the best pistol or small arm aboard her.

Article 6. Every man shall be at quarters, sober and ready for his watch prior to the sounding of eight bells or he shall lose the right to consume liquor for three days.

Article 7. Every man shall keep his arms clean and fit for an engagement. He who fails to do so shall be cut off from his share and suffer such other punishment as the Captain and Company think fit.

Article 8. All lights and candles shall be put out at night, and if any man desires to drink or converse after that, he shall do so on the open deck without light. If any man shall cause clatter after lights out, he shall receive Moses' Law, that being 40 stripes less one on the bare back.

Article 9. No man shall smoke tobacco below deck or carry a candle lighted without lantern. If he does, he shall receive Moses' Law.

Article 10. No man shall gamble with cards or dice aboard ship. If he does, he shall be cut off from his share and suffer such other punishment as the Captain and Company think fit.

Article 11. No man shall steal anything from another in the Company. If he does, he shall be marooned with one bottle of water, one small arm, one flask of powder, and a handful of shot.

Article 12. No man shall strike another in the Company whilst these Articles are in force, or he shall receive Moses' Law. Every man's quarrel shall be ended on shore by sword upon command from the Quartermaster. He that draws the first blood shall be declared the victor.

Article 13. If any man meets with a boy and meddles with him, he shall suffer death. If any man meets with a prudent woman and meddles with her without her consent, he shall suffer death.

Article 14. If any man runs away during an engagement or proffers secrets that bring hardship to the Company, his ears and nose shall be slit open and he shall be put ashore.

Article 15. If any man falls behind during an engagement, he shall stay behind.

Article 16. If any man suffers the loss of a limb in an engagement, he shall have 800 Pieces of Eight from the common stock. He shall receive proportionate amounts for greater or lesser hurts as the Company thinks fit.

Article 17. If any adversary invokes the right of parley during an engagement, no man shall harm him until the parley is complete.

Article 18. If any gentleman of fortune seeks to join the Company, he shall sign these articles and agree to abide by them, or be put ashore.

As you can see, the Code spelled out the rules for life aboard a pirate ship, and clearly explained the consequences of any action that was unacceptable. Because of this, the crew rarely felt pity when a guilty shipmate was punished for breaking a rule. As long as the code was applied equally to everyone – and enforced consistently – there were few problems.

Pirate codes were amazing social documents, as well. For instance, in the 1700's, commissioned naval officers were paid twenty to thirty times more than ordinary seamen, yet a pirate captain never received more than twice the smallest share. Likewise, the code guaranteed that a man injured in battle would receive a pension, even though it was common practice for a man wounded aboard a navy ship to be cast ashore and left there to beg or starve.

Smart captains recognized that New World colonists were their best source of supplies and alliances, and knew that violence against innocent citizens would destroy those crucial relationships. Therefore, rape and child molestation were strictly forbidden by pirate code, and individuals wishing to negotiate or do business with a pirate captain were protected by the rules of parley.

Finally, the code prompted on-board behaviors we don't readily associate with buccaneers – honor, respect, loyalty, courtesy, reliability, vigilance, safety, and compliance.

Your Code of Conduct

Your organization probably has a policy manual or employee handbook. In most companies, it is in a booklet or binder, and may very often be found sitting on a shelf collecting dust.

Find it. Read it. If it is too long, too vague, or too legal-sounding to serve as your group's code of conduct (or if no such handbook exists in your organization), your next order of business as a pirate captain is to create your own short and simple version of a Pirate Code of Conduct.

At a minimum, your code should outline your specific policies and expectations in the following nine areas:

1.   Compensation – including how and when wages or salaries are paid, plus all company-paid benefits that are provided.

2.   Attendance – including work hours, policies regarding vacation and other types of leave, and timekeeping procedures.

3. Use/Abuse of Company Resources – including all company-owned property such as computers, e-mail systems, telephones, tools, vehicles, and equipment.

4. Safety – including general housekeeping, maintenance procedures, hazard reporting, and use of protective gear – plus your organization's policy on workplace violence, firearms, and other weapons.

5. Accidents/Incidents – including incident reporting procedures, response policies, first aid, treatment options, and worker compensation claims.

6. Drugs and Alcohol – outlining your organization's policies and expectations relative to possession, use, or reporting to work under the influence.

7. Sexual and Other Harassment – detailing your organization's policies for the prevention, reporting, and investigation of workplace harassment.

8. Dress/Grooming – explaining any work attire or grooming requirements as well as any restrictions or limitations on clothing, jewelry, etc.

9. Employee Conduct – expectations (not covered above) for interacting with customers, other stakeholders, and fellow employees. This portion of your code may also list specific prohibited actions and behaviors, and the consequences of each.

Making It Work

As you establish your code, remember that some of your employees grew up in decidedly undisciplined environments.

Rules may have been vague or non-existent, and punishment was sometimes inconsistent (ranging from cruel to silly, depending on the maturity or sobriety of the person administering it).

Many employees will quite naturally resist your efforts to impose new rules. In fact, complaints about the new "code" may be widespread. Employee morale may decline – initially. Do not let that discourage or dissuade you. The objections will be temporary, provided you use the other skills and techniques presented in this book as you institute and reinforce the new code.

If your current environment is highly undisciplined, don't try to put the entire code in place all at once. Begin with just a few rules relating to a single key issue such as safety, attendance, or conduct. Resist the temptation to choose something easy. Start with an action or behavior that is currently a significant problem, and that will positively impact the results your team attains once compliance is the norm.

Be patient. It's worth noting that the primary purpose of U.S. Marine Corps recruit training (boot camp) is to teach discipline – and the process takes twelve weeks in an atmosphere totally dedicated to that purpose. Naturally, it will take a supervisor or manager more than a few days to influence behaviors and develop the degree of discipline that's appropriate for a regular workplace. Invest the time it takes.[1]

If you manage a work unit within a larger organization, a common question or complaint you will hear is, "How come we have to follow these rules when no one else does?" The answer will become apparent to your followers as you implement the skills in this book. The short answer (for now) is that your group is following a different course than all the others. You are trying to create a more positive and fulfilling employment experience for your followers. You are leading them to *treasure*.

The Quartermaster

The role of quartermaster aboard a pirate ship bears explanation. Out of their distrust for dictatorial rule, pirates placed a portion of a traditional naval captain's power in the hands of a quartermaster elected by the crew at large.

The quartermaster made work assignments, distributed supplies, oversaw the division of plunder, and helped maintain order. Both he and the captain had to agree on the punishment of a crew member before it was administered. In a union environment, the *shop steward* may fill a somewhat similar role.

On a pirate ship, the quartermaster was also responsible for learning (from the captain) everything the captain knew about running the ship – from hull repairs to battle tactics to celestial navigation. The quartermaster was expected to assume command in the event of the captain's death, or to receive a command of his own when training was complete and a suitable ship was taken as a prize in battle.

In the modern workplace, it is not generally possible (or advisable) to allow rank-and-file employees to elect an organization's management team (or to choose your successor). You can still adopt the concept of a quartermaster, however, if you ensure two things.

First, you must choose a person who is respected by the crew at large. Employees must feel that this individual is "one of their own." Second, you must confirm that whomever you select is committed to learning the key aspects of your job (and is willing to move into a formal leadership position someday). It is essential that your "quartermaster" have the personal desire and ambition to lead others at some point in the future.

Discuss everything with your quartermaster, and encourage this person to facilitate the sharing of information both up and down the "chain of command." This can be especially valuable when language or cultural differences inhibit your ability to have casual conversations with all of your employees.

A Good Start

Establish a code, and insist that your workplace pirates adhere to it. For Pirates of the Realm, the code was effective because it benefited the crew as a whole. It provided a framework of actions and behaviors that allowed a diverse collection of individuals to function as a team. After all, nobody wanted to work with a shipmate who allowed his own selfish interests to jeopardize the future well-being of everyone else. The same truth applies in modern workplaces.

As previously explained, this is not a "quick fix," but rather an extensive and permanent renovation. The important thing is to get started. Establish a few ground rules for the actions and behaviors that are most critical to your operation. Then, move forward by embracing achievement.

Embrace Achievement

TWO FUNDAMENTALLY DIFFERENT sets of operating principles – or "mindsets" – can shape everything an organization is and does. One is the pride of *achievement*; the other is the *resentment* felt toward those who achieve by those who do not.

Achievement and resentment are incompatible, yet they have coexisted throughout history. When a mindset of achievement prevailed, cultures flourished. When a mindset of resentment gained the upper hand, cultures declined and eventually perished.

Both mindsets were certainly present in the pirate culture of the New World. Pirate captains who embraced achievement were driven to create an abundant, overflowing life for themselves and their crews. Their goals were wealth and independence. In pursuit of these goals, they each made contributions, large and small, to the settlement of a new continent.

Consider the fact that literally hundreds of counties, cities, and schools – from the Carolinas to Texas – bear the names of men who were, at some point, declared pirates.[2]

On the other hand, the pirates who embraced resentment were motivated almost exclusively by their envy and hatred of those who were more self-disciplined and successful. They despised the civilization forming around them, and sought to destroy it through fear and violence.

The behaviors associated with achievement and resentment are often in conflict. When achievers produce a result, the resentful (being unwilling or unable to achieve anything themselves) are compelled to discredit or destroy the accomplishment in a twisted attempt to improve their own relative position. The most common tactic is to try to label the achievers and their achievements as being unethical, immoral, or somehow "wrong."

In a healthy organization, the resentful will be seen for what they are – undisciplined failures. Advancement and growth will continue.

In a troubled organization, however, this redefinition may be accepted. Resentment then becomes the "higher morality." Regulations and policies that once ensured productivity (by providing achievers with resources, support, and recognition) are reinterpreted to stifle growth and initiative. The new focus is a perverted form of "fairness" – where people who accomplish little and contribute nothing receive the same rewards and benefits as the achievers.

Many organizations are firmly in the grip of a resentment mindset. In a few cases, the resentment is so extreme that a "slum culture" has evolved – where slovenly dress, confrontational language, and violent acts are tolerated – even celebrated.

How did this happen? Most often, leaders simply *allowed* it to happen – by failing to "keep to the code."

In other cases, the balance was tipped toward resentment when someone in a position of authority caused physical, emotional, or financial harm to others (through ignorance, insensitivity, or an abuse of power). In those situations, the non-achievers became "victims" who gained widespread support and protection from coworkers. An "us" versus "them" scenario emerged – with everyone ultimately losing.

The balance may also have been tipped if an organization promoted someone from within a group of resentful employees, yet failed to train and develop that person into an achievement-focused leader. In such a case, resentment was given formal power and a platform from which to spread a negative message.

Is the scale tipped toward resentment in your organization? If not (that is, if your workplace is still achievement-oriented), what should you do as a leader when resentful actions occur? Absolutely nothing (provided those actions are expressed in a nonviolent and nondestructive way).

As long as leaders and achievers recognize resentment for what it is, it can do no harm in a healthy culture (other than perpetuating the failures of those who practice it). Passive resentment is utterly impotent. Of course, violent or destructive resentment should never be tolerated. Acts of hatred should be punished or prosecuted to the full extent of the law.

What if your organization already has a pervasive mindset of resentment? What is the best thing a leader can do? You must help those filled by resentment *learn to achieve.* How?

First, leaders at every level must themselves embrace achievement. This means personally striving to produce abundance, and it means feeling proud (without guilt) of the treasures you legitimately win for yourself and others. Everyone in a leadership role must aspire (and be held) to this higher standard. Achievers recognize that the greater the scope of one's individual accomplishments, the greater potential one has to positively impact the world as a whole.

Second, immediately reverse any policy or practice that allows resentment to be a profitable strategy. Resentment will continue as long as an organization subsidizes it by coddling those individuals who refuse to accept the discipline of work.

Achievement-oriented leaders must stop trying to win the favor of the resentful, and start requiring them to pull their weight. This will force the resentful to rely on their own capacity to achieve, however meager it may be.

Third, leaders must teach, train, coach, and mentor the resentful. You must give every employee the opportunity to become an achiever. This task is a genuine pleasure for any person who is already a true leader. In fact, one of the most rewarding pursuits in life is to develop a once-resentful (but willing to change) "loser" into a successful and productive "winner."

And what is to be done with people who are so filled with resentment that they are not willing to change? A leader can do nothing but carefully document the efforts that were made to help the non-achiever (as well as the person's resentful responses), and then "put the person ashore."

When you do, someone is sure to object and declare that the resentful must be "protected" – that is, carried on the backs of the achievers. Stand your ground. Fight the battle. As harsh as that may seem, it is the right thing to do.

Your crew (though smaller) will at long last be released from the shackles that chained them to their resentful and unproductive coworkers. They will finally have a real chance to excel. And when the misplaced charity of achievers dries up, the resentful will be forced to stop playing the "entitlement" game and become contributors to society.

Confirm Your Sources of Power

LEADERS POSSESS four distinctly different types of power. Each type has different qualities and carries a different weight in your efforts to lead workplace pirates.

Power of Position

The first type of power is *power of position*. This is power bestowed upon you by someone in authority. It gives you the right (and the responsibility) to plan, organize, guide, and monitor the activities of others.

The captain of a pirate ship had power of position. Captains who relied too heavily on this power to command a crew were often the victims of mutiny. Great pirate captains knew that their power of position was most useful when dealing with local governments, merchants, and other captains – and that it was the least effective type of power they had with their crews.

As a leader, your power of position (for example, the title of supervisor or manager) matters most when you are representing your team to others in the organization who have equal or higher authority, and when you are representing your organization to a customer, supplier, or other outside entity.

Power of position comes with two moral obligations. First, you must exhibit the courage to question the decisions and actions of those above you when necessary. Second, you must make it your responsibility to understand, support, and enact any lawful decision that's ultimately made.

Power of Competence

The second type of power is *power of competence*. Competence is the knowledge, skill, experience, and judgment necessary to achieve a desired result.

Pirate captains were among the most proficient ship handlers, navigators, and battle strategists of the era. They knew how to get a ship where it needed to go, and knew what to do when it got there. The more a captain demonstrated his competence, the more his crew respected and depended on that competence – making it a key source of power.

A business leader must likewise rely on the power of competence. In most cases, this is not a problem. People are usually promoted into managerial roles because they have visibly demonstrated a requisite degree of job-related knowledge, skill, and judgment.

When people are placed in leadership positions without adequate knowledge of the functions they manage, the result is an undeniable lack of respect. If the leader then tries to assert power of position to gain respect, a covert form of mutiny occurs where workers leverage whatever knowledge the boss doesn't possess.

Are you an owner or manager responsible for filling supervisory positions? If so, never let family, social, or political relationships force you to promote someone who is not functionally knowledgeable. If the person never worked in a store, don't bring him in as a manager. Give him a chance to learn the business from the bottom up – and to gain the power of competence.

Power of Personality

The third type of power is *power of personality*. Power of personality is held by those who are good listeners, effective communicators, and inspiring persuaders.

Great pirate captains were fully aware of the needs and concerns of their men. They kept them involved in major decisions, and gave them as much information as possible as soon as possible. They knew what to say to build courage and commitment.

Pirate captains also realized the importance of keeping other key stakeholders "in the loop" regarding their operations, and usually relied on their persuasive skills ("charms rather than arms," as one famous captain put it) to win the much needed support of territorial officials, local suppliers, and citizens.

Effective "people skills" were critical for the pirate captain – as they are for every business leader. The good news is that you don't have to be born with charismatic traits to have the power of personality. People skills, like the job-related skills that ensure power of competence, can be learned. (The essential motivation and communication skills for leading workplace pirates are presented later in this book.)

Power of Character

The fourth type of power is *power of character*. This is basically a leader's "credit rating" with other people. Is the individual perceived as trustworthy and believable, or is there a trail of broken promises and unfulfilled expectations?

In the somewhat lawless and cutthroat setting of the Golden Age of Piracy, a captain who was up front and honest, and who consistently did exactly what he said he would do, gained enormous and lasting power.

A crew did not always agree with the captain's position, but if the captain was a man of his word, the crew generally supported him (even when the task appeared impossible!). Knowing what to expect from their boss made the crew feel secure and confident. Surprises, especially ones with negative consequences, were something a pirate captain worked to avoid.

Power of character is also essential when dealing with people other than followers. A pirate captain who failed to deliver on promises to political backers, suppliers, or other supporters had a short lifespan.

Over the years, hundreds of English privateers were arrested for piracy and returned to London for trial (in spite of having valid Letters of Marque). Those who helped their patrons secure wealth and power in the New World rarely saw a courtroom. Many were knighted and sent back to the Americas in key government positions. In stark contrast, Capt. William Kidd was swiftly tried and publicly hung – primarily because his benefactors believed that he was operating in *his* best interests rather than theirs.

When a business leader is "hung" (i.e., demoted or fired), lack of character is almost always the cause. It is understood that a manager or supervisor will make operational mistakes, and most organizations accept those mistakes as a learning experience. However, when executives, stockholders, or other benefactors believe that they can no longer trust the word of someone they placed in a leadership role, that person's management career is over.

Do people trust you – or has your power of character been compromised (either by your past actions or the actions of other leaders in your organization)? Unless your integrity is beyond question, it is essential that you apply the techniques offered next to restore and strengthen your credibility.

Earn Trust

TRUST IS A MANDATORY ELEMENT for success as a leader, and it is always a two-way street. A pirate captain had to be able to trust his crew – and his crew had to be able to trust him. In an atmosphere where authority figures were generally viewed with contempt, this was much easier said than done.

In today's workplace, the same kind of mutual trust is essential – and some of the same barriers to establishing it may be found. Surveys show that roughly two-thirds of American workers do not trust their bosses![3]

When there is a lack of trust, there is also a lack of respect, responsibility, and commitment. Low levels of trust yield high levels of turnover, rumors, accidents, and mistakes. Trust affects every aspect of productivity and morale.

Consequently, when trust exists between you and your workers, your leadership role (developing individuals, building teams, and producing results) becomes much, much easier.

Several factors can challenge the process of building trust with your employees. For example, mergers and downsizing may have created instability, fear, stress, and paranoia. Adversarial relationships may exist between management and labor, and certain union practices may inhibit (or seem to inhibit) open communication between the two groups. Of course, executives or other managers in your organization may not be trustworthy themselves.

While you can't change these situations, you can start at the "grass roots" level to rebuild trust, one person at a time, with each individual you supervise or manage. In fact, if lack of trust between managers and workers is the *status quo* in your organization, then your personal integrity becomes more critical than ever.

As a leader, you have the ability to do many things that either build or destroy trust between you and your employees. Most of these actions seem like common sense, but a surprising number of bosses – from pirate captains to business executives – have failed to apply them, and subsequently failed as leaders. Be honest with yourself as you consider the true extent to which you are doing the following things.

Do you lead by example, and serve as a role model for other employees? Commit yourself to achieve excellence in your daily performance, and demonstrate the work habits and behaviors you want your followers to emulate.

Do you use your position, power, and influence appropriately? Use your power legitimately to achieve your organization's goals. Never use your authority or influence for personal gain.

Do you "walk your talk?" Your behaviors (the actions you take) must be consistent with your words (stated intentions).

Do you follow through on promises and commitments? Make it a habit to state what you will do – then do it, and *then* follow up to confirm that the result or benefit you promised was actually realized.

Do you communicate assertively? Assertiveness is the middle ground between submissive behavior (giving in to other people) and aggressive behavior (insisting that other people give in to you). Be open and honest with other people about what you can and cannot do, and then stick to it – yet work cooperatively to find a mutually acceptable option.

Do you move with a sense of purpose? People are always watching the leader, so stand up straight and walk like someone who has places to be. When you enter a room or work area, do so with an objective in mind. Don't wander about aimlessly looking lost or confused. You're a captain – look the part.

Do you convey poise? Poise is high energy enthusiasm balanced with relaxed self-confidence. In a stressful situation, when emotions are running high, how do you behave? Learn to maintain your composure and work through difficult issues with a sense of urgency and quiet confidence.

Do you greet people each day when you see them? Smile and make eye contact. Shake hands when it's appropriate. A good handshake is still a powerful way to convey trust and openness.

Do you talk with your employees? Don't rely on technology alone for communication. Choose the method (one-to-one conversations, group meetings, telephone calls, e-mails, etc.) based on the message and the outcome you desire.

Do you listen actively to others? Paraphrase and empathize to show you hear and understand not only the message content, but also the feeling behind it.

Do you give employees regular feedback about their performance? Feedback is perhaps the single most powerful tool for human development you have available (and it costs almost nothing to use!). Both praise (positive feedback) and constructive criticism (corrective feedback) are essential components in the performance coaching process, and each serves as a catalyst to increase employee competence and commitment.

Do you ask employees for their observations and input? Solicit (and consider) their perceptions about your performance as a leader and as a communicator. Make it "safe" for employees to be open and honest with you, and let them know when you implement their suggestions or take their advice.

Do you provide timely, accurate, and complete information to managers, customers, and employees alike? Keep people informed by sharing good news, and advise them of actions to address delays, errors, or other exceptions.

Do you provide the resources that you and your employees need to do jobs properly? Ensure that tools, supplies, equipment, and other resources are obtained, then used effectively (for the right purposes only) and efficiently (without waste).

Do you pay attention to factors that affect employee well-being such as health, safety, security, and family issues? Learn (and help your workers learn) about the programs and the benefits that your organization offers to assist employees.

Do you create an environment that encourages personal responsibility? Keep the group focused with common goals, shared decision making, and continual development and improvement.

Do you measure and acknowledge results? Find ways to "keep score" relative to your group's actions and achievements. Let them know the score and give credit where credit is due. Recognize and celebrate major milestones (not only accomplishments, but mistakes and the lessons learned from them, as well).

Do you have the "guts" to lead? To lead others, you need the courage to take reasonable risks, the confidence to admit your mistakes, the strength of character to do what you believe is right, and the wisdom to learn from your experiences. You will sometimes have to make decisions and enforce policies that your employees don't like. You will also have to "go to bat" for your people on occasion, presenting a message on their behalf that perhaps *your* manager doesn't want to hear. Can you do that?

Pirates of the Realm could easily recognize the difference between a captain who would put his own well-being on the line to fulfill a commitment to them, versus one who would play politics with their lives if he was backed into a corner. Workplace pirates (and all employees) respect and trust a leader who pursues a worthy objective with boldness, integrity, and selfless dedication.

Do you behave like their leader, or their friend? The inevitable problem that occurs when you behave like their friend is *favoritism*. Favoritism is by far the most frequent complaint that employees make about their supervisors – regardless of the size or type of organization. It's a huge threat to your credibility.

Favoritism occurs because there are naturally some people you like and enjoy spending time with, and some people you don't like and would rather not be around. No matter how hard you try to be unbiased, the people you *don't* like will always perceive that the people you *do* like (and with whom you prefer to spend time) are being treated much better, and therefore have an unfair advantage. And that may be true – after all, who is better positioned to know what you value and expect, and to understand your directions and guidance for achieving it: someone you like and spend a lot of time with, or someone you don't?

Some experts suggest that you simply avoid socializing with employees – but this can be impractical in many situations. The most important thing is to give your time equally. Treat all the people you encounter with dignity and respect. Create a work environment that is safe, fair, and productive for everyone.

Do you realistically assess your own strengths and weaknesses? Acknowledge the impact that both of these can have on other people.

The key to building trust is an accurate self-perception. You must be willing to "own up" to the actions and behaviors you exhibit, and realize how those actions and behaviors affect your credibility with others. Only then can you apply remedies that strengthen your integrity. Beyond that, later sections of this book will offer specific communication skills and techniques to help you build and maintain trust.

When you use daily communication to show that you trust others, and to show that you are trustworthy yourself, you will improve the quality of the relationships you have with your employees. You will gain the power of character, and begin to earn the confidence and respect of your workplace pirates – and everyone else.

Radiate Possibilities

EVERY WELL-TOLD PIRATE ADVENTURE includes an escape from a whirlpool or maelstrom – a violently spinning body of water that threatens to trap the ship and drag it down to Davy Jones locker.

While these phenomenon are more legend than fact, it is possible for a cavern (created during the ice age and now located beneath the sea bed) to crack open and temporarily create a free vortex – like opening the drain in a bathtub. If the cavern is large enough, the effect can draw floating objects inward and pull them under.

There is an equally dangerous force in today's workplace that threatens your ship – *negativity* (in terms of attitudes and conversations). The associated behaviors range from apathetic expressions and lethargic movements, to a steady stream of complaints about what's wrong, whose fault it is, and why it isn't fair.

Once the grumbling begins, other employees are compelled to join in (even the ones who are relatively happy seem powerless to resist) – and soon the entire organization is caught in the vortex.

When employees are dragged into this whirlpool of negativity, there is nowhere to go but down. Every factor by which a successful organization is measured will decline – morale, safety, efficiency, throughput, service – you name it, it will get worse.

Leaders may choose to deal with these whirlpools of negativity in one of three ways. In most cases, two of the methods won't work.

The first method is to "think positive" and encourage your followers to do the same. This essentially ignores the presence of a vortex. Organizations *do* have problems, however. They're not perfect, so most leaders find it difficult to pretend that nothing is wrong. Most employees find it insulting.

The second method is to swim down the throat of the vortex and close the drain – that is, to fix the problems. For supervisors or middle managers, this approach may be futile, as the problems are likely to be deeper than they can dive (i.e., beyond a manager's span of control). Even the most senior executive would be embarking on a "suicide mission" if he or she tried to address all the core problems that affect an industry or market in which an enterprise does business.

The third method (and the only viable one, really) is for the leader to do the same as any legendary pirate captain – get the entire group working together to break free of the whirlpool. You can't avoid the vortex or pretend it doesn't exist, and you can't change the natural forces that created it. You *can* help your crew sail out of it by *radiating possibilities*.[4]

Because workplace pirates have usually been stuck in some type of a vortex for their entire lives, they have trouble seeing the *possibility* of anything better. Nevertheless, the *desire* for something better is always there. The obstacle that keeps you from uniting your crew to pursue that treasure is the atmosphere of negativity – it can smother hopes and dreams like a wet blanket on a fire.

Think about the job candidates who apply for work at your organization. Each one is seeking "something better." For those who are hired, life is suddenly filled with possibilities. They got the job! When they report to work, their eyes are bright and their faces are literally beaming with enthusiasm. How long does that last?

Now look at the employees who work for you. Are their eyes shining and their faces beaming? Or do their expressions, movements, and conversations confirm that they are caught in the vortex of negativity? If it's the latter, you must ask yourself a very critical question: *"What am I doing (as the leader) that has caused my followers to give in and lose hope?"*

The leader's job is to radiate possibilities – to never forget (or let followers forget) that there is a treasure to be found. A leader must be the "keeper of the flame" and provide the spark that ignites the fuel in each follower.

Regardless of the situation, leaders can never allow themselves to be drawn into the whirlpool of negativity. When your coworkers or employees start to gripe, you cannot join in with negative comments of your own, no matter how justified their complaints might be (or how much fun it might be to commiserate with them for awhile).

You can, of course, listen. You can acknowledge (without blame or judgment) what employees already know – that conditions are less than perfect. You can also confirm that *changing* those conditions and fixing everything that's wrong is beyond your scope of power.

Your objective in doing this is to help your employees see the situation for what it is – like weather or gravity, the whirlpool exists. The problems are there. That's an undeniable reality. Yet like the force of gravity, the problems that exist may be viewed as a finite set of conditions that people can learn to *overcome* in order to achieve a goal.

When employees understand this, the leader can prompt them to make a decision. Do they simply want to give in to the complaints (and feel more miserable each day), or do they want to take control of their destiny and move toward something better?

In the Golden Age of Piracy, if ordinary citizens were marooned on a deserted island with no food or water, they would soon begin to talk about how they were going to die. More experienced and resourceful men in the same situation might talk about how they were going to survive. A captain would talk about how he was going to get off the island and get his ship back. That same relentless spirit of *possibilities* – believing that no matter how bad the circumstances become, desirable outcomes are still possible – is essential if you want to take command of a pirate workplace.

Less-than-perfect conditions for success and achievement *do* exist in most of today's workplaces. Organizations *do* have problems. Worse yet, it seems that each day brings another new crisis situation that threatens to send *everyone* into a downward spiral.

When such a problem occurs, you must continue to radiate possibilities. You must get employees to see the situation for what it is, inspire hope, and focus everyone on the goals that lie beyond the vortex. It is the critical prerequisite for escaping the whirlpools.

Of course, to be a great leader, you actually have to *break free* – which means being able to deal effectively with whatever problem or crisis has arisen.

Take Care of Crisis Situations

DAILY LIFE aboard a pirate vessel was often serene, if not outright dull. A portion of the crew's time was spent maintaining the ship and practicing their combat skills. The remainder of the day was devoted to rest and recreation – that is, until storm clouds or an enemy sail suddenly appeared on the horizon.

A typical workday in most organizations is very similar. Employees are engaged in a series of planned activities until a problem occurs – an equipment failure, a customer mandate, a reportable incident, or some other "crisis" that disrupts the normal routine.

For a pirate captain, the decisions made and actions taken during a crisis had a dramatic and lasting effect. In fact, they were often the defining events in a captain's career – the moments in which he truly earned the respect and loyalty of his crew – or lost his ship. The same is true for a supervisor, manager, or senior executive today.

Effectively managing a crisis is difficult, in part because leaders are often their own worst enemies when trouble looms. It is human nature, when things are going well, to want to maintain the status quo. When an impending problem appears, it is initially viewed as unwelcome inconvenience – something to be ignored or avoided. As a result, small and relatively easy-to-solve problems have a nasty habit of turning into full-scale crisis situations.

Once a problem grows to the point of being impossible to avoid or ignore, most leaders are willing to spring into action – but the action they take is not always productive.

A Common Mistake: Too Domineering

Some managers react to problems without consulting their followers. They unilaterally decide on a course of action, and then bark out orders for everyone to obey. Many employees will do exactly what the leader tells them to do.

At least some employees, however, will know more about why the problem occurred and how to correct it than the leader does. This faction will do what they think is "right," even though the action may be the opposite of what the leader instructed.

A third faction of employees will *think* they know more about how to solve the problem, but they'll be working with erroneous assumptions or without the critical "big picture" information the leader has.

What happens? Three different groups of employees pursue three different courses of action (and work against each other in the process). As a result, a problem that was manageable in the beginning grows into a major crisis before it is resolved.

After this occurs a few times, the domineering manager may conclude that problems are disruptive (rather than normal), and that they must be *prevented* (rather than resolved). The manager will then overreact to everything, and followers will be kept in a constant (and stressful) state of alert. When the inevitable next problem does appear, they will either try to hide it, or feel that they are being "blamed" for it. Either way, trust between the manager and employees will break down, the whirlpool of negativity will increase, and the manager will be powerless to lead.

Another Common Mistake: Too Reticent

Some managers are quick to recognize that the domineering approach taken by their counterparts is ineffective – so they allow (even encourage) employees to actively participate in problem solving.

That would be a positive thing – except when the manager leaves employees to do this without guidance, the group is still divided into at least three factions: employees who know how to solve the problem, employees who *think* they know how to solve the problem (but are relying on mistaken assumptions or incomplete information), and employees who don't know (and don't care).

Because there is generally more than one way to solve a problem, the first two factions may be further splintered, each arguing for his or her idea. The longer the argument goes on, the bigger the problem becomes. Ultimately, it may be the person with the loudest voice, the most charisma, or the most obstinate behavior that drives the decision – a decision that's often wrong.

After going through this very time consuming and frustrating process a few times, no group of employees wants to do it again. They then fall victim to "solutionism" – i.e., choosing the first proposed course of action that might possibly return things to "normal."

Because the first proposed solution usually deals with the obvious symptoms rather than the real underlying problem, the effect is the same as fighting a sea monster – cut off one head and two more appear. Cut off those two and four emerge.

It doesn't take long for employees to lose confidence in their manager, and for morale to plummet. If the monster (problem) doesn't get them, the resulting whirlpool of negativity will.

A Better Approach

An effective pirate captain provided leadership without hesitation, yet did not try to dominate his crew. He realized that his success at handling problems (and most likely his survival as captain) depended on his ability to make *other* people powerful. In a modern organization filled with workplace pirates, the same ability is required. There are five steps:

Step 1 – Accept that Change has Happened

Few scenes are as tranquil as a sailing ship on a peaceful sea. But weather changes, and in no time, thunderstorms can build and the waves can become monstrous. When this happens, the captain might curse the sky and swear at the ocean, but the sky and ocean don't care. If the captain doesn't respond quickly to the new conditions, the ship will be lost.

The first step in dealing with any new challenge is for you, as leader, to accept that things have changed. Whatever you might have *wanted* to happen, *planned* to happen, or *expected* to happen is (at least for the time being) off the table. You can't waste valuable time complaining. You have work to do.

Successful pirate captains never made the mistake of getting too comfortable when things were going well. They not only *accepted* change, they *anticipated* that changes and problems would be a part of their daily existence. They saw trouble-free hours as a rare gift (and of course, made the most of them!).

Step 2 – Get the Facts

The second stage of dealing with a problem or crisis is to ensure that everyone is looking at the *facts* about the situation – *all* the facts – and *just* the facts.

In a pirate culture, people tend to fill any void that is not covered by factual information with rumor and speculation. Because these speculations are almost always pessimistic and inaccurate, they only serve to increase the negative force of the whirlpool (generating even more rumors and complications as the situation evolves).

The leader must facilitate the discovery, presentation, and understanding of facts by everyone in the group. This is not the same as discussing everyone's opinions or solutions. The question is, "What do we *know* for sure (and have evidence to support)?" The leader must keep everyone focused on that and that alone, and steer the discussion away from what people *think* they know, how they *feel* about it, or what they believe they should *do* at this point.

The process of uncovering, compiling, sharing, and understanding factual information is an extremely constructive one. It enhances the group's willingness to work together toward a viable solution – i.e., a way to escape the whirlpool.

The leader cannot allow the team to skip this step and immediately begin arguing for a particular course of action before all the facts are examined. Also, the leader cannot lose patience with the process and unilaterally declare what the course of action will be. The result will be disappointing, and the destructive power of the whirlpool will expand.

Step 3 – Identify the Possible Outcomes

The facts pertaining to a situation are only "good" or "bad" relative to the expectations that existed before the situation developed. When a new situation emerges, a new set of expectations is needed. That's the third step in dealing with a problem or crisis – prompting the group to identify and explore alternative outcomes.

No matter how dire the situation, your fate is rarely sealed. There are at least several possible outcomes for any dilemma. The leader must ask the crucial question: "Given our current situation and the facts we have, how do we want this to turn out?"

The leader's objective is to have the group define the ideal outcome. Granted, the ideal outcome may or may not be feasible, but don't allow the group to start evaluating yet. The goal at this point is merely to describe the best possible (not necessarily the most probable) result.

When the best possible outcome is defined, the leader then prompts the group to identify other less ideal (but still desirable) results that might occur. It's very important that the leader focus the group on identifying possible *outcomes* rather than courses of *action* that might lead to those outcomes. In other words, don't ask "What should we *do* now?" Ask "How do we want things to *be* in the future when this crisis is over and no longer a concern?"

Imagine a pirate ship so badly damaged that it begins to sink near a deserted island. After accepting that the situation has happened and gathering the facts, the crew might identify four possible outcomes: (a) being safely aboard a friendly vessel en route to their home port, (b) being in control of a captured enemy vessel and back in the "pirate business," (c) surviving long-term on the island, or (d) for those without hope, choosing the time and manner of death.

Until the group considers where they want to go, it's too soon to discuss what they need to *do* to get there. When the group is focused on defining a variety of possible outcomes, they are less likely to get caught up in the whirlpool of negativity. They are also less likely to jump to solutions that are easy (but ineffective), or solutions that are costly and impossible to implement (and therefore a waste of time).

Step 4 – Analyze the Options

The fourth step in dealing with a problem or crisis is to identify a path to each desired outcome, analyze and compare those paths, and choose the best option. This is the step in which the leader truly makes other people powerful.

The leader must help the group examine each desired outcome in turn, consider the facts, and ask "How might we get there?" Group members should not argue for or against any one idea at this point, but instead, collaborate on finding as many viable paths to each result as possible.

For example, if the marooned pirates in the previous example were discussing outcome (b), one path to that outcome might be to use their derelict ship to build a raft (in order to pursue and sneak aboard an enemy vessel), while another path might be to use the ship as a decoy (and draw the enemy to them).

Once all the paths (options) are identified, each is analyzed on the basis of its probability for success and the consequences of its failure.

For instance, the crew would likely agree that the probability of successfully overtaking an enemy vessel by raft and capturing it was low (given the limited number of men and weapons it could carry), and that the consequences of failure would be severe – whereas the probability of successfully drawing an enemy to them with a decoy would be better, and the consequences of failing to attract an enemy ship (or failing to capture it) would be less severe. In most cases this discussion will quickly lead to a group consensus.

Step 5 – Create the Desired Result

Once a group agrees on a path or option, they are empowered to pool their collective knowledge and carry out the actions that create the desired outcome.

A wise leader will never underestimate the importance of a clear objective or the power of collective knowledge. A well-facilitated team with a common goal will always be "smarter" than a single individual. They will find better solutions more quickly (if properly facilitated), and be more fully committed to ensuring that the outcome they decide upon is realized.

Summary

Pirate code ensured that each man had an equal voice in the affairs of the ship. Nevertheless, when a challenge arose, a smart captain did not call an all-hands meeting and ask the crew at-large what they wanted to do. He provided a framework for the crew's input, and then used that input to compile facts, identify possible outcomes, analyze the options, and take control of the future.

To take command as a supervisor or manager, you must effectively handle the crisis situations that arise from day to day. As a true leader, however, you'll do even more. You'll guide your crew to a destination that lies far beyond the whirlpool of negativity. You'll lead them to treasure – to the ultimate prize. That journey begins with a vision.

Part III.
"Eyes on the Prize"

Vision

Realize the Value of a Vision

EFFECTIVE LEADERS consistently produce desired results. A *vision* defines the ultimate desired result. It's the *treasure* your work unit or organization is seeking – captured in words, pictures, and stories that everyone can understand.

Consider this illustration. If time and money were no object, what would be your dream vacation? People usually respond to that question with a single phrase, for example, "a cruise," "a villa in Tuscany," or "playing golf all day and poker all night." Yet unless you already shared a similar dream, nothing about those statements would entice you to want to go along on one of those trips – much less help pay for it.

Imagine, however, that a person described a luxury villa in detail – the elegant rooms, the beautiful views from the terrace, the fragrant scents, and the perfect weather. Suppose she had a colorful brochure to accompany her description. Suppose she talked about the friendly neighbors and helpful servants who would be eager to make her feel welcome and comfortable. Suppose she described how she would take the Ferrari for a quick drive through the rolling hills. And all of this within the first hour of arrival!

Even if you'd never dreamed of a vacation in Tuscany, this trip might begin to sound intriguing.

No one follows a leader (at least, not with enthusiasm) to a place they don't want to go. No one follows unless they are convinced that the leader has a plan to get there. No one who has limited information about a future destination is capable of being any more inspired or excited about it than the leader is.

A rich, compelling vision convinces people to sign up for the trip they never knew they wanted to take. It assures them that the leader knows exactly where he or she is going. Vivid descriptions create enthusiasm and generate action.

Pirate captains knew the backgrounds of their crew members, and understood each man's personal hopes and desires. For some, the desire was to return to Europe. For others, it was to bring their families to the New World. For still others, it was to have a ship of their own – or a farm or store. Some just wanted freedom and a peaceful life they had never known.

With the crew's desires in mind, the captain created a grand vision for the ship, and carefully linked its realization to the hopes and dreams of every man on board. He spoke of it frequently, and used it as a reason for everything – from maintaining shipboard discipline to fighting bravely against a larger and more powerful ship.

A vision brings a dream into sharp focus and transforms it into a definitive, desirable result that can be attained. This transformation is critically important because of the way the human brain functions. A dream resides in the unconscious mind. A vision resides in the conscious mind. A wonderful thing about the brain is that it automatically sorts through the billions of pieces of incoming information we receive every day in an effort to find things that will satisfy the conscious mind.[5]

The brain doesn't actively search for things to fulfill our unconscious dreams – only things that help us realize a conscious vision.

Consequently, the scope of our vision directly affects the scope of our accomplishments. If our vision is vague and limited, the brain will provide vague and limited information. If our vision is detailed and grand, the brain will sort through and provide "breakthrough" ideas. It works like a magnet to attract the knowledge, people, and resources we need. The clearer the vision, the more powerful the magnet.

It is also important to know that the brain's "sorting" mechanism doesn't recognize the difference between dreams and nightmares, or goals and fears. Whatever we envision most clearly is what the brain is working to create. It is the essence of the so called "self-fulfilling prophecy."

If our business vision is to be number one in customer service, and we have a detailed description of what that involves, we will very likely achieve it. If, on the other hand, we have an overriding fear of rising costs and possible layoffs, our brain will likely feed us the very information that leads to those problems.

The message here is not to just "think positive" and ignore your fears. The message is to choose your vision wisely, and to actively manage the associated risks. (Only the most arrogant, vain, or disturbed leaders – be they pirate captains or politicians – embark on difficult missions with no more than an optimistic belief that something good might happen once the journey begins.)

If an organization has an inherently grand purpose (saving lives, curing cancer, etc.), formulating a vision is relatively easy. But what if the organization does something far less glamorous?

The story of Seattle's Pike Place Fish Market is well known. The work is grueling and the hours are long, yet employees bring high levels of passion and energy to the job every day.

Hundreds of companies have tried to emulate the success principles taught in "FISH!" seminars around the country.

Many fail solely because they overlook the fact that the *vision* of success was the catalyst that started it all. Owner John Yokoyama's vision: to make his fish stand "world famous."

Imagine what it was like the first time a group of fishmongers (the epitome of workplace pirates, at the time) heard John's vision. Even John admits to thinking, "What a stupid thing to say!"[6]

Not so stupid, as it turns out. Today, Pike Place Fish is a major tourist attraction. The fish-throwing employees are often featured in magazines, on television, and in motion pictures. They provide fresh seafood to customers around the globe. Some workers have been with the store for many years – and there is a waiting list of eager applicants.

The point is that there is nothing mystical about a vision. Any type of work unit or organization can create one and offer a path of redemption for workplace pirates. All it takes is ten simple steps:

1. Identify the Organization

2. Clarify the Mission

3. Note the Challenges and Opportunities

4. Assess the Risks and Rewards

5. Recognize the Core Values

6. Determine a Distinctive Difference

7. Describe the Ideal Outcome

8. Tell the Story

9. Adopt a Rallying Cry

10. Spread the Word

The following chapters examine each step in detail.

Identify the Organization

THE FIRST STEP in developing and communicating a vision is to identify the specific organization for which you are creating the vision.

Is the organization a single work unit, a cross-functional project team, or an entire enterprise? Is it a business, government agency, or non-profit entity?

The organization you identify must be one for which you have at least some functional authority and accountability. In other words, if you supervise the janitorial staff at a local high school, the organization you'd identify would be that functional group of workers, not the school system as a whole.

Regardless of the size or type of organization you manage, you must clearly describe the organization's main purpose – that is, its basic reason for existence. To do this, consider the following questions.

What output (products and/or services) does the organization provide?

Who benefits from the output provided, and in what ways?

Who would miss the organization if it ceased to exist? (Consider not only customers, but others who benefit – directly or indirectly – from the organization's presence. Examples might include vendors or suppliers, the surrounding community, charities to which the organization contributes, etc.)

What key standards or expectations must consistently be met by the organization as it provides output? (These objectives may relate to productivity, profitability, quality, service, price, regulatory compliance, customer integration, or any number of other performance areas.)

Once you have clearly identified the specific organization you are leading, you can clarify its mission.

Clarify the Mission

THE SECOND STEP is to clarify the one prevailing objective that unifies all of the organization's efforts – i.e., its mission. There are four basic types of missions: target-driven, competition-driven, model-driven, and transformation-driven.

Organizations with *target-driven* missions are in pursuit of specific measurable or attributable results. Generally, the results involve outcomes that can be independently ver_fied, not merely "hyped." A pirate captain pursuing the grand flagship of the Royal Navy would be on target-driven mission – as would a health clinic seeking national accreditation for the various rehabilitation programs it offers.

Organizations with *competition-driven* missions are seeking to overtake or dominate rival organizations in one or more key performance areas. A pirate captain striving to acquire the most treasure, become the fastest ship, or command the fiercest crew would be competition-driven – as would an outpatient facility that is working to become its city's largest provider of physical and occupational therapy services.

Organizations with *model-driven* missions are seeking to benchmark an exemplar in another industry. A pirate captain representing himself as "the Robin Hood of the high seas" is model-driven – as is a network of family health clinics with a mission to become "the McDonald's of immediate care."

Organizations with *transformation-driven* missions are seeking to reshape their functions and redefine the way they are perceived. If a notoriously cruel buccaneer sought to ally his ship with a respected colonial government, his mission might be considered transformation-driven. A clinic striving to use advanced Internet technologies in order to institute remote diagnosis, eliminate waiting rooms, and provide fast, convenient, patient-focused treatment for non life-threatening illnesses and injuries would likewise be transformation-driven.

If you are a supervisor or mid-level manager, examine the mission of your company, division, or agency when you clarify the mission of your work unit. If you lead an *operational* unit, you may have the same type of mission (in other words, if the larger organization is transformation-driven, the operational units within it will likely be transformation-driven, as well). If you lead a *support* unit, your mission may be different – for example, the achievement of a transformation-driven mission by a support unit may be necessary to enable a target-driven corporate mission (and vice versa).

What is your organization's specific mission? Which type of mission is it? Who or what is driving it? (Was the mission chosen by stockholders, managers, customers, regulatory officials, or someone else? Was it the result of economics, geography, or some other factor?)

Clarify the mission – then continue on.

Note the Challenges and Opportunities

THE THIRD STEP is to examine the changing conditions (internal and external) that affect the organization and the mission you have identified.

Pirate captains could not predict the formation or path of a hurricane. But a good captain knew when and where hurricanes were the most probable, and he constantly watched for warning signs that signaled their approach. This diligence allowed him to keep his ship out of danger – and at times, to use the storms to his competitive advantage. In doing so, he earned the trust and respect of his crew.

You can't predict the future, but you can recognize and prepare for the changes that are most likely to affect your organization. The key is to ask the right questions up front.

How might your customers and beneficiaries change in the future? What changes might occur to the markets or methods through which you provide output? What changes might occur in the economy? How might emerging technologies affect your organization? What emerging legal or regulatory issues could influence your operations? What social issues could change the way your organization is perceived? What kinds of regional, national, or global events could impact your workforce or processes?

How might the ownership or management of your organization change? What changes might occur in your workforce, labor pool, and job market?

What changes might be made to the products and/or services you provide? What new outputs might be developed or offered? What changes might affect the processes through which existing outputs are created and delivered?

Yes, the answer to some of these questions may be, "It depends." That's the point – to consider all the possible scenarios you may face.

In 2008, rising oil prices and stress in the housing market impacted almost every type of organization – from small school districts to giant retailers. Those events were not without precedent or warning, however – and organizations that recognized and prepared for them were in a much better position to weather the storm.

Which community leaders do you trust and respect more – the ones who have the foresight to plan for contingencies, or the ones who don't (and then have to raise your taxes to fund a reactive response)?

Who will your workplace pirates trust and respect more – a leader who anticipates challenges and opportunities, or one who doesn't (and has to cut jobs, hours, or benefits)?

Once you have considered the changes that the future could hold for your organization (and have listed the various possibilities), you can narrow the list.

Assess the Risks and Rewards

FOR EACH SPECIFIC CHANGE SCENARIO you listed, examine the *probability* of its occurrence in the foreseeable future. Assign a "low," "medium," or "high" probability rating. Remove from your list any items that have a "low" probability. (There isn't enough time or money to build your vision around improbable events.)

For each "medium" or "high" probability item that remains, consider the impact it would have on your organization if it actually occurred. Assign a "minor," "moderate," or "major" impact rating, as well as a "+" (positive impact) or "–" (negative impact) indicator. Remove items from your list that have "minor +" or "minor –" impacts.

Examine the items that remain. If the rated impacts are almost all negative, you may have had an overly pessimistic view of the future. Likewise, if the rated impacts are mainly positive, your outlook may have been too optimistic. In either case, revisit the questions in the previous chapter to create a more balanced list. You want to identify not only the "storms" you'll need to ride out, but also the "wind shifts" that might provide your organization with unique opportunities.

Divide the list into three groups. The "A" list contains items that have a "high" probability of occurring and that will have a "major" impact on your organization (positive or negative) if they do. These are the changes you can't ignore, because your ideal future depends on handling them appropriately. Your organization's vision must reflect how it will survive the likely challenges and take advantage of the likely opportunities.

Next, examine the items that did not make the "A" list (items with a "medium" probability of occurring, or a "moderate" potential impact on your organization). Estimate the amount of time, money, and effort required to prepare your organization to take advantage of the opportunity (if the potential impact is positive), or to survive the challenges (if the potential impact is negative). If you can afford to make those preparations (i.e., if the cost and effort would be minimal), place the item on the "B" list.

If you cannot afford to make those preparations, place the item on the "C" list.

You *must* prepare for the "A" list items. They have a high probability of occurring and will have a high impact if and when they do.

You *should* prepare for the "B" list items (with a medium probability and/or a moderate impact). However, if you lack the time, resources, and money to do so, then it's more rational to sacrifice one of the "B" list preparations than one from the "A" list.

You'd *like* to prepare for "C" list items, but simply don't have the capacity at present. Even so, review this list regularly. Conditions change, so something you initially assess as having only a medium probability or moderate impact (i.e., a "C" list item) may suddenly belong on the "A" list.

Recognize the Core Values

VALUES DEFINE WHAT IS IMPORTANT to team members as they work to address the challenges and opportunities they encounter.

A pirate captain had to recognize the core values of his crew, and incorporate those values into shipboard life. For instance, pirates placed a high value on taking care of their own. Consequently, most pirate captains provided a sizable pension to any man who was severely injured in battle – even though (as previously noted) it was common practice in the age of piracy for a man wounded aboard a naval ship to be cast ashore and left there to survive as a beggar.

When you consider the core values of your organization and personnel – and then integrate those values into your vision and mission – you begin to create the same *esprit de corps* that permeated the brotherhood of pirates, and all other highly successful organizations.

The best way to discover your employee's core values is to ask them these specific questions about their workplace desires and expectations:

What factors or characteristics would you expect to find in an ideal working environment?

What would you most like to see relative to the amount of control or autonomy you have when performing your job?

What is important to you regarding the manner in which people interact with one another at this organization – or in any workplace?

What would you expect from an "ideal" organization in terms of stability, security, and personal safety?

In what areas should this organization be more attentive to moral, ethical, legal, or regulatory issues – in order to do the "right thing?"

What do you want for yourself in terms of personal growth or advancement? How would an "ideal" organization be helping you?

As you discuss these questions with your employees, do not make promises or guarantees. Help them understand that even the most senior leader in your organization can't magically create the ideal work climate overnight. It will take time – but the process can only begin when you understand their perception of "ideal."

Gaining this perspective will not only allow you to build trust, it will provide you with the insight you'll need to connect each person's hopes and desires to the realization of the vision.

Determine a Distinctive Difference

THIS STEP IS MUCH SIMPLER than the previous three. It only requires you to identify the skills, behaviors, or other qualities that distinguish this group of people (your unit) from all others.

Is there an area where your workforce excels? Is there a function they perform better than anyone else? These are obvious areas around which to build a vision of the ideal future.

Be aware that not all distinctive differences appear positive – at least, not at first. At Pike Place Fish, John Yokoyama had a group of employees who were often described with words like "goofy," "loud," and "rebellious" – not exactly the traits that a retail store owner with an upscale customer base might wish for. John could have tried to ignore, tolerate, or drive out those behaviors (as many owners do), but instead he embraced them and made these behaviors a critical part of his strategy for becoming "world famous."

What if your group has no distinguishing characteristics you can build on? Not to fear – you have all the ingredients of a genuine American success story. In books and movies – and in real life – this nation cheers for ordinary people (and groups of people) who do something extraordinary. There's nothing wrong with a vision where the underdog, the "regular" folks, or the "little guys" come out of nowhere to win.

Of course, even the most impossible underdogs always have one skill or character trait that seems insignificant at first, and then suddenly emerges as the pivotal element of success when conditions change. Don't underestimate the potential that may be hiding within you and your group.

Effective pirate captains understood the power of this potential, and seldom underestimated it. In fact, it is a characteristic of all successful leaders to rely on the capacity of their followers to achieve whatever they envision.

Describe the Ideal Outcome

EXAMINE THE ORGANIZATION'S PURPOSE, and review all the various options the organization could pursue to fulfill its mission.

For each option, consider how the organization might successfully address the "A" list challenges, capitalize on the "A" list opportunities, and manage the relevant "B" list items in both categories. Then, for each option, explore ways to integrate the core values and apply any distinctive differences you identified.

The preferred option is the one that yields the most credible and desirable future for the organization. Create a vivid description or mental picture of that outcome or "end state" – this is your "vision" statement. It should be realistic enough for people to accept as achievable, yet extraordinary enough to be inspiring.

In the late 1950's, the United States and Soviet Union were openly engaged in a cultural, technological, and ideological rivalry. The economic and military implications of controlling outer space were significant, and the USSR already had an active satellite program.

In 1961, President John F. Kennedy determined that "landing a man on the moon and returning him safely to the Earth" by the end of the decade would demonstrate that, even with a four year head start, the Soviets were no match for America's scientific and engineering capabilities. He and his advisors felt that this single accomplishment would do more to win global respect and ensure peace than any other political, economic, or military action under consideration.[7]

President Kennedy's vision statement unified the thoughts and efforts of government, commercial, and academic institutions across the country. Eight years later, the vision was achieved.

A vivid description generates enthusiasm and commitment. It provides the rationale for pursuing a goal. It creates meaning in workers' lives by clarifying a worthwhile endeavor.

Your vision statement answers an important question that workplace pirates ask themselves regularly: *"Why should I go to work today?"* The answer will not only be *"to earn a paycheck and stay out of trouble,"* but also, *"to help create a better future for the organization – and for me."* A promising future gives workplace pirates a reason to get up in the morning and bring their best efforts to work.

Don't worry that the steps for arriving at that future are not fully planned. While the leader needs to have some idea of how the outcome will be achieved, it isn't necessary to have every detail in place when the vision is formulated. To start the journey, your followers only need a clear picture of where they are going and what they have to do *next* in order to get there.

Once they are enrolled in the vision, achieving it becomes a matter of getting each person to "buy in" to each next step, and then to complete the task or action associated with that step. To do that, you'll need to understand human motivation and behavior – covered in *Part IV* of this book.

But first, there are still three more critical steps for creating the vision.

Tell the Story

MOST PIRATE CREWS had no concept of true *freedom*. The captain had to help them envision what life would be like when the hold was filled with treasure, nations were at peace, and colonists welcomed them ashore. To do this, he'd use the art of storytelling.

If no enemies were in sight, the captain would assemble the crew on deck in the evening and tell a colorful tale of a legendary pirate who attained wealth and independence. He would then ask a few of the crew members to talk about what they would do with the money and freedom they sought, once it was in their possession. Rather than laughing at someone's idea, the captain would encourage others to expand on it, and to share their own goals for the future.

Over time, the captain became familiar with every man's hopes and dreams. He learned to understand the desires that motivated every person, and was able to link the fulfillment of those desires to the realization of the vision. You can, too.

Some companies spend considerable time and money to forge a corporate vision, and yet mistakenly believe they are finished when they complete the previous step (describe the ideal outcome). They hash out the perfect wording, have it printed and framed, and then place it in strategic locations for all to see. To the majority of employees, however, the vision is merely a bunch of words on the wall. Leaders have to give those words meaning and bring them life. Storytelling is an excellent tool for doing that.

A regional dairy operation (farm, processing, transport, and retail outlets) defined its ideal outcome as being the region's "first choice for high quality dairy products, while conducting business with the utmost integrity, and delivering a profit to owners." A lead herdsman recognized the need to bring this vision to life for his farm-based crew of workplace pirates.[8]

The leader explained that fulfillment of the vision started with the cows – in fact, it was impossible to achieve *without* the cows. The best cared-for cows would always produce the highest quality milk. By really caring for the cows properly, the operation would never have any integrity issues (no need to hide or cover up anything). Finally, by producing the highest quality product and doing the "right" thing every day, the company would be profitable.

The lead herdsman noted that small agri-business operations like theirs rarely outperformed corporate farms and mass producers – and when one did, it usually got immediate and very favorable attention from investors and the industry alike.

"One day," the leader explained, "people will travel from all over the world to see the special way you take care of our cows. Competitors will try to lure you away with more money to take care of their cows. Our company, instead of looking to cut jobs or hire cheaper labor, will truly appreciate you and place a great value on the important work you do. Take care of the cows, every minute, every day – and everything else will fall into place."

Most people want *something*. What they often lack is (a) a good reason to go after it, (b) a plan to get it, and/or (c) the self-confidence to believe that they will succeed. Storytelling can help them discover all three.

Adopt a Rallying Cry

YOU'VE DESCRIBED the ideal future. Your team has connected it to their personal hopes and desires through storytelling. Now, you need to create "brand recognition" for your vision.

Think about the following phrases:

"Take a bite out of crime."

"Melts in your mouth, not in your hand."

"A mind is a terrible thing to waste."

"Keeps going and going and going..."

Most people can immediately link each of those "tag lines" to a related event, organization, or product. The phrases trigger visual images, emotional responses, and tangible information.

The brotherhood of pirates did not have a universal flag. Every pirate captain and crew created a unique version of the "jolly roger" for their ship. These almost always had a black background, and included a symbol and slogan that reflected the ship's purpose and the "public image" the crew wanted to project. The embedded symbols and slogans eventually found their way onto clothing, tattoos, and weapons – which unified the crew and helped to spread their reputation and message.

That's the goal of your rallying cry. You want a short phrase that captures your team's ideal future and summarizes the challenges you'll face together to achieve that future. If you can supplement the words with a mascot or characterization (like McGruff the Crime Dog or the Energizer Bunny), that's even better.

For the dairy farm described in the previous chapter, the rallying cry became, "It's all about the cows!" ("What's it all about?" the leader would ask at the start of each day – *It's all about the cows!*" would be the rally cry response.)

In some cases the rallying cry may be less direct, and more symbolic or metaphorical in nature. Consider this example:

A struggling factory was overwhelmed with regulatory findings, product quality issues, and labor relations problems – and on the verge of having to close its doors.[9]

With a transformation-driven mission in mind, the general manager asked each department to assign one person to a troubleshooting team. Department managers generally appointed the people they could most easily afford to lose – so the team leader ended up with a group of true workplace pirates. In spite of this, the team identified a vision of "financial stability, regulatory compliance, employee pride, and product quality."

Most felt that achieving the vision would be impossible, as it required a systematic analysis of every operational process and procedure (including some that had been in place for more than 50 years) in order to uncover and correct long-hidden problems. As one team member phrased it, "We have to drain this primeval swamp and find all the crocodiles."

The next day, the team leader came to work in a khaki shirt and shorts (a la *The Crocodile Hunter*, Steve Irwin). When asked to explain his attire, he summed up the team's purpose in one sentence: "Crikey, we're draining the swamp and trapping the crocs, mate!" Just like that, a rallying cry was born.

Over the next several weeks, the team held a series of "crocodile hunts" which were basically interviews and investigations to analyze key processes and identify problems. Team members brought toy crocodiles to work (rubber and stuffed animal versions) to represent each newly discovered problem or issue that arose – the bigger the perceived problem, the larger the toy crocodile that was chosen to represent it.

As the project evolved, team members began a practice of placing a toy croc on the desk of the person responsible for the next action item – along with a sticky note (usually in the croc's teeth) reminding the person of what needed to be done to solve the problem and move the action forward.

When a solution was implemented (and its success verified), a small celebration was held and the toy crocodile representing the problem was placed on the edge of the decorative fountain in the atrium of the administration building (where every employee entered and exited the plant). This became a visible way for team members, employees, managers, other stakeholders to observe the progress being made.

In spite of the commitment and creativity displayed by the team, not everyone in the organization supported their efforts. Progress reached a standstill with 37 critical action items still pending. The team leader asked the general manager to join him on a different kind of crocodile hunt – one where they physically tracked down the missing toys to see where each action item had stalled.

Remarkably, 35 of the 37 missing crocodiles were found piled in the corners of two middle manager's offices. The bottlenecks to progress (and as it turned out, the root cause of many of the company's difficulties) were suddenly apparent. The general manager appointed himself "game warden" and declared that anyone who delayed an action item (kept a crocodile in his or her office) would be considered a "poacher." Progress resumed.

This "drain the swamp" rallying cry captured a vision of organizational transformation. Even better, it inspired a team that was initially apathetic (or even hostile) to actually have *fun* dealing with the messy and difficult business of finding and implementing the process improvements that were needed to get a struggling operation back on track.

The rallying cry and crocodile characterization also clarified the vision for the rest of the workforce in general, and ultimately helped the team overcome two areas of resentful resistance.

Of course, not every vision affects the entire organization, and not every rallying cry "catches fire" and spreads the way this one did. In such cases, it is easy for those outside your group of followers to intentionally or inadvertently get in your way because they are simply unaware of your intent to do something good. That's where the final step in formulating a vision comes in – spreading the word.

Spread the Word

ONCE YOU HAVE A CLEAR DESCRIPTION of the ideal future, accompanied by stories and perhaps a rallying cry that your followers have embraced, you must spread the word. This means communicating the vision to anyone who may eventually have a stake in the outcome, or in a process for reaching that outcome.

Senior managers often view these stakeholders as a captive audience – "we talk, they listen." Indeed, there is plenty of talking, but people rarely listen and get the message. Supervisors and lower tier managers, lacking a captive audience, sometimes fail to talk at all. Again, no one gets the message.

A leader at any level has to promote the vision in a way that cuts through the masses of information that people receive daily. You have to grab their attention. Once you have their attention, you have to "sell" them in order to win their support or cooperation – just as you would any other customer. That's why these final steps in formulating a vision are handled like a promotional effort rather than a corporate edict.

A "grassroots" approach will be more effective than "mass marketing." Instead of making a big presentation or sending a broadcast memo, schedule small meetings with specific groups and communicate the vision in a way that demonstrates its relevance to that group. Be sure to answer the questions, "*So what? Why should I care?*" and "*What's in it for me?*"

Don't just *announce* the vision. Pirate captains talked about it daily, and you can, too. Use creative formats to deliver the message continually. Notes, signs, bulletin boards, banner ads, webcasts, and other technologies can keep the information flowing.

Casual conversations also provide a daily opportunity to spread the word. Create an "elevator speech" (30 seconds or less in length) that encapsulates what the vision is about and why it is important. Whenever you are with other people – in the parking lot, break room, or lunch line – talk about the treasure that you and your employees are seeking.

If you do find yourself in a position to speak to a captive audience, don't rely on descriptive words alone to spread the word. Share the symbols, pictures, and stories you developed in the previous steps.

Remember, too, that for a vision to be credible there has to be some real "steak" with the sizzle. You can't just *talk* about the vision. All of your daily decisions and actions have to reflect your personal commitment to *achieving* it. After all, this is not a fanciful discussion about a dream vacation you'll never take. This is a real destination and the ship is sailing now! You want to describe the future in such rich detail that the people around you can hardly wait to sign aboard and get underway.

You have a worthy treasure and a pirate crew that is eager to pursue it. Will they maintain their enthusiasm once you set sail, or become discouraged when the first storm cloud appears? Will they stick with you for the long haul, or "jump ship" to another organization? Will they assume the role of "passengers" (merely along for the ride), or will they truly become active participants, committed to doing the work it takes to succeed? Your understanding of *motivation* will help provide the answer...

Part IV.
"That's the Spirit!"

Motivation

Solve the Mystery of Motivation

IT'S A SOMEWHAT GRAPHIC LINE, usually attributed to John Wayne: "If you've got them by the balls, their hearts and minds will follow." Perhaps – but only for as long as you can hold on.

Most leaders in the 1700s had the resources to dominate their followers and the power to manipulate them. Pirate captains were no exception. In fact, several of the more infamous captains nurtured a climate of intense fear among their crew members, and treated their men with unbelievable cruelty. Their careers were generally measured in months.

The pirate captains who were effective over a long period recognized that crew members gave their best effort to complete assigned tasks not when they were afraid of punishment (or were allowed to do as they pleased), but rather when they were fully committed – heart, mind, and spirit – to achieving a shared goal. Today's workplace pirates – and in fact, most employees – are no different.

How do effective leaders get this type of total commitment from their followers? They truly understand people. And (very important) even if you don't consider yourself to be much of a "people person," and perhaps have struggled with the human relations aspect of working together with others over the years, this is still a skill set you can master.

The first key to understanding people is to recognize that all people are naturally motivated. You may have heard someone say, "He's just not motivated." Yet even the person who does absolutely nothing is motivated – to do absolutely nothing.

The second key is to realize that people are motivated for *their* reasons, not yours. Outside of a police state, it may be possible to force another adult do something that he or she really doesn't want to do – but you will need an unlimited supply of energy, patience, and implements of torture.

The only reliable way to get anybody to do anything with full commitment is to influence the person to *want* to do it.

How do you get your followers to want to bring their hearts, minds, and spirit to work each day? Ah, that's the mystery of motivation. The greatest pirate captains solved the mystery, and soon, you will know all of their secrets – and more!

Satisfy Their Basic Needs

THE PROCESS of understanding your people (whether they are workplace pirates or peak performers) begins with understanding their needs.

A "need" is something that is physically, mentally, or emotionally required for human health and well-being. Of course, every living person shares a common set of basic needs.[10]

Our most fundamental needs are for air, water, food, sleep, and shelter. We also need to feel (and be) safe from physical harm. These are *practical* needs. When all of our practical needs are being satisfied, a second level emerges – the need for acceptance and belonging, and the need for love and affection. These are *social* needs. When all of our practical needs and social needs are being met, a third level arises – the need for mastery, contribution, and self-actualization (i.e., to be all we can be). These are *ego* needs.

As human beings, we instinctively strive to fulfill our lowest level of unsatisfied needs. For example, if we don't have enough to eat or don't feel safe, we will work to address those needs (and ignore our higher level social and ego needs). Only when our practical needs are being met do we strive to find our place within a group. And only when we have a sense of acceptance and belonging (the feeling that we are in the "right" place) do we truly focus on mastering a skill, making a contribution, and pursuing a dream.

As already described, conditions for seafaring men during the Golden Age of Piracy were brutally primitive. A common sailor on a royal ship-of-the-line struggled just to have his practical needs fulfilled, and to survive for another day.

Pirate captains recognized (years before most naval commanders) that providing a crew with adequate food and water, better "working conditions," and a relative degree of safety and security had two advantages.

First, it reduced turnover. If the crew's practical needs were being met, they were less likely to betray the captain, jump ship, or otherwise risk getting into situation where those needs might not be met. Lower turnover meant a fully staffed, well-trained, and highly efficient crew.

Second, the fulfillment of practical needs allowed the next level (social needs) to emerge. As the name suggests, the *Order of the Brethren of the Coast* was a true brotherhood in which many disconnected and disenfranchised individuals found a new family. Pirate captains capitalized on this to build teamwork and *esprit de corps*, which further enhanced retention and operational effectiveness.

Early studies on human motivation collectively referred to the practical and social needs described above as *hygiene factors*. Over the years, it became clear that employees must have safe working conditions, plus the compensation and benefits necessary to meet their basic practical needs. Even without a legal obligation to do this, it makes sense. After all, employees can't focus their full capabilities on a job task until they find their "place" within the group. And they can't do that if their prevailing concern is personal safety, money to feed their families, or whether or not they'll still have a job tomorrow.[11]

Clearly, things are much improved in today's workplaces. Yet modern studies have confirmed what many pirate captains knew long ago: The presence of a hygiene factor is not a motivator, but the absence of a hygiene factor is most definitely a "de-motivator."

In other words, if employees already feel that a workplace is generally safe and that they are adequately compensated, there's nothing wrong with striving to make them feel safer and pay them even more – but you should not expect it to cause their performance or output to increase. On the other hand, if employees begin to feel that a workplace is unsafe or that compensation is grossly inadequate, *those* conditions can cause performance or output to *decline*.

Some employers are not quite able to grasp that concept. If your firm has job vacancies and is not attracting an adequate number of qualified applicants, it's a safe bet that you are not offering enough in terms of compensation or working conditions. How much is "enough?" Whatever it takes to draw the types and numbers of candidates you need, and to maintain a minimum level of output.

If you're filling your job vacancies easily, but you regularly lose qualified people, the problem might still be with compensation or working conditions. One example is wages that don't keep pace with the cost of living. If eight dollars an hour was "enough" when a person was hired, paying the person $8.25 would not have motivated him to work harder. Yet, if the cost of living has increased by three percent and you are still paying eight dollars, not getting that extra twenty-five cents can be a major de-motivator.

Many organizations offer an annual "merit" increase tied to a performance appraisal or other type of scoring form. In most cases, this policy does nothing more than reinforce resentment and negativity.

Employees should receive a periodic pay raise to keep pace with the cost of living. They should never expect a *scheduled* increase for anything else. In most cases, additional compensation should only come with (a) demonstration of greater competence, (b) acceptance of more responsibility, or (c) a direct contribution to the achievement of the organization's mission or vision. (Each of these is indicative of an employee working to fulfill ego needs – and to be all that he or she can be.)

If you are certain that your compensation system is in order, yet you keep losing qualified people, the problem is most likely related to other first-tier or second-tier needs – e.g., safety and health, work schedules, job security, or the feeling (expressed by many departing employees) of simply not "fitting in" (the cause of which is very often a single unsatisfactory manager or team member).

Problems with these hygiene factors are easy to identify. They are also comparatively inexpensive to correct in all but a few geographic locations, and for all but a few unique or highly dangerous occupations. These factors must be attended to.

Don't assume that because you are "only" a supervisor or mid-level manager that these problems are not *your* problems to solve. They are, and it's part of your role as a leader (building trust up and down the organization) to initiate the action necessary.

Make it your personal mission to have a workplace climate that fulfills the employment-related practical and social needs of every employee. And then, go after their *full* commitment!

Gain Their Commitment

COMMITMENT IS the willingness and confidence to put one's very best effort into the completion of an assigned work task.

When practical and social needs are being met, people strive to fulfill their ego needs. How they choose to do that, however, is totally up to them (remember, people are motivated for *their* reasons, not yours).

So (you might be asking), what's the point of satisfying their basic needs if employees are ultimately going to do whatever they want anyway? It's a fair question, since companies with above-average compensation packages and exceptional work climates have workplace pirates just like everyone else.

The answer is that until employees have their basic needs met, they are not "leadable." When their practical or social needs are at risk, people tend to feel attacked or victimized, and often react irrationally. They are unable to commit to anything beyond that lower-level need, and you are stuck trying to "manage" the resulting behavior.

Consider this example: When a pirate captain spotted a potential prize on the horizon, a lot of activity ensued to prepare the ship for battle. Every crew member had a specific job to do. If a crew member was being denied food and water, however, or if he felt disliked and mistreated by his shipmates, then the situation provided an irresistible opportunity to perform his task in a way that sabotaged the operation. On the other hand, if a crew member's basic needs were being met, the same situation prompted a decision: He could give his very best, simply "go through the motions," or even "blow off" the assignment altogether.

Once the basic needs are satisfied, energy is no longer focused on the de-motivating elements of the employment relationship. Instead of having their behavior driven by resentment, motivated people are in the position to *choose* how they act. (By the way, if you lead volunteers, rather than employees, you may assume that their basic needs are being met – and that volunteer work is part of their personal strategy for mastering a skill, making a contribution, or otherwise fulfilling their ego needs.)

On a pirate ship, when everyone made the choice to give his very best (full commitment), the mission was successful. When most gave their best and a few didn't (partial commitment), the mission was often less successful, and had a higher cost. If too many tasks were left undone or done poorly (lack of commitment), the mission failed – sometimes with extreme consequences. The same is true in your workplace.

Look at it this way: Pay and benefits get people to show up for work. Your "code" ensures that they show up on time and sober. Beyond that, how willing they are to perform the task at hand, and how much effort they put into it, is a decision they actually make themselves from minute to minute.

To gain full commitment, a leader must be able to influence that critical decision. That means understanding how and why people make the conscience choices they make in any given situation.

People decide with their hearts, minds, and spirits. Full commitment requires you to win all three.

Win Their Hearts

THE "HEART" is the emotional component of any decision. To choose a specific course of action and "put their hearts into it," people have to emotionally "buy in" to whatever you've asked them to do. What causes this? Two factors – desire and trust.

To perform a task "whole heartedly," the person must have a *desire* for something associated with the completion of that task (or be so discontented with the current situation that anything different – any change at all – would be a change for the better).

So what about money? People want that, right? For people working on commissions or bonuses, the desire for money might be a factor in winning their hearts (salespeople who haven't met their quotas do seem more motivated at the end of the month). For almost anyone else, however, money is a basic need – not a true motivator. The fact that you pay people to do a job doesn't mean that they will give it their best effort. There has to be something else they want.

So what else do people want? They want to be "winners," for one. Humans are born with the desire to learn, improve, and excel. (If you don't believe it, think of all the questions that young children ask in order to satisfy that learning instinct.) As living creatures, we are natural students, curious explorers, and born achievers! Over time, the forces of resentment and negativity can stifle those desires and inject a feeling of apathy or hopelessness. Yet, the condition is reversible in most cases.

The previous section of this book focused on formulating a vision, gaining a preliminary insight into people's hopes and dreams, and connecting the realization of one to the other. In a healthy, achievement-oriented culture, people want to be part of a winning team. Giving people a chance to get something they all want is the first factor in winning their hearts.

Trust is the second factor. No matter how much people want something, if they don't trust you, they simply cannot "buy in" to what you're asking them to do. To commit to an action, emotionally, they have to believe that you are being honest with them, that you know what you're talking about, and that what you are asking them to do is in their best interests.

An earlier chapter of this book was dedicated to building trust and credibility. If your integrity is still a little shaky, keep working at it – trust takes time. Invest all the time it takes, however, because truly winning their hearts means earning their trust.

Win Their Minds

THE "MIND" is the intellectual component of any decision. To choose a specific course of action and "set their minds to it," people have to *intellectually* "buy in" to whatever you ask them to do.

What creates this buy-in? Two factors – knowledge and confidence.

To "mentally" commit to a task, the person has to know (a) *what* to do, (b) *how* to do it, (c) the *outcome* that is expected, and (d) *why* the outcome matters. The person also has to believe that the outcome is *feasible*, and have the *confidence* that he or she can complete the task successfully (i.e., produce the desired outcome).

To ready his ship for battle, a pirate captain would issue the command, "Clear the decks!" The order meant that any item on any deck that was not needed to engage in combat was to be securely stowed.

Each man was responsible for putting away the items in a specific area. To complete the task, a man had to first know exactly *what* he was supposed to do.

Second, he had to know precisely *how* to do it. Navigational instruments had to be handled carefully. Barrels containing food, water, and supplies had to be moved in a certain manner to very specific locations and secured with the correct ropes and knots.

Third, a crewman had to know what *outcome* was expected. No matter how violently the ship pitched or rolled, items could not spill out of drawers, lockers, or bins. Everything had to remain secure.

Fourth, he had to know *why* that outcome mattered. Between the ocean's waves and the ship's maneuvers during battle, anything not properly secured could break free. Small items loose on a deck could cause a crew member to trip or slip. A large item that came loose could block a passageway, crush a sailor, or seriously damage the ship itself.

Finally, to put his best effort into performing an assigned task, a man had to believe that it was *possible* to do the job, and have the *confidence* that he could do it properly (for example, moving a heavy barrel safely and tying the appropriate knots).

It all seems fairly straightforward, doesn't it? And yet, in a modern workplace, things so often go wrong here.

If an employee is absent, who covers his task? If a new member joins your crew, do *you* assign all the work, or do other crew members rush to "delegate" parts of their jobs? Who teaches people how to perform new tasks? Are they being taught properly, or have shortcuts been introduced and key steps omitted?

Do people know how to "check" their work? Are errors identified and corrected before significant problems occur? Do people recognize the importance and relevance of each task, or do they assume that some things are just "busywork?"

Are people confident in their skills, or do they hesitate to complete urgent tasks (or constantly need help from others)? Or at the opposite extreme, are some workers overconfident, resulting in distractions or careless mistakes?

If your employees lack the knowledge or confidence to intellectually commit to a task, you will have to develop it (*and guidance on this aspect of leadership is provided in Part VI*). For now, however, back to the topic of motivation...

Win Their Spirits

THE HUMAN SPIRIT is the esoteric component of any decision. It's the "wild card." It can make the most impossible dream a shining reality – or turn the most ridiculously simple "to-do" item into an unholy disaster.

More often than not, it is this third component of total commitment that leaders fail to capture. Any decent organization can make adjustments to meet its employees' basic needs. Any manager can eventually put the pieces in place to win the hearts and minds of followers. To win their spirits, however – and truly gain their full commitment to an assigned task – a higher level of leadership proficiency is required. The great pirate captains attained it, and soon, so will you.

"Spirit," as defined here, is simply a person's excitement or enthusiasm regarding a task. When you see people who love their work, that spirit is obvious and their commitment is absolute.

Granted, the functions that you supervise or manage may involve a lot of work that's "hard to love." So how are you supposed to get people excited about it?

First, recall the fish market example from earlier in the book, and the fact that having an inspirational vision of the future really helps. Second, understand that it is not the task itself that generates excitement, enthusiasm, or passion. It is the performance of the task that either ignites the spirit – or breaks it.

There is nothing mystical here. The capacity for a person to feel excited or "jazzed" about doing something (or to absolutely dread it) is comprised of four distinct behaviors or "spirit factors" – dominance, involvement, stability, and compliance. Relative to performing a specific task:

- *Dominance* is the extent to which the person wants (and is allowed) to be in control, have autonomy, and take risks to achieve results.

- *Involvement* is the extent to which the person wants (and is allowed) to meet, influence, and interact with other people to achieve results.

- *Stability* is the extent to which the person wants (and is allowed) to have a predictable routine, follow a proven process, and fill an established role as part of a larger group to achieve results.

- *Compliance* is the extent to which the person wants (and is allowed) to analyze the facts and data, and pursue the most logical, accurate, and "correct" course of action to achieve results.

Almost every job or occupation requires (and provides) each of the four behaviors or spirit factors to some degree – but for any *one* task associated with a *specific* job, a single factor is usually essential to success.

Likewise, every human being seeks at least some measure of all four factors. In a particular work setting, however, there is usually one specific factor that matters *more* to the individual than the other three. That is the element in which the person literally thrives – thereby enlivening his or her spirit.

To better understand this concept, consider the following example. The job of taking a longboat ashore alone to "requisition" supplies from an enemy camp is best suited to someone who thrives on dominance (control, autonomy, risk), while the job of ship's cook is best suited to someone who thrives on stability (predictable routines, a proven process, an established role within a larger group). In each case, the person who is a great fit for one job would probably be a terrible fit for the other.

Consider the major job tasks that are normally associated with the following occupations:

- Test Pilot -   - Police Officer -   - Brain Surgeon -
- Sales Clerk -   - Advertising/Marketing Specialist -
- Carpenter -   - Teacher -   - Assembly Line Worker -
- Forensic Scientist -   - Financial Analyst -

Each job requires some measure of dominance, involvement, stability, and compliance. Yet for each key task associated with those jobs, one of those four elements is practically *mandatory* and crucial to success. For example, success as a test pilot requires extensive risk-taking (dominance). Success as an assembly line worker requires one to repeat a proven and predictable routine (stability).

To win the spirit of a particular follower, the leader tries to satisfy the strongest of the four preferences in that individual – either by assigning a task for which that same factor is most essential, or by defining the task in a way that allows the person to make the most of that behavior during task completion.

To keep from "breaking" someone's spirit (and losing his or her commitment), a leader should try to avoid making assignments where an employee's strongest preference and the essential behavior demanded by the task are a mismatch.

Of course, it is not always possible to make a perfect match, or to avoid a mismatch. Sometimes, you have to assign people to jobs that are outside of their comfort zones in order to expand their skills and capabilities – and sometimes, there is simply no one else available to perform the task.

Although every task we are paying someone to perform is important, some are more critical than others to the accomplishment of your mission. For mission-critical tasks, identify which of the four factors is most essential to success, and then try to make good matches when assigning those tasks to employees.

When you have no choice but to assign a task that you know is a mismatch, discuss it with the employee. Acknowledge your awareness that some elements of the assignment are less-than-ideal for that person. If possible, redefine the task to allow the person to apply his or her strengths, and to potentially spark some enthusiasm.

At worst, employees will be highly committed (heart, mind, and spirit) to the most critical tasks, and at least marginally committed to the tasks of lesser importance. That's probably an improvement over the way things have been up to now – especially with your workplace pirates.

Of course, to do this you'll need a method for "reading" people and recognizing which of the four factors – dominance, involvement, stability, or compliance – is most likely to help you win each person's spirit.

Coming right up...

Understand Their Behaviors

WHEN A PERSON'S COMMITMENT is strongly affected by one of the four "spirit factors" (dominance, involvement, stability, or compliance), the behavior that he or she exhibits is usually consistent with that same factor. Consequently, to appreciate, motivate, and communicate with people, it is necessary to understand the behavior they exhibit.

Behavior is the way people act in any given situation. Behavior is *not* the same as personality. Every human being has a unique personality. Each person is truly one-of-a-kind – so the goal is not to categorize or "pigeonhole" your individual followers. This is not about *who* people *are* (personality); it's about *what* people *do* (behavior).

Behavior is external and *observable*. You can't see an employee's personality, but you can see how he or she acts in a wide variety of situations. And if you think about it, in any given situation there are only a limited number of different ways you can behave.

With that in mind, behavior is *situational*. An employee is the same unique person at work, at home, or out with friends – yet that person may *behave* very differently depending on where he is and who he is with (as the saying goes, "There's often a thin line between Saturday night and Sunday morning!").

Behavior is *predictable*. You have probably told someone, "I just *knew* you were going to do that." All people have *patterns* of behavior that they rely upon to meet their needs.

Assuming that a person is not suffering from a mental illness or disability – or operating under the influence of a behavior-altering substance – you can learn to anticipate what he or she will say and do in a variety of situations.

Finally, behavior is *dynamic*. While it can be predicted, every human being has the power to choose a different behavior at any time. When you understand your own behavior, it gives you the power to make adjustments – to consciously act, rather than react. When you understand the reasons behind other people's behaviors, it gives you the power to influence those behaviors – and to improve your relationships (and results) with other people.

Pace and Focus

The two most recognizable dimensions of human behavior (characteristics you can easily see in your employees) are *pace* and *focus*.

Every person has a *pace* at which he or she is comfortable going through life. Some people are relatively fast-paced (they seem to be in more of a hurry, speak rapidly, and make quick decisions). Some people are relatively slow-paced (they are more "laid-back," speak more slowly, and are more deliberate in their decisions-making). One pace is not better than another. They're just different.

You can watch the way any person performs almost any job, and within a minute or so, determine that person's preferred pace. In general, faster-paced people are perceived as being more impatient, spontaneous, and verbally expressive. Slower-paced people are seen as more patient, structured in their approach to work tasks, and more reserved in their communication style.

Faster-paced people tend to speak conceptually ("big picture") and like a lot of variety on the job. Slower-paced people are generally more detail-oriented and tend to prefer a more stable and predictable work setting.

Faster-paced people are driven to reshape the environment around them. Slower-paced people are more likely to look for ways they can work effectively within the existing environment.

The second major dimension of human behavior, besides pace, is *focus*. In almost every situation, a person tends to focus more on either building relationships or completing tasks. Relationship-focused people are able complete tasks by connecting with others. Task-focused people are able to create relationships by getting things done. Again, one behavior is not better than the other. They're just different focuses, or approaches, to work and life.

It is important to emphasize that relationship-focused people really do care about the tasks they perform – they just prefer to accomplish those tasks by creating harmony and leveraging the rapport they have with others. It's equally important to note that task-focused people really do care about their relationships – but they often prefer to develop and nurture those relationships by establishing reliable processes and producing measurable results.

As with the *pace* dimension, you can watch a person in a given setting and determine if his or her *focus* leans more toward tasks or relationships.

Relationship-focused people are typically more intuitive and sociable, while task-focused people often come across as being more logical and distant. Relationship-focused people can be somewhat "flexible" when dealing with numbers and time, where task-focused people are usually more precise and accurate.

Finally, relationship-focused people tend to see the rest of the world as supportive – that given the opportunity, other people would help them. (Extremely relationship-focused people are often considered "gullible.") Task-focused people tend to see the rest of the world in a more skeptical way – that given the opportunity, other people might try to take advantage of them. (Extremely task-focused people are often considered to be overly suspicious of others.)

Remember that behavior is situational. A person may be faster paced and task-focused in one setting, yet slower paced and relationship-focused in another.

Simply by observing the pace and focus of your employees, you can "read" their behavior preference (identify their strongest "spirit factor") in that setting. People who are faster paced and task-focused tend to have a Dominance ("D") spirit. People who are faster paced and relationship-focused tend to have an Involvement ("I") spirit. People who are slower paced and relationship-focused tend to have a Stability ("S") spirit. People who are slower paced and task-focused tend to have a Compliance ("C") spirit.[12]

The FOUR BEHAVIOR or "SPIRIT" TYPES

FASTER PACED

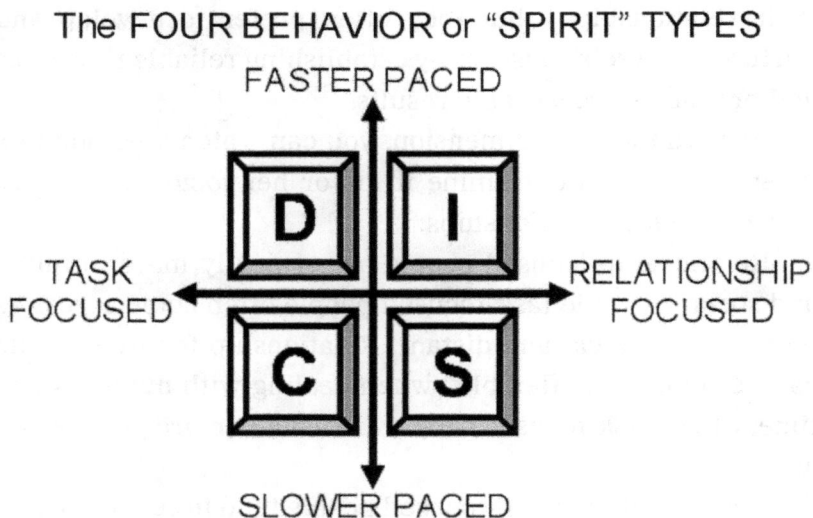

SLOWER PACED

Understanding the D-Spirit

The goal of a person with a Dominance preference (or D-spirit) is to gain control over a situation in order to produce results quickly. Because they see themselves as capable of reshaping their environment, and because they initially perceive every environment to be somewhat hostile, these employees seek *control* to get the outcome they want (and to keep others from taking advantage of them).

D-spirits have a *bias for action* and like to make things happen. They don't mind directing others and they are comfortable with aggression.

D-spirits like some *variety* on the job. Performing a repetitive task day after day is not for them. They also want *autonomy* (no one looking over their shoulders). They are drawn to tasks that involve unique challenges, require rapid action and decisions, and allow a person to work independently.

D-spirits prefer *direct* styles of communication (bottom line, get to the point). To them, the only real purpose of conversation is to get things done. They also tend to prefer work situations that offer opportunities for high-impact achievements and formal advancement.

As part of a group, D-spirits are decisive, focused, and persistent. With these strengths come certain limitations – specifically, they can seem very impatient, insensitive to the feelings of others, and so wrapped up in the task at hand that they become too busy for anything or anyone else.

Understanding the I-Spirit

The goal of a person with an involvement preference (or I-spirit) is to connect with other people. I-spirits are "people people." They tend to initiate contact with others, and create new relationships quickly. Because they see themselves as capable of reshaping their environment, and because they initially perceive that most environments are supportive of them, these employees look for ways to entertain, persuade, or *influence* others in order to gain support and produce the desired outcome.

I-spirits want to look good and make a *positive impression* on others. They enjoy casual conversation. They like to express their opinions, and they try to be *active participants* in any situation.

I-spirits prefer work settings that are lively and fun. They enjoy working in groups, and like to meet new people. They need opportunities to *verbalize*. They struggle with tasks that involve working alone or analyzing details. They are drawn to tasks that rely on interaction skills, and that offer some form of public recognition for a job well-done.

As part of a group, I-spirits can be enthusiastic, inspiring, and fun. One of their limitations is that they can appear superficial and even fickle at times. Also, they are typically more disorganized than their slower paced and task-focused counterparts. Finally, they sometimes lack follow-through – they can get so excited about the *next* big thing that they often neglect to finish the *last* big thing.

Understanding the S-Spirit

The goal of a person with a Stability preference (or S-spirit) is exactly that – stability. They seek to create a comfortable, secure routine – and then maintain the status quo. They are not as comfortable with ambiguity, direct styles of communication, and potential conflict as their faster paced counterparts, yet they do see the world as a generally supportive place – so they seek situations where they can join in, find their place, and feel a strong sense of "belonging."

S-spirits strive to build ever-closer relationships with the people they know. They need to *emotionally connect* with others and "feel the love." To them, coworkers are like a second family.

S-spirits prefer work tasks involving established processes and shared responsibilities. They often develop a *specialized skill*, and then apply that skill to make a contribution. Their goals are usually modest – to "do what needs to be done" (and they expect others to do the same). They are drawn to tasks where public recognition is focused on the group at-large, rather than one individual (but they do appreciate a sincere acknowledgement of their contributions – in private).

As part of a group, S-spirits are natural team players – reliable, patient, loyal, and empathetic. Because they seek stability, one of their limitations is that they can be resistant to change and unwilling to take risks. Because of their slower pace and desire to avoid conflict, their communication style can be too indirect at times, and they can be indecisive in the face of a confrontation or crisis. In these circumstances, others may see them as "wishy-washy."

Understanding the C-Spirit

The goal of a person with a Compliance preference (or C-spirit) is to meet his or her own standards of what is "right." They are driven to conform to their environment rather than reshape it, yet they perceive the environment to be a somewhat arbitrary and hostile – so their goal is to set and meet a *high set of standards*, so no matter what else happens, they can feel assured that they are doing what is right.

C-spirits think *analytically*, apply systematic approaches, and examine details. They are normally tactful in their communications with others, and show respect for any established lines of authority.

C-spirits are drawn to work tasks where the emphasis is on quality, accuracy, and *attention to detail*. They prefer a highly functional or business-like atmosphere, where procedures are followed and performance is measured. If a job is worth doing at all, they expect there to be enough time to do it right. They tend to pursue careers that use proficiency testing and qualification processes to acknowledge expertise.

As part of a group, C-spirits are usually thorough, accurate, and diplomatic. Because they seek compliance to a high standard, one of their limitations is that they can seem stubborn and inflexible. Also, they may spend more time perfecting something than it is really worth in the overall scheme of things. They prefer written forms of communication, and sometimes fail to see the value of casual conversation. This, combined with an intense drive to be "right," can give the impression that a C-spirit thinks he or she is just slightly superior to everyone else.

Summary

Recognizing the key "spirit factor" that drives a person's behavior allows you to solve the mystery of motivation – why people do the things they do. With that knowledge, you are now ready to communicate, manage performance, and build teamwork in a way that will bring out the very best your workplace pirates (and all employees) have to offer.

Part V.
"Now Hear This"

Communication

Communicate Skillfully

IN THE GOLDEN AGE OF PIRACY, a captain needed four distinct sets of skills. *Technical* skills were necessary to help him navigate and maintain the ship. *Administrative* skills were necessary to help him manage the resources on board. *Conceptual* skills were necessary to help him recognize the potential consequences of a decision. *Communication* skills were necessary for – well, everything.

The same is true of leaders in a modern organization. They need technical, administrative, and conceptual skills that relate to their specific industries, the types of jobs they manage, the policies and procedures of their employers, and the levels of responsibility they hold.

A production supervisor, for example, needs a higher degree of technical skills pertaining to product assembly than the company president. The company president, on the other hand, needs a higher degree of conceptual skills pertaining to stockholder reports. Both need administrative skills (though not the *same* administrative skills) and both need communication skills.

All leaders, regardless of their actual job titles, need a well-rounded set of communication skills. A single technical mistake, administrative blunder, or conceptual misjudgment on the part of a manager rarely "sinks the ship." However, if there is a "failure to communicate" by just one person in a key leadership role, the consequences can be extremely serious.

Consider any significant event, in any era, in any setting. If you change what was communicated, when it was communicated, how it was communicated, and by whom – you change history. On a battleground or in a workplace, skillful communication can turn potential losses into huge victories. Likewise, miscommunication can turn a sure win into a stunning defeat.

Are you a skillful communicator? If you're like most people, you've spent every day of your life interacting with others. You've completed at least twelve years of formal education, a significant portion of which was focused on speaking and writing skills. Even so, the role of a leader presents a unique set of communication challenges – and may therefore demand certain proficiencies that you have not yet developed.

In addition, everyone has a communication "style," and that style includes certain habits. Your style and habits usually help you get what you want. If you're honest, however, there are times when just the opposite occurs – when your style "gets in the way" and actually *keeps* you from achieving a desired result.

When you communicate as a leader, you represent more people and cover a far broader range of topics than you ever do as an individual. This makes good communication even more difficult – and the consequences of miscommunication more severe.

Fortunately, communication is a skill. And while it's a difficult skill to master (there are about a half-million books on the subject), there are a few essential tricks and techniques that any leader at any level can learn quickly and apply easily in order to communicate with greater skill and confidence.

The next several chapters will outline the key "how to" steps for leadership communication.

Adjust Your Pace and Focus

IN THE PREVIOUS SECTION (*Part IV*) of this book, you were introduced to four "spirit factors" (Dominance, Involvement, Stability, and Compliance). As you recall, a person's spirit is largely driven by two dimensions of behavior, pace and focus. Each person has a preferred pace for going through life (some faster, some slower), and each person has a tendency to focus on either task completion or relationship building to meet his or her needs in a given situation.

People who prefer a faster pace and a task focus are considered dominance-driven or "D-spirits." People who prefer a faster pace and a relationship focus are considered involvement-driven or "I-spirits." People who prefer a slower pace and a relationship focus are considered stability-driven or "S-spirits." People who prefer a slower pace and a task focus are considered compliance-driven or "C-spirits."

What does all this have to do with effective communication? Quite a bit, actually. The manner in which a person communicates is influenced by his or her pace and focus preferences. Consequently, even though two people share a common goal, they may communicate about that goal in very different ways.

In the television series *Home Improvement*, Tim "the Tool Man" Taylor was portrayed as a D-spirit, while his assistant Al Borland was an S-spirit. When approaching new projects together, Tim (being faster paced) wanted to jump right in and get results quickly. Al (being slower paced) wanted to discuss the plan first, and then follow a proven process to ensure safety and to produce a high quality, predictable result.

Tim (being task-focused) enjoyed talking about *things* (cars and tools, for instance). He obviously cared about the people in his life, yet he was not comfortable discussing those feelings. Al (being relationship-focused) considered it perfectly normal to openly share how he felt about the important people in his life, and to confirm how they felt about him. He was often frustrated or hurt by Tim's apparent lack of sensitivity, and Tim was genuinely confused by Al's reactions.

Each episode depicted, with great humor, the misunderstandings and conflicts that occur when two people interact at a different pace, and with a different focus. In a real workplace, however, there is usually nothing funny about it.

How do you discuss a detailed safety checklist with your "Tim the Tool Man" employee? How do you convince an "Al Borland" coworker to sign off on a new initiative that needs to be implemented quickly?

The secret is to adjust the pace of your communication to match the comfort level of the other party, and shift the focus of your message to mirror the other party's emphasis on either tasks or relationships. Remember, people are motivated for *their* reasons, not yours. So communicating effectively means interacting with the pace and focus the *other* person prefers, not the pace and focus that *you'd* prefer.

Changing Your Habits

The first step in adjusting your pace and focus is to recognize your own style or "spirit" – and then modify any habits or behaviors that could undermine your ability to interact effectively as a leader.

If you're a D-spirit (faster paced, task-focused):

Recognize that your style of communication often has a "do it, and do it now!" tone. You are probably seen by others as straight-forward, action-oriented, and good under pressure – but also blunt, controlling, and a poor listener.

Be more patient when communicating with other people. Tone down your directness. Ask more questions to learn what others think. Smile, and encourage conversation by listening more actively. Face the speaker and give the person your undivided attention. Paraphrase by putting what they say into your own words, and empathize by labeling the emotion they feel ("how-to" guidance on each of these verbal skills is presented in detail in subsequent chapters). In general, slow down the pace of your communication and pay more attention to the relationship-building aspects of it.

If you're an I-spirit (faster paced, relationship-focused):

Recognize that your style of communication often has a "can do... whatever it is" tone. You are probably seen by others as enthusiastic, flexible, and poised – but may also be seen as disorganized, superficial, and perhaps more interested in looking good than in getting results.

Work to better organize your thoughts before you share them with others. Offer more facts – fewer opinions and "gut" feelings. Listen more attentively to details in meetings and conversations. Take time to discover and present key supporting data, and provide others with the more detailed information they need about events or situations. Be specific when praising, disagreeing, or empathizing with others. In general, slow down the pace of your communication, and focus more on the task-related details.

If you're an S-spirit (slower paced, relationship-focused):

Recognize that your style of communication often has a "leave things as they are" tone. You are probably seen by others as sincere, a good team player, and an excellent listener – but also too submissive, afraid of risk, and slow to act on difficult issues.

Learn to cope with change more easily, and look for opportunities to initiate action or accept risks that will increase your security and stability in the long run. Be assertive when interacting with others. Be honest and direct when communicating your thoughts or expressing your feelings. Don't allow the burden of everyone else's problems and concerns to overwhelm or sway you – be empathetic, yet firm. In general, pick up the pace of your communications, and become more action-biased.

If you're a C-spirit (slower paced, task-focused):

Recognize that your communication style often has a "You know I'm always right" tone. You are probably seen by others as highly proficient, detailed, accurate, and objective – but also overly cautious, inflexible, and possibly a bit arrogant or aloof.

Be more tolerant and accepting of other people and their approaches to problems. Encourage and support their creativity and intuition. Be sure you are looking at the "big picture" from a variety of possible perspectives – not just your assessment of what's "right." Build your conversational skills. As much as you may dislike doing it, practice "small talk" by participating in more casual interactions and providing more information about yourself. In general, speed up the pace of your actions and decisions, and focus more on relationship-building in daily conversations.

Adapting to Others

The second step in adjusting your pace and focus is to recognize and overcome the behavior-based communication habits and barriers of *other* people. Books and seminars often refer to individuals who possess such habits as "difficult." In reality, they are merely exhibiting an extreme pace and/or focus.

Interacting with an extreme D-spirit
(unusually fast-paced and task-focused):

Speed up your own pace, and stay focused on bottom-line results. Stick to business and minimize small talk. Be specific about what is needed and who will do it. Get to the point immediately – don't ramble. Expect them to argue or object, and give direct answers in response. Clearly present your bottom line (*what* you want), but don't tell the person *how* to do it. If there are constraints that must be followed, incorporate them into goals rather than adding them as restrictions.

Also remember that D-spirits need control. Under stress, they tend to get pushy, and if they still don't get their way, they may permanently withdraw. Look for opportunities to give up some control so they can feel "in charge."

Interacting with an extreme I-spirit
(unusually fast-paced and relationship-focused):

Converse at a rapid pace and be more focused on expanding the relationship and enjoying the exchange. Create a friendly, sociable environment and give the person lots of chances to verbalize. Build in some fun by talking about things that support the person's interests. Avoid descriptions of detailed processes. Instead, provide relevant examples that outline the actions taken by people who did something similar (and were recognized for it). Name-dropping is definitely permitted!

If information needs to be written down, remember that I-spirits prefer verbal communication and expect that anything *really* important will be discussed with them face-to-face. Recognize that I-spirits often make decisions based on emotions and intuition. In fact, your enthusiasm and commitment while communicating something may influence them more than the actual content of your message – so let your feelings show.

I-spirits often talk themselves into a course of action before they take it, so give them plenty of opportunities to do that. Don't tell them what they should do – use open-end questions to help them discover the answer for themselves. Finally, keep in mind that I-spirits under stress may appear disorganized and emotional, and often tend to vent their frustration verbally – but the anger is usually very temporary and they will quickly work to rebuild the relationship once they get whatever is bothering them out of their systems.

Interacting with an extreme S-spirit
(unusually slow-paced and relationship-focused):

Relax your own pace, and pay more attention to nurturing the relationship. Create a casual, supportive environment for your discussion. Show sincere personal interest. Clearly define what you would like the person to do. Carefully outline the action steps they can take to get results. Be patient. Ask questions to draw out their concerns, and then listen and respond empathetically.

If an S-spirit feels threatened by change, divide the action you are requesting into small steps, and ask for commitment to the first step only. Make the person's responsibility clear – no ambiguities. Then provide ongoing reinforcement (as the person proceeds through each step) by confirming the successful outcomes – and then by asking the person to commit to the next step. Show how immediate action minimizes risk and creates stability and security in the long run.

S-spirits tend to communicate indirectly. They often use questions to express concerns or objections. If you simply respond to their questions as asked (rather than probing into their underlying concerns), you may miss an opportunity to resolve the key issue and win their support. Remember, too, that S-spirits under stress may use "victim" or "martyr" language, a clue that you have not yet acknowledged whatever is bothering them. Ask probing questions, and then listen *patiently* to discover their concerns.

Interacting with an extreme C-spirit
(unusually slow-paced and task-focused):

Be slower paced yourself and focus more on facts and details. Prepare all the information and data that is relevant to your discussion in advance – never try to "wing it." Be ready to explain why a particular decision or course of action is "right" using logic and credible data. Take your time. Discuss step-by-step approaches to achieving a goal. Stay organized, on topic, and business focused – don't drift or skip over details.

Help clarify the "bigger picture," especially if the person is focused on perfection or bogged down in detail. Show respect for the person's knowledge, qualifications, and accuracy. Use patience, hard evidence, and diplomacy to address disagreements. Disagree with items of information, not the person (for example, "I have a different number." rather than "You have the number wrong."). C-spirits have a driving need to be "right," and can get very defensive if they feel personally attacked or criticized.

C-spirits make decisions by researching, analyzing, and reflecting. They are good readers, and assume that anything important will be supported and communicated in writing. Never push them to make a verbal commitment without giving them a chance to read and reflect on the facts involved. C-spirits under stress may become overly-defensive, sarcastic, or critical of others. Any of these reactions can make communication more difficult, but don't give up. If you have to, begin at the beginning by reaching an agreement on your common goal – then work from there.

Summary

Adapting your communication style to fit the pace and focus of the other person may seem like a lot of effort initially, but once you begin "reading" people in terms of their pace and focus, it will become easy to recognize the behavior or "spirit" that drives them. This knowledge will allow you to "customize" your conversations, and get more of what you want by giving other people more of what they want from each interaction you have.

Enhance the Self-Esteem of Others

THE MORE EFFECTIVELY YOU COMMUNICATE with other people, the more quickly and completely you will attain the results you desire as a leader.

The good news is that you don't have to be born with a silver tongue or a golden pen to be an effective communicator. Yes, *exceptional* communicators (people who most likely earn a living by speaking or writing) may have a special gift – but *effective* communication for a person in a leadership role requires no more than basic proficiency at a specific set of learnable skills.

A single core principle underlies all of those skills: Enhance the self-esteem of other people (and if you can't do that, at least *maintain* their self-esteem).

As a leader, you are at your most powerful if people feel good about themselves whenever you are around. Look for ways in every interaction to make others feel proud of themselves and proud of the organization they are a part of.

Always treat people with dignity and respect. Never embarrass, humiliate, or criticize someone in front of other people, and never say or do anything solely for the purpose of destroying someone's self-image. Those are the actions of a "bully," and if a leader bullies people, it will create fierce resentment.

Even when a person with whom you are interacting "has it coming" for something he or she said or did to you first, avoid the instinctive desire to retaliate. To do so shows a lack of poise and self-control – plus once something damaging has been said or written, it can never be taken back. You can not effectively influence or interact with someone you have insulted or disgraced.

Along those lines, be careful with electronic forms of written communication (e-mail, text messaging, etc.). Do not say anything in an electronic message that you wouldn't say face-to-face. When in doubt, imagine that the person is sitting across from you. Would you really *say* what you are about to send?

In every communication, put yourself in the other person's situation, and view the exchange from his or her perspective. What does the other person understand, believe, and feel? What would you *like* for the person to understand, believe, and feel (about the topic, and about you)? Plan your communication and present your message with that goal in mind.

Give the other person the same courtesy and attention you would want. Not everyone can speak or write clearly, and strong emotions or language barriers can make it even harder for some people to express themselves. Make a sincere effort to help the other person get his or her message across by looking beyond the actual words to find the true meaning.

This is especially true when you feel attacked, offended, or annoyed. Don't assume that this was other person's intent (and then make a challenging situation even worse by overreacting). Respond in a way that maintains or enhances the other person's self-esteem, and you will be surprised at how often you stop yourself from saying or doing something that would have undermined your effectiveness as a leader.

Does all this mean "if you can't say something nice, don't say anything" to people? Absolutely not!

Offer Useful Corrective Feedback

DESTROYING ANOTHER PERSON'S SELF-ESTEEM is never useful. Even so, people do make mistakes, break the code, and fall short of expectations at times. They cannot, however, be allowed to keep making the *same* mistakes – and yet, they will, unless you tell them about it.

Telling them about it can be tricky, because everything associated with criticism is potentially negative. Consequently, most managers postpone these discussions for as long as possible. And when they finally discuss an issue, they almost always do it badly – and often make the problem even worse.

Fortunately, there are three simple guidelines you can observe, and a basic 3-step process you can follow, that will allow you to confidently offer useful corrective feedback to others. First, some important guidelines:

To be useful, corrective feedback must be given as soon as possible after the person makes a mistake or does something wrong. Supervisors often wait too long, which suggests that it wasn't that important to begin with (and makes the person feel "picked on").

Corrective feedback must also be given in private. As already discussed, criticizing someone in front of other people is deeply humiliating.

Finally, corrective feedback must be given in person if at all possible. Criticizing someone over the phone or in writing omits key aspects of communication (facial expressions, tone of voice, etc.) and reduces the odds of your message being accurately received.

With those guidelines in mind, there is a very basic 3-step process you can use to give *anyone* corrective feedback in virtually any situation:

1. Tell the person what he or she did;

2. Tell the person what he or she might have done instead to be more effective;

3. Explain why the action you are suggesting would be better in the future.

When telling the person what he or she did, be specific (describe exactly what you observed) and be factual (don't exaggerate, and don't criticize or "label" the individual – for instance, don't call the person "lazy" or "stupid"). Likewise, do not attempt to inject humor in order to "lighten" the mood.

When telling the person what he or she might have done to be more effective, define the action that you would have preferred.

When explaining why the action you are suggesting would be better in the future, highlight the benefits that the action will provide, or the problems it will help avoid (emphasize the effect on the individual or the organization as a whole – not just you).

This style of feedback essentially says, "Here's what I saw, here's what I think would have been better, and here's why." You're commenting on an event, as opposed to criticizing the person. Consequently, the person is more likely to hear and consider your suggestion without becoming angry or defensive.

When you give corrective feedback to your employees for problems relating to job performance or behavior, you will add two more steps to ensure their commitment and to keep the problem from happening again. (*These steps are explained in Part VI.*)

Praise People Daily

EVEN WHEN CORRECTIVE FEEDBACK is delivered properly, some people still have trouble admitting their mistakes. Workplace pirates have an especially difficult time accepting criticism from someone in a position of "authority."

One reason is because people in authority have been catching them doing things wrong for their entire lives. Great pirate captains were keenly aware of this, and recognized that the only way to overcome it was to spend more time "catching" people doing things right!

When you praise people's performance, behavior, and other actions on a daily basis, it builds trust and makes it much easier for them to admit that there may be room for improvement in certain areas. Praise gives them a "credit balance" to draw on. Without a daily "deposit" of praise, you run the risk that any serious corrective feedback you offer will plunge the other person straight into the red.

When people do something good, they like hearing that it was noticed and appreciated. Not just employees – everyone (business associates, family members, service people, anybody). Praise takes only a few seconds and costs nothing. In fact, praise may be the single most powerful tool that leaders have to inspire enthusiasm and commitment in others.

So why aren't more supervisors and managers using it? Some don't think it's necessary to praise people for doing what they're being paid to do anyway. Others are afraid of looking "soft." Most simply don't realize how important and beneficial it is. It has never been a part of their organization's "culture."

There is a basic 3-step process for giving another person praise (also called positive feedback):

1. Tell the person what he or she did;

2. Explain why the action was important or helpful;

3. Ask the person how he or she completed the action or achieved the result (if appropriate).

When you tell people what they did, be specific (don't just say, "Good job" – state what you observed), but keep it brief and sincere. When explaining why the action was important, highlight the benefits gained or the ways in which the action was helpful. When asking people how they did it, give them a chance to talk about the accomplishment. This makes them feel good, and gives you an insight into what motivates them (and lets you determine if they were competent – or just lucky).

When you complete the steps, *thank* the person and walk away – never tag another message or request onto the end of praise. That would be "manipulation."

It's easy to catch people doing things wrong. It takes a conscious effort to catch them doing things right. Create a "system" where, on the way to work, you think of one thing to watch for that day that people are supposed to be doing (don't tell them what it is, and choose something different each day). Then try to "catch" people doing it – and when you do, praise them.

Praising people daily may feel awkward at first. Some workplace pirates may react with suspicion. Acknowledge that fact. Tell them that you're going to try it for three weeks – but after that, you'll go back to the way things were if they want you to. If you're following the process above, they won't!

Listen Actively

TO PARAPHRASE the Greek philosopher Epictetus, "Leaders have two ears and one mouth, and should endeavor to use them in that proportion."

Listening is *the* essential skill for effective verbal communication – one in which most people have had little or no training.

When another person speaks, *passive* listening simply allows you to hear sounds. *Active* listening allows you to receive and process the message. To listen actively, you must overcome nine obstacles.

Talking Too Much

Most leaders talk too much. A leader's job is not just to pass information along to his or her followers. It is to know what followers think and feel, and (perhaps more important) to have a reasonably good idea what they will *do*. Listening is the key.

Put your ego on hold. Give the other person the "starring role" in any conversation, while you take on a supporting part. If you have the urge to interrupt or change the subject, practice holding your tongue through at least one more sentence. Over time, your desire to dominate the interaction will decline.

External Distractions

The second obstacle is external distractions. These may include environmental noise, a ringing telephone, activity outside the door or window, or the presence of another person or issue that is demanding your attention.

When listening to another person, avoid interruptions (to the degree possible) – hold your incoming calls, or move to an area free of phones, equipment noise, and other people. If you have a weakness for gazing out the window, close the blinds. If you are working on something else, stop – face the speaker, lean forward slightly, and maintain eye contact. Offer your undivided attention. External distractions can be very distressing to someone who is trying to communicate with you, and if you don't eliminate them, the other person might fail to tell you something that you really need to know!

Internal Distractions

The third obstacle to effective listening is internal distractions. These are the mental "detours" and daydreams that occur when someone is speaking. These happen because you can think from four to ten times faster than a person can talk. Distractions creep in from everywhere to fill that void. Sometimes, when you are bored, you open the door and invite them in!

Avoiding internal distractions means constantly monitoring and controlling your own "brain traffic," and pulling yourself back from the natural diversions. This requires a high degree of awareness, and the ability to exercise self-discipline.

If self-discipline is difficult for you, try to handle internal distractions by approaching every conversation as a chance to learn. Pretend you are gathering information to present in a report. Listen to each statement and decide if it expresses a verifiable fact or a personal opinion. This will give you more insight into the message and improve your concentration, even if the speaker and topic are dull.

Improper Distance

The fourth obstacle is improper distance. When the speaker is too close or too far away, it can make it difficult for the listener to focus on the message (you may recall the "close talker" from a classic episode of the TV series *Seinfeld*).

To the degree possible, seek the ideal distance between you and the person speaking.

For one-to-one business or social conversations, the ideal distance is from 18 to 42 inches. Anything closer than 18 inches is considered "personal space" for most Americans, and is only appropriate for intimate conversations (of course, this varies by culture, so keep that fact in mind in a diverse setting).

Distances of three to twelve feet are ideal for business or social conversations involving multiple people.

For presentation style interactions, listeners should be twelve to 25 feet from the speaker (it may be more with audio/visual reinforcement).

Misunderstanding the Purpose

The fifth obstacle is misunderstanding the purpose of the message. People talk to leaders for many reasons, and many times, key information is missed or forgotten because the leader failed to realize the speaker's primary objective.

Always ask yourself, "Why is this person talking to me?" It may be to complete a task, or it may just be to build the relationship. The person may be trying to inform you, persuade you, or get your permission. The person may be trying to amuse you, bond with you, spark your interest, or gain your sympathy. The content of a message, and how you handle it, depends on the reason it is being presented to you in the first place. Be sure you know.

Prejudice

The sixth obstacle to effective listening is prejudice. Sometimes you don't listen because you don't want to listen. Prejudice is a natural human emotion. It's normal to encounter certain people who are more difficult to like, trust, or understand. Yet, as a leader, you have to create an atmosphere where you can communicate constructively with everyone – which means you must listen without prejudice.

Prejudice is not just a racial phenomenon. Everyone you encounter is subconsciously classified by gender, age, religion, physical build, manner of dress, education, job type, where they grew up, and a variety of other factors. It is easy to assume that a person will reflect the same beliefs, values, opinions, and perspectives as someone else from that same group. To listen effectively, however – in fact, to *lead* effectively – you have to "turn off" all the subconscious filters through which you process incoming information, and hear what the person is saying – without prejudgment.

Jumping to Conclusions

The seventh obstacle is jumping to conclusions. For leaders, experience and time pressure often contribute to this barrier. It can be especially easy to jump to conclusions when you have heard a similar message before, know where the speaker is going with this one, and feel certain that you can skip to the bottom line – and save everyone a lot of time.

There are two problems with this. First, you can't know for sure what people are going to say unless you let them say it. Second, while *you* may have heard it all before, the message is unique and important to the person speaking. He or she will not feel listened to and valued if you do not allow the message to be delivered intact.

Hear the person out. If you're too busy to do so at that moment, explain that you really want to give the person your full attention, and ask if you can get back to him or her at a specific time – and then do so. (If the matter is urgent and can't wait, use the rapport building skills in the next chapter to accelerate the process of getting to the bottom line.)

Emotions

The eighth obstacle is emotions. When a person has strong feelings (positive or negative) about the message he or she has to communicate, it can be much more difficult to express the message clearly. (People often say, "I'm speechless!" when overwhelmed.)

It is inevitable that you will deal with emotional people and situations as a leader. When you do, it is important that you do not allow those emotions to interfere with the message – or cause you to lose control of your own emotions.

Many leaders treat the emotions of a speaker like a distraction, and attempt to set them aside. This is one approach, but another more effective method is to acknowledge what the speaker is feeling.

Anger, hurt, disappointment, and frustration are often expressed because the person subconsciously wants you know that he or she feels that way. Appearing to ignore it may only make the situation worse. Yet once you openly acknowledge the emotion (saying, for example, "I can tell that you are upset."), the person is more likely to be able to clearly explain why, and you are more likely be able to listen without getting upset or defensive yourself.

Linguistics

The ninth obstacle is linguistics, a technical term that refers to the way a person speaks – including voice tone, pitch, volume, rhythm, accent, dialect, and pronunciation. Not only can these characteristics make a speaker difficult to understand, they can either conceal or reveal the true meaning of the words.

Read aloud the statement, "I didn't throw a rock through that window." Your tone of voice can make the same words sound hostile, sarcastic, sly, or defensive. Emphasize a different word in the sentence and you change the meaning. If you pay attention to those nuances as a listener, you will be able to spot subtle inconsistencies that will allow you to probe for more information and avoid miscommunications.

A pirate captain's native tongue was often different than the language spoken by the majority of his crew. To overcome language barriers, pirate captains invented many of the nautical terms and sailing commands that are still in use today. In fact, Creole languages are, in part, an integration of the English, French, Dutch, Spanish, Portuguese, and West African dialects spoken on pirate ships. It may benefit the leaders of modern organizations to create and adopt a similar kind of "work language" – or at least a set of commonly-used terms – for a multilingual workforce.[13]

Summary

It takes extra effort to listen actively, and to overcome the obstacles that impair good verbal communication. Make the effort, however, and you will quickly develop new habits that make your day-to-day interactions easier and more effective.

Build Rapport

RAPPORT IS A FEELING of being totally "in sync" with another individual. In your personal life, you've probably had an instant rapport with certain people. As a leader, you must be able to establish some degree of rapport with *everyone* you encounter.

The communication skills presented so far can help you build rapport over time. Beyond those skills, there are eight powerful techniques you can apply in any almost situation to immediately create rapport.

Paraphrasing

The first technique is *paraphrasing*, which means restating the content of what someone said in your own words. This lets the person know that you were listening, and that he or she was heard and understood. For example, "So what you're saying is the delivery may be delayed due to weather, right?" Of course, if that isn't accurate, the person will correct you, and a misunderstanding will be avoided.

Empathizing

The second interaction technique is *empathizing*, which involves recognizing and labeling the emotion someone is feeling. This lets the person know that you understand not only the *content* of the message, but also how he or she *feels* about the situation. To say, "I know how you feel" is not enough. You must *label* that feeling. For example, "I can tell that you are *upset*." What if you choose the wrong label? If "upset" did not reflect the person's true feelings, he or she would likely say so – either way, the person will know that *you* know how he or she feels.

There is one critical thing to remember when empathizing. Do not follow an empathy statement with the word "but" – for example, "I can tell that you are upset, *but* weather delays are a fact of life this time of year." This unravels the empathy statement, and suggests that even though you *understand* the person's feelings, you really don't *care* about them.

If it is necessary to elaborate after an empathy statement, make it a separate comment. "I can tell that you are upset. Weather delays are a fact of life this time of year." This way, both statements can stand equally, and you have a better chance to move forward together toward a solution.

Probing

The third technique is *probing*, or posing an open-end question to gain insight or information about a success or a problem. This lets people know that you respect their abilities, and gives you insight into what *they* think (before they know what *you* think).

Open-end questions cannot be answered with a "yes" or "no." An explanation is required. Effective probing questions often begin with the word "How...?" For example, "How did you assemble that so quickly?" These are natural conversations starters, because they invite people to talk about something they know.

Avoid asking questions that begin with the word "Why...?" Workplace pirates attempt to justify their actions when they hear it. If you really want to know the reasoning or rationale behind a person's actions, ask "How come...?" or say, "Tell me about..."

Reacting

The fourth interaction technique is *reacting*, which involves demonstrating interest (both verbally and non-verbally) in what the other person is saying.

Reacting includes using your body language and facial expressions to convey an appropriate response to the speaker's message – for example, nodding your head to show agreement. Verbal reactions can range from simple comments ("Oh, I see") to a specific acknowledgment ("Great idea!").

Exploring

The fifth interaction technique is *exploring*. This involves helping the person think through the benefits and drawbacks of an idea or suggestion by asking relevant questions. For example, "What would be some of the advantages of choosing that course of action?" or "What are the risks associated with that option?"

Exploring allows the other person to see that you are fully considering his or her idea. By asking the right questions, it also allows you to guide the decision-making process. For instance, you can ask leading questions about the positive aspects of an idea to help it build momentum, or you can ask leading questions about the drawbacks to help the person discover the reasons why a suggestion might not be workable.

Asking questions that help people discover the shortcomings of an idea for themselves is far better than an outright rejection (e.g., "No, that won't work.").

Expanding

The sixth technique is *expanding*, which means offering your suggestion or idea in the form of a question. This lets other people know what you are thinking, yet allows them to consider your input as a possible alternative (rather than assuming that because it's your idea, that's what has to happen).

For example, if the boss says, "I think we need to pick up the order ourselves," then that's probably what will occur – whether it's a good idea or not. By asking "What if we arranged to pick up the order ourselves?" the boss can learn the pros and cons.

As the name implies, expanding allows you to place your ideas alongside those already proposed by other people – without making it seem as though you are overruling them. In fact, if you do this skillfully, the people who eventually support your solution won't remember who thought of it – it will seem like *their* idea, and they will work much harder to implement it.

Relating

The seventh technique is relating – helping the other person see that you share a common interest, concern, or benefit. This involves using the words "we," "us," and "our" instead of "I," "me," and "you" wherever possible in conversation. (Every discussion begins with an "I" and a "you" participating. When you transform the relationship to "we," you change the dynamics.)

Acknowledging

The final technique is *acknowledging*. This is simply saying, "thank you." It lets the person know that you value his or her communication with you.

Be thankful for every interaction you have as a leader – even the ones that bring challenges or bad news. If you don't thank people for taking the time to share important information with you, you will eventually find yourself in an information vacuum.

Respond Assertively

ASSERTIVENESS IS AN ESSENTIAL SKILL for interpersonal communications, performance management, and team leadership. It is a skill that can also be applied at home and in social situations. Assertiveness can do wonders for the respect you command in the workplace, for the service you receive as a customer, and for the impressions you create in every walk of life.

In every situation, we have the choice to be submissive, aggressive, or assertive.

Submissive behavior involves giving in to the other person when you know you should be standing up for your position. Why would you do this? Most often, it is either because you want to be liked, or you wish to avoid a confrontation. As a leader, you need respect, and *submissive behavior is the sworn enemy of respect*. Submissive behavior will always result in your requests or viewpoints being ignored, and in your rights being neglected. You will feel undervalued and resentful – which is stressful and counterproductive.

Aggressive behavior involves doing whatever is necessary to get your way or make yourself heard. The typical view of aggressive behavior is a person who comes in with "guns blazing," slamming doors, banging desks, and shouting orders. But there are other less demonstrative styles of aggressive behavior – for instance, a person who uses emotional manipulation, guilt, or deceit to get his or her way is exhibiting a more subtle form of aggressive behavior. Either way, the advantage of aggressive behavior is that you don't get taken advantage of, and that you may get what you want – at least, briefly. A lot depends on how much people fear your aggression. Even if you *do* get what you want, aggressive behavior does not win the help and cooperation of others. When you are aggressive, people begin to react defensively, withhold information, and become covertly aggressive themselves in return.

There is a middle ground – *assertive* behavior. Assertiveness allows you to receive the attention and respect you deserve from other people. It allows you to be emotionally honest about how you feel, and to deal openly and fairly with other people. It means looking people in the eye and treating them with respect, but without fear or manipulation. It encourages them to treat you the same way – adult to adult.

Assertiveness gives you the best chance of resolving a conflict or situation satisfactorily. Sometimes, there is no satisfactory solution. Even then, assertiveness allows you to select an appropriate course of action while leaving the door open for a fair and honest discussion when the next issue arises.

Being assertive means balancing your needs and the needs of others. This varies in every context, according to who you are dealing with (a follower, peer, boss, customer, supplier, etc.) and the substance of the issue. Consequently, there is no script you can follow to be assertive. There *are* three useful guidelines.

- Be honest (about what is relevant)
- Know what you really need (and stick to it)
- Interact as equals.[14]

Be Honest (About what is Relevant)

Honesty is the most important component of assertiveness. Unless you are honest with yourself and with other people, you will never be able to achieve a balanced transaction.

So what prevents people from being honest? Normally it's the fear of what might happen if you tell the truth. One way to overcome this fear is to ask yourself, "If I am honest with this person, what is the worst thing that can happen?" When you come up with the answer, divide it in half.

It is a law of the universe that honesty is never as dangerous as you think it's going to be. Still, it can be a worry. If you are a bit submissive, you imagine that honesty will lead to confrontation – and disaster. If you are a bit aggressive, you imagine that honesty will lead to a loss of control – and disaster.

The truth is that honesty breeds honesty. It makes communication possible because everyone can finally learn what everyone else really thinks. Your position may be right, it may be wrong – but at least people will know where you stand. Of course, it is important not to get so carried away with your enthusiasm to "tell it like it is" that you become rude or insensitive. So *keep it relevant.*

You only need to be honest about what's relevant. Some facts and emotions have a direct impact on the issue at hand, and are therefore relevant. Other facts and emotions are not. Be especially careful of emotions. If a person has caused you a lot of trouble or pain, it may be relevant to state the facts of the situation and the feelings you have – but irrelevant to compare the person to Darth Vader or a bad dentist.

Know What You Really Need (and Stick to It)

You have to decide, in any interaction, what you really need from the other person. You have to know (relative to your goals and values) what is negotiable and what is not. You'll want to determine (in advance) which things are *not* negotiable, and then commit to firmly and diplomatically "standing your ground," no matter what. Making this decision ahead of time will help you deal with any pressure to "give in" later.

A failure to follow this rule is one of the major causes of misunderstandings between people. If you are not absolutely certain about what you really need and value, how will the other person know? When you hesitate or "waffle" on your key position or core principles, you weaken your credibility and send out a mixed message. From then on, people may assume that with you, *everything* is negotiable.

How do you stand your ground without becoming aggressive? One technique is called the "instant replay" technique. With this technique, you calmly state your position and continue to repeat it – politely, yet firmly – each time the other person attempts to make you compromise or concede. By knowing in advance what you will not compromise, you can refuse another person's request without making it feel like a personal rejection.

Imagine that a coworker rushes in and asks you to provide sales data (data that you maintain) to him by noon for an urgent meeting. You have already promised to complete a task for another coworker, and your bottom line is that you are not going to break that promise. You say, "I'm sorry, I can't get you the data by noon."

Your coworker insists, "But I have to have it! My career is on the line!"

You repeat, "I'm sorry, I just can't get you the data by noon."

Your coworker asks, "Why not?"

You reply, "I promised to have this report to Holly," and then repeat, "so I'm sorry, I just can't get you the data by noon."

Your coworker gets more aggressive. "Just call her and tell you you'll be late with her report."

You repeat, "I'm sorry, I just can't get you the data by noon." And then suggest what you *can* do to help. "I can get it to you by 4:00."

Sensing that you might be giving in, you coworker insists, "But I need it by noon!"

You repeat, "I just can't get you the data by noon." Then suggest another way you might help. "What if I give you temporary access to the database so you can pull together the sales figures you need?"

The instant replay technique makes your bottom line clear. Repeating it calmly and nicely, and offering other ways that you can help, allows you to be assertive, yet keeps you from appearing rigid or uncaring.

Interact as Equals

The instant replay makes it clear what you are *not* able or willing to do. Once this is established, everything else becomes negotiable.

As you negotiate, try to interact as equals with a common goal – finding a solution that achieves both of your objectives. To do this, put yourself in the right mental state to interact as an equal. Control your emotions and stay calm. Be firm, yet friendly and helpful.

Use the rapport building techniques in the previous chapter to establish common ground and to encourage the other party to offer ideas of how you might work together to solve a problem. Demonstrate that you have a sincere interest in reaching a practical solution.

You may find it difficult to do this if the other person is being belligerent or rude. When someone behaves aggressively or emotionally towards you and you are tempted to retaliate, try to imagine that the individual has just received terrible news, and that you are the first person he or she has come into contact with. Imagine, for example, that the person just learned that his or her child was diagnosed with a very serious illness.

It may not be true, but if you respond as though it were, you will keep your own emotions under control. And if something stressful *did* just happen to the person, you will have behaved with maturity and sensitivity – and will have nothing to regret or feel embarrassed about later. This approach may not totally diffuse a confrontational situation, but at least your actions will keep it from escalating.

Summary

Assertiveness doesn't guarantee that you will always get what you want. Nothing can. Assertive behavior does give you the best possibility of finding a mutually satisfactory solution to a challenging situation, and it helps you earn the respect you deserve as a leader.

Ask Wisely

A LEADER NEEDS THINGS from other people. For a pirate captain, taking things by force or deception was always risky. The same is true today. Leadership is easier when people are willing to *give* you what you need.

Ask, and you shall... *what*? The answer is not a closely-guarded secret formula. Almost everyone can fill in the blank. "Ask, and you shall receive."

The phrase is not "*bully* and you shall receive," and it's not "*manipulate* or *cheat* and you shall receive." It's also not "*whine, gripe,* or *complain* endlessly and you shall receive." *Asking* is the key.

In spite of this, most people *don't* ask for (and thus, don't receive) what they need. Why not? Often, it's because they fear the word "no."

An effective leader understands that when someone says "no," it simply means that a person who was not giving the leader what he or she wanted is *still* not giving the leader what he or she wanted. That's it. It doesn't mean that the leader or the goal is any less worthy or deserving of help.

You have nothing to lose by asking. Asking works. Asking *wisely* works even better. Use the following eight guidelines to ask wisely.[15]

1. *Be polite.* Make a courteous *request.* Don't presume or *demand* that others help or assist you.

2. *Be specific.* Explain exactly what you want, and why. People are more responsive to specific requests.

3. *Be reasonable.* Don't ask for more than you'd be willing to give if the situation were reversed.

4. *Demonstrate your commitment.* People want to see that you have dedicated a substantial amount of your time, energy, or resources to whatever you're asking them to support. After all, why should they help you if you haven't done anything to help yourself?

5. *Focus on individuals who have the ability to help.* Identify the people who are in a legitimate position to fulfill your request, and then approach them directly one-to-one. Don't broadcast your appeal to a mass audience, and don't ask people who couldn't provide the help you need even if they wanted to.

6. *Create value first.* Do something to make yourself valuable to the other person – or to make the other person see value in your goal. People will help you either (a) because you helped them first (and they "owe" you), or (b) because they recognize that helping you will also help them get what *they* want.

7. *Ask until...* one of three things happens: (1) you get what you need, (2) you get advice, feedback, or referrals that can help you get what you need elsewhere, or (3) the person tells you to stop asking. Be persistent, but not pushy or obnoxious.

8. *Say thank you.* Whatever occurs, be grateful. Say thank you, and when appropriate, show your gratitude with a thank you note, a small gift, or any valuable help you can offer in return.

The simple act of asking wisely can fill many of your basic needs. When more complex issues are involved, you can call upon the power of persuasion...

Persuade Convincingly

MOST LEADERS rely on the power of persuasion more often than any other communication skill except active listening and praise (positive feedback).

There is no magic to persuasion. You don't have to cast a spell over people or trick them into going along with you. In fact, you will only be able to convince people to give you their total commitment if they feel completely in control of the decision, and if they are convinced that what you are asking them to do is in their own best interest.

The formula for this is simple: prepare, probe, sell, and close.[16]

Prepare

Too often, leaders ask for something without considering why other people should listen or care. Before you meet with people to try to persuade them, consider two questions.

1. *Are they aware of the problem or the opportunity?* If the other parties are not familiar with the issue, you will have to first convince them that a problem or opportunity exists before you can persuade them to take a specific course of action to address it.

2. *Will they do something about it?* If the other parties are aware of the problem or opportunity, but don't believe that it affects them, then you must be prepared to show how it does. If they don't think they

have the ability to do anything about it, then you
must be prepared to change their minds.

Obviously, if the people you are trying to persuade are both
(a) aware of the problem, and (b) willing to address it, then
your job is easier.

The next part of preparation involves focusing on what the
people you are trying to persuade can gain from granting your
request or agreeing with your idea. To convince the other
parties, you must be prepared to show what's in it for them.
Once you identify what they want, you have to demonstrate
how your plan will help them get it.

To connect your plan to their interests, brainstorm the
benefits they would gain. Identify as many advantages as you
can (so you have plenty of persuasive points to work with).
Then pick the top three benefits to feature in your proposal.
Don't overwhelm your audience with too many promises.
Three key points is the maximum that most listeners can
process and recall.

Finally, determine whether any of the parties have had a
positive or negative experience with a course of action similar
to the one you are proposing (or any positive or negative
experiences with other options that your proposal may be
competing against).

Probe

The best way to persuade is not to push your ideas onto
other people, but to let them discover for themselves the
benefits of agreeing with you.

Begin your presentation by clearly and briefly stating what
your proposal is ultimately intended to accomplish – ideally in
terms of the three key benefits you identified during

preparation. Then ask your listeners a series of questions to uncover their individual needs. If their responses confirm the same needs that you identified during your preparation, then you are right on track. If not, you will need to explore the new responses and uncover the related benefits.

When you are certain that your proposal will satisfy the needs of the parties you are trying to convince, ask questions of those who have experienced similar situations. Your objective here is to reveal specific instances where following a course of action like yours was successful, and where not doing so was problematic.

Opening your presentation with questions gets people involved and encourages them to think about what you have to offer. Once they are engaged, it's time to make your pitch.

Sell

If you have completed the first two steps properly, at least some of your listeners may already be sold. To win the rest, you need to link their needs to a specific feature or benefit of your proposal. You must show them how your idea matches their specific goals or desires.

In most cases, they will be looking to "fix what's broken" or "build on a past success." Identify which it is, and then demonstrate how your idea helps them meet that objective.

There are three ingredients that will make this portion of your argument more convincing – logic, credibility, and passion.

To persuade someone, what you are requesting must make sense. You can lend *logic* to your argument by using documented evidence, verifiable statistics, observed events, and specific examples that either you or other participants have experienced.

To give your proposal (and yourself) credibility, people must find you *believable*, and feel that you are *qualified* to make the points you want them to accept. Your sources of credibility include trustworthiness (a successful "track record"), credentials, work experience, and association (the endorsement of other authorities who are already accepted as credible by the people you are trying to convince).

Your argument may be logical and credible, but it won't be convincing unless your *excitement* shows. Passion creates interest in your message, and it's contagious. To radiate passion, constantly remind yourself of why the issue is important. Let your listeners hear the passion as you vary the tone and volume of your voice. Support your message with non-verbal communication. For example, smile, make eye contact, and use natural facial expressions and hand gestures to emphasize critical points.

Another key concept to remember when selling is to manage your listener's choices. Although every problem has a variety of possible solutions, most people prefer an "either/or" decision to a complex analysis (even when they know the issue is not that simple).

If you are guiding others to explore alternatives and choose a preferred course of action, you want them to consider all the possibilities. But if you have already *made* a decision and are trying to persuade a group of people to *support* that decision, you want to limit the number of outcomes they have to consider. Give them only two choices – the positive result of accepting your proposal and the negative outcome of rejecting it. Few will choose the downside.

As you describe the two choices, influence the decision with the words you select. Use strong verbs and adjectives to show your listeners how much they have to gain by adopting your proposal, how much they have to lose by rejecting it, and how narrow the window of opportunity is. Compare the outcome that people fear the most to the one that they desire the most.

Close

When you can see that you have won over the people you are trying to persuade, stop selling! End your proposal with a direct request for action. Never leave anyone wondering what's supposed to happen next. If the "ball is in their court," make it clear what you want them to do with it.

If you need group members to accept action items in order to implement your proposal, explain exactly what needs to be done and by when. Identify who is going to do it, and ask for that person's firm commitment to complete the action. If someone is unwilling to commit, you may have to go back to stage two and ask more questions before you can close. A person who is unwilling to commit to action has not been persuaded yet.

If you only need the group's agreement and approval so you can proceed with action items, you might try the *assumed close.* You "close the deal" by outlining what you will do next to move the proposal forward, as though they have already agreed. This can be very effective if you have a few people in a group who are still against your proposal or "on the fence" – because they will have to speak up with a specific objection to keep it from moving forward.

If the group needs time to review your proposal or wishes to discuss it in private, set a follow-up date to return, answer questions, and get a firm decision.

If you have clearly addressed all the concerns and issues, but still cannot get a firm commitment, consider using a *reduced risk close* – also called a "puppy dog close" by sales professionals. (A pet shop owner allows the customer to take a puppy home for the weekend with no risk – "simply bring it back on Monday for a full refund if you're not happy." The puppy joins the family, licks a face, does something adorable, and the deal is closed – not by the pet shop owner, but by the puppy!)

You can adopt this technique by asking your listeners to make a partial commitment – to agree to a smaller portion of whatever you are proposing so they can see for themselves how beneficial it is before they agree to the entire plan. Then make certain they receive the interim results you promised. Once you confirm that they have, ask for a larger commitment.

Summary

Persuasion is all about presenting choices, and then guiding your audience to select the choice you want. To do that, you must know your audience, identify their interests, and demonstrate the benefits of your idea. It takes planning to build a logical, credible, and passionate presentation. When you go to that effort, however, you expand your effectiveness and greatly increase the amount of influence you have within your organization.

Meet Productively

IN THE U.S. LAST YEAR, the average professional spent 61.2 hours in meetings. Over half of that time was considered unproductive – key attendees were missing or late, necessary resources were not available or not functioning, and participants were daydreaming, dozing, or focused on unrelated activities.[17]

Conservatively, the American workforce wastes more than 1.4 billion hours in meetings each year (by contrast, it took roughly 42 million hours of labor to construct the Hoover Dam). The cost of unproductive meetings in the U.S. exceeds the Gross National Product of three-quarters of the nations in the world.[18]

In addition to this direct cost, unproductive meetings have many indirect consequences: confusion, misinformation, incomplete action items, and delayed decisions to name a few.

So your meetings are probably no worse than anyone else's. Consider this, however. A meeting, if conducted properly, is one of the best tools available to make your organization more effective and efficient.

Pirate captains certainly understood that a meeting was the fastest way to communicate something to the entire crew, and to ensure that the same message was heard and understood by everyone.

So what makes a meeting "productive," and how does a leader conduct such a meeting? The task of running a meeting can be separated into two sets of proficiencies – managing the *administrative* aspects of the meeting, and managing the *people* who attend.

Managing the Administrative Aspects

From a purely administrative perspective, there are five keys to running an effective meeting: Planning, Preparing, Structuring, Informing, and Recording.

The first key is *planning*. A productive meeting is one that accomplishes its desired purpose without wasting time or resources. Leaders often have unproductive meetings because they hold them without any clear sense of purpose other than "It's our weekly meeting." Be clear in your mind about the purpose for holding a meeting and outcome expected from it.

Meetings are held for many reasons – to give and receive information, to make decisions, to solve problems, to complete a collective work task, to maintain a routine, or to present an image. The purpose of your meeting may include one or more of these reasons, but before you schedule it, know exactly what you want it to achieve. Then verify that a meeting will be the most effective and efficient way to communicate and achieve those desired outcomes. Review the potential topics to be covered and eliminate those that could be addressed more quickly with one-to-one conversations, phone calls, or e-mails. If there is no need to have a regularly scheduled meeting, cancel it.

The second key is *preparing*. The single largest administrative cause of unproductive meetings is the lack of a useful agenda. The agenda is the product of good preparation, and the catalyst for an effective and efficient meeting.

To prepare an agenda, begin by examining the topics you outlined in the preparation stage. Create a clear yet brief summary of each topic, as well as the related outcome you expect to achieve. Determine who needs to be present at the meeting to accomplish that outcome, and ensure that they are able to arrive on time (a meeting of ten people that starts just six minutes late has already wasted an hour of staff time!).

Identify any background information or special materials that will be needed by participants. Finally, determine the amount of time each topic will take to discuss and complete. Allow ample time for important items (key to your mission) and significantly less time for announcements and routine matters.

The third key is *structuring*. For a meeting to be productive, agenda items must be placed in the proper order. In a typical staff or work team meeting, announcements will be the first items on the agenda. Progress reports are next. Adhere to strict time limits for each progress report, and do not allow participants to discuss problems while a report is being delivered.

Once the progress reports are complete, allow time to discuss any problems or questions that arose, and then proceed to new items or issues. For each item on the agenda, list the goal or desired outcome, the time allotted to achieve that outcome, the person responsible for leading the discussion, and any methodology that will be used such as polling, brainstorming, or criteria rating. Conclude the meeting with a summary of action items (including who will take those actions, and by when).

The fourth key is *informing*. Circulate the agenda to ensure that everyone knows in advance that a meeting is being held. Highlight any pre-work that's required, and supply any background information necessary. Provide a reminder notice of the meeting in two formats, one verbal (phone call or voice message) and one visual (bulletin board notice or e-mail). Keep the agenda posted where it is visible during the meeting, or ensure that all participants have a copy in front of them.

The fifth key is *recording*. Write down all decisions made during the meeting as they occur, including any assigned action items. Action items should include the task to be completed, the outcome expected, the due date, and the person responsible. Ensure that the agenda for the next meeting includes time for progress reports on each new action item. Distribute the action points within 24 hours of the conclusion of the meeting.

As you can see, most of the administrative tasks associated with a productive, well-run meeting are actually done before and after the meeting. A good agenda keeps you from having to manage structural details while a meeting is in progress. Your key function then is to manage the participants.

Managing the People

A meeting leader has to deploy a wide range of human relations skills. In a meeting, you must guide, listen, interpret, solicit facts, verify understanding, survey, summarize results, balance the participation, and ensure that each person feels respected, valued, and involved. Nobody expects a leader to be a psychologist. Your goal is to hold the meeting together and keep it moving constructively by uniting, focusing, and mobilizing the participants.

Uniting the group means getting everyone to work together. The principal threat to achieving unity in a meeting setting is aggression. Aggressive behavior provokes arguments, and arguments trigger emotions.

Because disagreements are inevitable, it's pointless to say, "Let's keep feelings out of this." They are already there. The trick is to allow people to let off steam without letting them get carried away. Don't be afraid to ask people what's bothering them. Encourage them to get their feelings into the open by describing the problems or difficulties they experienced – not by attacking or assigning blame to someone else.

Once the person opens up, don't take sides or get personally involved. Also, keep others in the group from interrupting, reacting, or responding initially. Let the person have his or her say.

Once you and the group have listened to the person, bring in the others and broaden the debate. Aggression often conceals a positive desire to make something right. Find out if there is a legitimate problem that needs to be rectified, first by asking the person what the real problem is, and then by engaging the other participants – especially those who are unbiased (not actively involved in the issue).

Don't jump to conclusions or try to find a solution yet. Prompt people to stick to the facts that help clarify the issue. Discourage opinions (an opinion without factual evidence merely prolongs the agony, since it is likely to either favor or oppose the aggressor). It often helps to ask specific questions rather than general ones. "How many times did that happen last week?" rather than "Does that happen often?" The less subjective the question, the more likely you are to get answers that help lessen any tension.

Remember that not all people express dissatisfaction in the same way. A person who is pouting or sulking can be just as big an obstacle to group unity as one who is screaming and shouting.

Focusing the group means keeping the meeting on schedule by keeping participants engaged in the topic at hand. Everyone is prone to rambling, especially when it leads to lighter topics such as good places to eat or last night's television. Some lightness and humor can be helpful, especially if the issue under discussion is difficult, and the group needs a mental break to refresh and refocus. The secret is to not go too far, and to get back onto the original track quickly.

It's also possible for meetings to veer off track when participants are struck by the apparent similarity between what a speaker is saying and their own experience with the matter (everyone has a travel-related "horror story," for instance). Suddenly, each person feels that he or she has to have a chance to express a viewpoint or experience, whether it's relevant to a decision or not. In these cases, the leader needs to keep a hand on the wheel and remain attentive to the time allotted on the agenda for each discussion.

Meeting participants are often poor listeners. As leader, you can take notes and periodically summarize the main points people are making. Listen and observe to keep important contributions from being overlooked by others in the group.

Ensure that people are not jumping in too quickly with their own comments, or going over old ground – both signs that they were merely waiting for their turns to talk, rather than seriously considering the information offered by others. Paraphrase what the last speaker said when bored or blank expressions are evident, and ask participants to comment.

Always test your assumptions by asking questions. It's easy to misunderstand what someone else is saying, or to miss the point of why they are saying it. Usually, people will act as though they understood a speaker's contribution rather than ask about something they fear might be obvious to others. As a leader, ask follow-up questions on behalf of the group as necessary.

Finally, to keep a group focused, begin the meeting on time, follow the agenda, and end on time. If you are undisciplined yourself, or too tolerant of time wasters, you will lose the respect of others in the group.

Mobilizing the group means moving everyone in a positive direction, together. In any meeting where there are problems to solve, a potential "vortex" or whirlpool of negativity exists. Some participants may want to elaborate on how much they have suffered and whose fault it is. They may ignore or belittle the contributions of others. Another threat is "solutionism" (where people jump too quickly to one course of action simply to get the discussion over with and move on).

Leadership is essential here. Participants must be guided to concentrate on what is being said and to explore the positive aspects of every idea that may contribute to a positive outcome. Make sure everyone who has something to say gets to say it, and that everyone else listens. Otherwise why have a meeting?

Individuals who are faster-paced may tend to dominate the meeting (they are comfortable "thinking out loud"). Ensure that once they have had their turns, others get to speak without interruption.

Drawing out the quiet people is just as important as restraining those who always jump in quickly. If their silence is caused by apathy or hostility, set aside time for a general discussion about how your meeting process might be improved. (Of course, sometimes people say nothing because they have nothing to say.)

Write down all suggestions and contributions during a meeting, preferably where everyone can see them. The ideal method is to use a flipchart or marker board. Using a visible display encourages everyone to be more positive, especially if you write down each suggestion. Recording every idea also reassures contributors. Once they see their suggestion recorded, they don't feel they have to keep restating it.

In the end, you want the group to *agree* to action items and solutions, rather than you *assigning* them. When a group consensus can be reached, even those initially opposed a course of action will help make it work – if their viewpoints were given a fair hearing.

Finally, never try to compete with an abusive or sniping participant (someone who takes "cheap shots" at you or others), but don't ignore the behavior, either. Call it into the open by questioning the person on his or her facts. Bring other participants into the discussion and ask for their input and observations. Do not be pulled into a one-on-one argument. If necessary, have a private word (using corrective feedback) after the meeting with anyone who makes an insulting or insubordinate remark.

Summary

Perfection is not the goal. To ensure that the meetings you lead are more productive, you don't have to master *everything* that's suggested here. Doing just *one or two* things more effectively – starting a meeting on time, steering a discussion back on track, or paraphrasing a key point that others missed – can save your group an hour or more each week, and save your organization thousands of dollars a year.

Write Powerfully

FOR MOST LEADERS, verbal communication skills are far more critical than written communication when interacting with followers. Writing skills become more important when the message contains instructions, policies, or resource commitments that are being transmitted up the chain of command, across departmental boundaries, or outside the organization to customers or other stakeholders.

Do you prepare formal correspondence, reports, proposals, or other official materials on behalf of your organization? Is written composition a key function you perform to produce desired results? If so, there are a number of exceptional books and courses on business writing that are well worth the cost.

Are you a leader who writes primarily to document, report, or clarify activities relating to your work unit? Are most of your written communications informal in nature (e-mails, for example) – and are your readers mainly people with whom you deal on a regular basis? If so, the most important thing you can do to improve your written communication is to write more powerfully. In a work setting, powerful writing has five essential qualities – it's (1) clear, (2) coherent, (3) concise, (4) conversational, and (5) correct.

Be Clear

In school, the purpose of most of your writing was to demonstrate how much you knew in order to get a grade. As a leader, the equivalent of your "grade" is whether or not your readers take the action you want them to take. So before you begin writing, be clear in your mind about what you want your readers to *do*.

Even if you are sending an e-mail that is strictly FYI (for your information), consider what you want the readers to *do* with that information, once they read it. If the answer is just to read it and forget it, then save everyone time by not writing it in the first place. If the answer is to know something so that the knowledge can be applied in a specific situation, explain that up front.

A common mistake that many leaders make is putting too much detail at the very beginning of a message – before the reader understands its relevance. Instead, start off by clearly stating the intent of your message and the action (if any) that is being requested. Indicate the date by which the action is expected. Then provide the facts necessary to support the action.

If the action you are seeking includes a reply or response from the reader, make it as easy as possible for the reader to take that action immediately. Build in a "response mechanism," like a postage-paid reply card (or a hyperlink, for electronic correspondence) so the reader can complete the action at that moment, rather than setting it aside and forgetting about it. Also, indicate the consequences of non-response (i.e., what you will assume or do if there is no reply).

Be Coherent

Once you know what you want your readers to do, decide what they need to know in order to be convinced and capable of doing it. In most cases, this means organizing the information in some coherent manner. There are "boilerplates" for organizing the content of many types of business writing, and you may find those helpful when preparing official documents. For other more general business correspondence, there are five common methods for organizing information.

1. A *chronological* method organizes information in the sequence it occurred. (A description of the events leading up to an accident might be structured in this manner.)

2. A *priority* method organizes information in order of its importance. (A presentation on the accomplishments and results of a special project might be structured this way.)

3. A *problem-cause-solution* method organizes information into what's wrong, why, and how to fix it. (A proposal to improve employee morale could be structured using this method.)

4. A *compare-contrast* method organizes information into the similarities and differences between two or more issues or multiple courses of action. (A recommendation to buy a specific service plan from among three vendor's offers could be structured like this.)

5. A *pros-and-cons* method organizes information into the advantages and disadvantages associated with a single issue or action. (The argument to upgrade a software product – or not – could be structured in this manner.)

Be Concise

In school, you were often required to write a minimum number of words on a subject. Even when you weren't, you realized that using more words often resulted in a better grade. Although you could have covered everything you had to say in thirty words, you found a way to stretch it into 200.

Good business writing is just the opposite. Once you know what you want your readers to do, and have assembled and organized the supporting information, tell them exactly what they need to know to be willing and able to take the desired action. Nothing more. Granted, if your audience is comprised of ten readers, two of them may want all the associated information. You can provide it to them as an attachment, or when they ask for it. The other eight will find it much easier to read (and will be more likely to take the desired action) if you keep the message as brief as possible.

Be Conversational

One way to keep your writing brief is to use short words, short sentences, and short paragraphs. After you have written something, read it aloud. Is that really the way you would say it if you were talking to the reader in person? If not, consider revising it.

In school, you were taught to replace simple, conversational language with lengthy, colorful prose. As a leader, most of your writing is likely to be either informational or action-oriented. Use simple words and short phrases to get the message across.

Also, use active voice, rather than passive voice. For example, "It has been requested that the form attached herein be completed by all employees and submitted to the appropriate supervisor not later than the last day of June" might sound official. Yet, "Please fill out the attached form and give it to me by June 30" is half the length, and the call to action is much clearer.

Be Correct

For the writing assignments you completed in school, "correct" most often meant grammatically perfect. Good grammar is often interpreted as a sign of intelligence and attention to detail, so it would be improper to suggest that it doesn't matter in your business writing. It is not the most critical factor, however, on the internal correspondence you send to your followers, peers, or boss.

What *is* absolutely critical is accuracy. Names, dates, times, dollar amounts, and other figures must be correct. A spellchecker can't help you with the typos that often occur in names and number sequences. These of mistakes can be costly and embarrassing. Double check all names and numbers before sending anything.

Also, verify the facts that you present. Virtually all forms of written communication, even e-mails, become permanent (and legally discoverable) since computer files are backed-up redundantly. It is almost impossible to destroy all evidence of something you commit to writing – so never assume, exaggerate, or fabricate facts or evidence to support your position.

Be Conscientious

E-mail, instant messaging, and other forms of text-based electronic interaction have revolutionized business communication. In many organizations, e-mail is the lifeblood of the operation.

E-messaging is easy to use, but the sheer volume can overwhelm recipients. Before you send a blanket message, ensure that every addressee really needs the information. Before you forward a message, consider if sending your summary (of the relevant portion) would be better than passing along the entire message.

E-messaging has an informal feel – making it an ideal way to send and receive written information that is clear, concise, and conversational. Yet the informality and ease of use also causes people to forget that the reader only has the actual words to work with. People cannot see the body language or hear voice tone of the writer. Therefore it is critical that a supervisor or manager be especially conscientious when using any form of electronic messaging.

Never debate a topic by e-mail or text messaging. If you receive negative feedback or detect confusion in an electronic message, refrain from responding to it with more written text. Instead, follow up by telephone (or in person) to discuss the facts verbally. This will help minimize the potential of either party becoming frustrated or being misunderstood.

E-mail may seem like a highly efficient way to deal with difficult, emotionally-charged issues. In truth, however, if you fear that controversial viewpoints or challenging behaviors will make someone hard to speak with face-to-face, that's enough evidence to tell you that you must deal with the issue in person. For a leader to handle difficult people or tough situations in any other way is cowardly and immature.

Likewise, do not coach or develop people via electronic messaging. Corrective feedback, praise, coaching, and discipline should be handled in person. In addition, do not deliver "bad news" messages electronically. In those cases, a phone call, person-to-person meeting, or formal letter is preferred.

Finally, remember that you have no rights or expectations of privacy in the world of electronic messaging. Anything you send can be misrouted, forwarded to someone else, saved permanently, stored redundantly, and even produced as evidence in a court case. It is a wonderful tool – just use it conscientiously.

Apologize Gracefully

AN APOLOGY is an expression of remorse (either verbal or written) over an action that caused problems, harm, or inconvenience for another person.

Leaders are human. They make mistakes, and when they do, an apology is necessary. Employees also make mistakes, and at times, it is essential for their leader to apologize to someone (a customer, for instance) on their behalf. The captain is always accountable for the actions of the crew.

Failing to apologize in these situations sends a message that you are either clueless (which is seldom the right message for a leader to send) or that you just don't care (which is even worse than being clueless).

Nevertheless, it's important to recognize when an apology is appropriate (or not). For some, apologetic phrases are an unconscious verbal habit. A leader should not offer an apology unless he or she has some level of responsibility for the problem that occurred (empathy, perhaps – but not an apology).

In general, an apology should be offered as soon as you are aware that one is necessary. When possible, make the apology in person, face-to-face. Not only is this perceived as more sincere, it avoids the creation of a document that could be used against you later.

A graceful apology has six key stages, and all six stages are mandatory.

1. *Acknowledge the consequences*. When making an apology, begin by showing that you clearly recognize the problem,

harm, or inconvenience the other person felt or experienced by stating it in your own words. It is important that the other person knows that *you* know what he or she is going through.

2. *Explain that the consequences were unintended.* Some people jump to the conclusion that others are *trying* to hurt them. So once you acknowledge the consequences, state very clearly that you did not mean for those consequences to occur.

3. *Accept responsibility.* Tell the person that you accept responsibility for the outcome. Do not offer any explanations or excuses. (Say, "I'm responsible for the delay you experienced." Do not add, "...but I had three people out sick that day.")

4. *Express regret.* Say "I'm sorry it happened." Do not talk about how bad *you* feel (Don't say, "I'm really upset about that"). Also, don't apologize for how the other person feels (Don't say, "I'm sorry you're angry"). Remained focused on the consequences you acknowledged initially.

5. *Repair the damage.* Summarize the action you'll take to ensure that the problem doesn't occur again. Also, state what you intend to do to rectify the current situation. If you're unsure about how to "make things right," ask. If the person is unresponsive, explain how important the person is to you. Emphasize that you do not want to lose that valuable relationship, and then ask again.

6. *Follow up.* Take the action you promised, and then contact the person regularly – both to confirm that the situation has been resolved, and to rebuild any loss of trust. Be patient and persistent, but if the person insists on holding a grudge, all you can do is let go and move on.

Present a Strong Visual Image

ANY FACE-TO-FACE COMMUNICATION contains three key elements – the actual words that are spoken, tone of voice, and non-verbals (or "body language"). Each of those three factors contributes differently to our "liking" the person who is speaking to us: the words account for 7 percent, voice tone for 38 percent, and non-verbals for 55 percent.[19]

What this means is that you can say the *words* a leader should say, and speak them with a "leader-like" *tone of voice*, but if you don't *look the part* (i.e., if your appearance is incongruent with your words), a substantial portion of your message may be lost. Consider the following suggestions to present a strong visual image.

Look Your Best. Be clean and well-groomed. Dress appropriately – which usually means better than your employees, without overdoing it. Wear safety or protective equipment as required (set an example).

Pirate captains dressed a little "fancy" (given the nature of the occupation), but their attire matched that of other naval captains and gentlemen of the era. Clothes made the man (or woman). Even in today's ultra-casual workplace settings, 91 percent of workers say that their boss' appearance influences their perception of his or her professional competence.[20]

Make an effective entrance. The way you walk into a room makes a powerful statement about who you are. When someone in a position of authority enters a work area, all eyes are on that person (even if people appear to be focused on their jobs). Leaders are always "on stage," so avoid tentative entrances. Before you walk in, think about where you'll go and what you'll do. Move with a sense of purpose – smoothly and quickly. Don't look lost, hesitant, or absent-minded.

Establish eye contact with people immediately. Avoiding eye contact is almost always perceived as a sign of weakness or deception. When you approach anyone to communicate, look the person in the eyes. This accomplishes two things. First, it is a genuine token of openness and honesty. Second, eye contact instantly transmits positive energy.

Charismatic people are often described as having a "sparkle" in their eyes. Actually, *everyone* has that sparkle, but it is rarely noticed because most people do not make full eye contact when they meet or speak, and full eye contact is required to make the sparkle visible.

Smile. A "poker face" is a great asset – if you're in a poker game. In a workplace, however, it is usually perceived as hostile, threatening, and cold. This perception sets up a communication barrier. A grim, frowning leader rarely inspires or influences others. A smile, however, tells your followers, "We'll be okay."

Your smile is also an invitation to *connect*. A leader who never smiles may as well have a sign that says, "Leave me alone. I have nothing to give you, and you have nothing to offer me that I care about."

For some people, a smile comes naturally. If you're not one of those people, you'll have to consciously think about smiling in situations where you need to build rapport. Don't try to force a fake smile. Instead, relax your facial muscles, and then reflect on your feelings about a pleasant person or an enjoyable situation. Allow your normal smile to develop.

Shake hands. In the golden age of piracy, every father took his son aside and carefully taught him the importance of a good handshake. That rite of passage may seem quaint today, but physical touch still makes a powerful impression on people – and a handshake is about the only socially acceptable form of physical contact you can initiate in the workplace.

Fortunately, it is not difficult to deliver a hearty handshake that conveys warmth, openness, and a willingness to communicate. Grasp the other person's hand fully (your palms should touch, not just your fingers). Squeeze *moderately*. A firm handshake does not require a bone-crushing grip, but it should not be a "dead fish," either. While giving the handshake, do not look down at your hands, but rather into the eyes of the other person. Start talking *before* you let go: "It's great to meet you" or "How is it going today?"

Etiquette used to state that a man only shook hands with a woman if she offered her hand first. This is no longer the rule. If a woman wishes to be treated as an equal in a business setting, she will always shake hands (failure to do so is often interpreted as arrogance or a lack of self-confidence). Bottom line, a good handshake still matters to people in the 21st century.

Think before you sit. Making an entrance often concludes with taking a seat. How and where you sit gives everyone who is present a clear signal about your attitude and approach to work.

Don't rush to your seat. Take your time. Make eye contact and greet people. If others in the room are already seated, the process will give you a few moments to be "looked up to" – literally. This creates a strong impression in others that you are very much in control of the world around you (even if you're not).

Give some thought to where you sit. If you have a choice, choose a firm chair that allows you to maintain an upright posture. Avoid a sofa or soft chair that "swallows" you up. If there is natural light (from a window), having it behind you will help convey power and authority. Having the light on your face will help you convey honesty and sincerity.

If you are sitting at a rectangular table, be aware of the psychological geography. The greatest power position is, naturally, at the head of the table. The second most dominant position is at the other end of the table. The third dominant position is at the midpoint of either side of the table. The middle seats are also the most influential positions from which to build collaboration and consensus with other participants. The least favorable position is to the immediate right of the head of table (or the recognized leader), followed by the seat to the immediate left of the head (or the leader). Of course, not having a seat the table (but instead, sitting along a perimeter wall) is the weakest position possible.

If you are attending a session in a classroom or auditorium, sit near one end of the front row. People sit in the back so they can observe or slip in and out unnoticed. Great leaders are not observers or people who slip in and out – they are active participants, and always sit up front where the action is!

Be on time. You can toss out almost everything covered up to this point about "looking the part" if you arrive late. To make a powerful visual impression, always be on time – or better yet, be a couple of minutes early in order to give yourself an opportunity to connect with others.

Part VI.
"Full Sail"

Performance Management

Direct the Work

PREVIOUS SECTIONS of this book explained how to take command, formulate a vision, motivate, and communicate. Each of those skills will support your ability to lead other people. This section explains how you actually guide those people to consistently produce desired results. This is performance management.

In many organizations, the term "performance management" equates only to annual appraisals or disciplinary discussions. In the context of effective leadership, however, performance management is not a singular event. It is a continuous cycle of planning, organizing, and executing that involves regular conversations between leaders and employees.

To manage performance (and ultimately, to produce desired results), the leader must do two major things – direct the work to be done, and develop the people who do that work.

A leader's obligation to *direct the work* does not mean barking out orders or micromanaging every activity, but rather, providing a structure that will allow competent, committed employees to consistently do the right things the right way.

A leader's obligation to *develop the people* ensures that employees are competent to perform the work (i.e., knowledgeable, skilled, and experienced), and committed to doing it (i.e., confident, motivated, and enthusiastic).

The next three chapters in this section outline the specific steps you can take to direct the work. Subsequent chapters provide the skills and techniques you'll need to develop employees into highly competent and wholly committed peak performers.

There are three key components to directing the work: (1) setting goals, (2) planning actions, and (3) establishing standards.

Setting the goals for your employees means identifying the specific results you want. *Planning the actions* means defining the work activities that will be required to accomplish those results. *Establishing the standards* means specifying the key requirements and expectations that govern the manner in which work activities are performed.

There is a logical sequence to the three key components of directing the work (you obviously have to know what you want before you can determine the actions required to achieve it). Nevertheless, most organizations add or modify goals, revise plans, and update standards on routine basis. So, for leaders, directing the work is not a step-by-step process, but rather an iterative and ongoing system of management.

HR managers and EEO coordinators (who often investigate employee complaints of discrimination and harassment) suggest that as many as 95 percent of the employee complaints they receive are a direct result of a supervisor or manager who has arbitrarily and subjectively evaluated a worker's performance (instead of setting goals and establishing standards).[21]

When unacceptable work is the boss's *opinion*, it's easy for the non-performing employee to believe that he or she is being victimized. Goals and standards allow you to manage each employee's performance on the basis of *fact*.

Set the Goals

THE EFFECTIVE PERFORMANCE of any job or task begins with a goal. An organization without goals is like a ship drifting on the ocean – the crew is hopelessly trapped and bound for nowhere.

Three Levels

Most organizations set goals at three levels: strategic, tactical, and operational.

Strategic goals are broad objectives (usually two to five years in scope) that bridge the gap between an organization's current situation and its vision or mission. Strategic goals are typically set by senior managers.

Tactical goals are the specific outcomes to be achieved during a budget cycle (such as a quarter or fiscal year) in pursuit of a given strategic objective. Tactical goals are typically set by middle managers.

Operational goals are the results to be accomplished day-to-day and week-to-week in pursuit of a tactical goal. (Many organizations make a distinction between *operational* and *support* goals at this level, where operational goals are results that *directly contribute* to the mission, and support goals are results that sustain or *enable* those daily operations.) Goals at the operational (or support) level are typically set by supervisors and first-line managers.

All the goals within an organization should be aligned such that operational goals explain how a tactical goal will be achieved, and tactical goals explain how a strategic goal (and ultimately, the vision) will be attained. Likewise, a tactical goal should explain why an associated operational goal is being pursued, and a strategic goal should explain why a tactical goal exists.

Four Purposes

Goals may be set for four different purposes: achievement, maintenance, elimination, or prevention.

Achievement goals are set to attain something desirable that the organization doesn't yet have.

Maintenance goals are set to preserve something desirable that the organization does already have.

Elimination goals are set to reduce or eradicate something undesirable that the organization has.

Prevention goals are set to avoid something undesirable that the organization doesn't have (and doesn't want).

Three Types

At the operational level, there are three types of goals: recurring goals, project goals, and ad-hoc goals.

Recurring goals are pursued and attained repeatedly, usually on a cyclical basis. For example, "having a restorable backup disk for each computer hard drive" in an office might be set as a goal to accomplish at the end of every workday or every week.

Project goals are pursued and attained once, and involve a unique outcome or deliverable. "Having an application program upgraded to release 9.1.3 on all computers" in an office by the end of the week would be an example of a project goal.

Ad-hoc goals are also temporary in nature, but are set "on the fly" (in contrast to project goals, which are set and planned in advance). Ad-hoc goals are most often necessary when an unforeseen problem or obstacle delays progress on a recurring or project goal. For example, it might be necessary to "have a new video driver installed" on one older computer to allow a scheduled application upgrade to be completed – a condition that was unknown when the upgrade project was planned.

Two Methodologies

Goals (of all types) may be set in either a directive or a collaborative manner.

Directive goals are decided upon by a leader and then communicated to the employees. This is most appropriate when the leader personally has all the relevant information, experience, and expertise.

Collaborative goals are decided upon jointly by the leader and the employees. This is most appropriate when pertinent information, experience, and expertise are shared among all of the parties involved.

Seven Qualities

A goal should reflect seven qualities, regardless of the level to which it pertains, the type of goal it is, or how it is set. Every goal should be (1) outcome oriented, (2) verifiable, (3) achievable, (4) time-bound, (5) integrated, (6) official, and (7) noteworthy.

Outcome oriented – An effective goal should describe a result – something that a beneficiary will *have* or *be* when an activity is complete. ("Having a recoverable backup disk" is an example of an outcome. "Back up the hard drive" is an activity, not a goal.)

Verifiable – An effective goal, and the interim progress toward it, should be measurable – or at least capable of being objectively confirmed by observation. (For example, a backup disk either exists or it doesn't, and progress toward creating that disk can be readily quantified.)

Achievable – An effective goal should be physically possible, and the work required to attain it should be feasible. (A goal that can never be reached is frustrating.)

Time-bound – An effective goal should have an explicit deadline for completion. ("Having a restorable backup disk by 5:00 p.m. Friday," is an example.) A goal without a deadline is merely a "wish."

Integrated – An effective goal should be congruent with the other goals that impact the same people. In other words, the employee should not have to sacrifice one assigned goal in order to attain another.

Official – An effective goal should be legal, ethical, and sanctioned or supported by the organization. It should not exist to serve a personal motive or private agenda. The goal should also be documented. Stating a goal in writing dramatically increases the probability that it will be achieved.

Noteworthy – An effective goal should be worth the effort required to accomplish it. Employees (especially workplace pirates) only give their best effort when they understand why the outcome is worth achieving.

Once effective goals are set, your next step is to define and plan the actions for achieving them...

Plan the Actions

A GOAL IDENTIFIES A DESIRED OUTCOME. A *plan* describes the actions required to attain that outcome. Planning is a leadership responsibility, though (like goal setting) it may be done in a directive or collaborative manner, and may involve people from various levels of an organization.

Once you have set a goal, there are eight steps you can take to define and plan the actions that will be necessary to achieve it: (1) work breakdown, (2) task definition, (3) resource identification, (4) duration estimating, (5) cost estimating, (6) activity sequencing, (7) scheduling, and (8) budgeting.

Work Breakdown

When the achievement of a goal is expected to involve more than one person – or when it will require more than one day to accomplish – the outcome may be broken down (subdivided) into a series of *interim results* or *component deliverables*.

For example, the goal of having a ship repainted would involve multiple people for several days. An interim result for that goal might be that at the end of the first day, a section is prepped and ready for primer.

Performance is more manageable when large goals are broken down into a series of smaller and shorter-term outcomes that meet the seven qualities outlined in the previous chapter. This type of breakdown also helps you confirm that whatever employees are working on at a given point in time has a legitimate purpose, and is aligned with the vision and mission of the organization.

Task Definition

The next step in planning the work is to define the series of activities or *tasks* that are required to produce each interim result or component deliverable.

A task is an element of work that generally involves one person (or multiple people working as one unit), and can be completed in a day or less without interruption (i.e., without being diverted to a different goal, and without acquiring additional resources).

For recurring goals, the major tasks may be pre-defined in the form of operating protocols, standard procedures, etc. For project and ad-hoc goals, you will create a list of work tasks based on past experience.

Resource Identification

Next, for each task defined above, you identify the resources that will be required to complete that task. You also determine when those resources need to be available (relative to the start of the activity), and where they will be located when the task begins.

The resources to consider include not only facilities, equipment, materials, and supplies – but also the human resources necessary to perform the task. You may choose to identify an actual employee at this point, or simply identify the knowledge, skills, and qualifications needed – and assign the individual later.

Duration Estimating

Your next step is to estimate the amount of time it will take to complete each defined task (given the resources that you just identified).

Task durations that are associated with a recurring goal can be estimated using past performance as a guide. Some repetitive tasks may have standard completion times built in already.

The duration of a unique task, performed in support of a project or ad-hoc goal, can be more difficult to estimate. You may have to base these on expert judgment, the time required to complete similar activities elsewhere, and/or a statistical estimating methodology.

Cost Estimating

The fifth step in planning the work is to estimate the costs that are associated with all resources required to complete each defined task.

If a task will involve the lease or purchase of equipment and materials, the cost of that lease or purchase is projected. If the task will consume supplies from stock, an estimate may be made on a pro-rata basis. You may estimate the cost of human resources (labor) using task durations and pay rates – although many organizations prefer to use a standard labor rate that includes the cost of benefits and overhead.

Activity Sequencing

To achieve a desired result, some tasks must be performed in a specific order (for instance, a surface must be prepped before it is primed, and primed before it is painted). Activity sequencing identifies dependencies among interrelated tasks.

If the work you are planning involves multiple task dependencies (the start of one task depends on the completion of several others, or vice versa), you may wish to create a network diagram to visualize the logic.

Scheduling

This step in the planning process analyzes all of the resource requirements, duration estimates, cost estimates, and activity sequences to determine the exact dates or times that work will begin and end on each task, and who will be performing that work.

In most cases, adjustments and "trade-offs" are necessary to reduce slack time, prevent bottlenecks, and avoid the over-scheduling or underutilization of key resources. Work management software can be a helpful tool for analyzing and preparing complex work schedules and for managing work assignments.

Budgeting

The final step in planning the work is budgeting, but what this entails depends on the goal and on your position within the organizational hierarchy.

If you need approval from higher up to pursue the goal, budgeting is the process by which you justify and request the money and resources necessary for a specific fiscal period. If you are the "approving authority" in this situation, budgeting is the process by which you authorize the work to be done during the period, and allocate the money and resources to do it.

In most organizations, money and resources are limited, so planning is often an iterative process – you may need to repeat the earlier steps in order to revise a goal, redefine the associated tasks, modify the resources required, and adjust the duration, cost, sequence, and schedule of activities in order to meet resource, time, or budget constraints.

As the work is planned, performance standards should also be established...

Establish the Standards

GOALS DEFINE THE RESULTS to be achieved. Plans describe the work required to reach those goals. *Standards* explain how the results will be confirmed and measured. Standards also describe the processes and behaviors that must be observed or practiced as a job or task is performed. In essence, standards enable everyone to agree on what constitutes "good work."

The same standards apply to *everyone* who works on a specific goal (except those who are still being trained). Leaders may set different *targets* for different employees (more about that later), but the same minimum standards apply to everybody. Granted, some may struggle to meet a certain standard, while others exceed it easily. Nevertheless, if employees are doing the same job in support of the same goal, then they are subject to the same standards.

Three types of standards are needed: output standards, process standards, and behavior standards.

Output Standards

Output standards define (and provide a way to confirm and measure) the results produced by a given work task.

Output standards normally include: quantity expectations (defining how much should be done); budget expectations (defining how much it should cost to do it); quality expectations (defining how "good" it should be when it's done); schedule expectations (defining when it should be delivered).

Process Standards

Process standards define (and provide a way to confirm and measure) the methods used to complete a given work task.

Process standards may include: *compliance* expectations (defining legal, regulatory, and procedural guidelines that should be followed); *risk management* expectations (defining actions that should be taken to prevent incidents, accidents, or other negative events); *integration* expectations (defining how the task "fits in" with everything else the organization is doing); *information* expectations (defining the data or other details that should be collected and compiled as the work proceeds); *communication* expectations (defining the reports or other notifications that should be made).

Behavior Standards

Behavior standards define (and provide a way to confirm and measure) the actions people take while completing a given work task.

Behavior standards represent a broad array of characteristics: responsibility; flexibility; dependability; service; integrity; respect; initiative; collaboration; interaction; optimism; perception; judgment. It is essential that you identify *specific* expectations for each relevant category. For example, "Prompt" is too vague. "At work on time" is better. "Actively working on the day's first scheduled task by 8:00 a.m." defines exactly what's expected, and it's a behavior that can be objectively observed and verified.

Stakeholder Perspective

Standards in all three of the above categories should be considered and established from a variety of perspectives, not just those of the leader, manager, or crew members. This can be done by asking four questions:

1. What outputs, processes, and behaviors are most important relative to satisfying the *owners'* or *stockholders'* needs and expectations (or for an entity in the public sector, the expectations of sponsoring politicians and taxpaying citizens)?

2. What outputs, processes, and behaviors are most important relative to satisfying the *customers'* needs and expectations (or for an entity in the public sector, the needs of the agency's beneficiaries)?

3. What outputs, processes, and behaviors are most important relative to helping the *work unit* or *team* excel at its function or purpose?

4. What outputs, processes, and behaviors are most important relative to helping the *individual* learn and increase the value of his or her contribution to the organization?

Application, Congruence, and Primacy

Some standards are applied universally, to every employee in a company or organization. Other more specific and/or more stringent standards may apply only to a particular department or work unit.

For example, an organization could have a process standard regarding the disposal of used dry cell batteries from portable devices. This standard would apply to all employees in the workplace. A more specific set of guidelines for transferring those used batteries from the workplace to a sanitary landfill or recycling center would exist for the work unit (within the organization) that was charged with that unique responsibility. However, both sets of standards would exist to support the same environmental, safety, and health goals.

Standards should be congruent (in harmony) with one another. Workplace pirates are superbly adept at identifying non-congruent standards and using them to their advantage – very often by pitting one standard against another. Examples of this would be the employee who asks, "Do you want me to do it *fast*, or do you want me to do it *right*? Do you want me to help the customer or make the stockholders rich?"

The answer in each case, of course, is *both*. Your standards should not create an "either-or" situation. Employees must be capable of meeting *all* expectations.

Even so, in the real world, there may sometimes be unforeseen circumstances that cause certain standards to be in conflict temporarily. For instance, if a seal on a production machine suddenly begins to leak, it might place the output standards for an assembly task at odds with process standards for that same task. It may truly be impossible for the employee running that machine to meet quantity and schedule expectations while fully complying with safety and environmental standards.

To address provisional episodes like these, every employee should know what the "prime directive" is for a given action or job task – the one standard and stakeholder perspective that is *never* to be comprised when that particular task is being performed.

As goals are set, actions are planned, and standards are established, you can begin to focus more of your effort on the *people* who perform the work...

Develop the People

YOUR ROLE AS A LEADER is to develop the competence and commitment of your people – whether they were hired yesterday or have worked there for years.

Competence is the knowledge, skill, experience, and judgment to perform a job task. *Commitment* is the confidence, motivation, and enthusiasm to perform that job task as well as possible. Both elements are essential to good performance.

It doesn't matter how competent a person is if he or she lacks the confidence or motivation to apply those capabilities. Likewise, the most enthusiastic person in the world cannot excel at something that he or she knows nothing about. Outstanding job performance requires high levels of both competence and commitment relative to the key skills and major tasks that pertain to the job.

As previously explained, pirate captains often had to take whatever crew they could find – which meant setting sail with men who were neither competent nor committed. To succeed (and survive), a captain had to *develop* the skills of each crew member.

Similarly, modern day leaders who are unable to hire people who are competent and committed to begin with must *develop* the employees they have. Employee development is the heart of performance management.

You may have heard the term "learning curve." The path of employee development follows a "U" shaped curve – much like the half-pipe used in extreme sports.

The horizontal dimension (from left to right) represents an employee's level of competence. The left end of the curve reflects the "potential" state – little or no knowledge, skill, experience, or judgment relative to the specific job. The right end of the curve reflects the "developed" state – expert knowledge, advanced skills, broad experience, and keen judgment.

The vertical dimension (from bottom to top) represents an employee's level of commitment. The upper ends of the curve indicate high commitment – a willingness to perform the job, and a feeling of confidence that it can be done well (or learned). The bottom of the curve indicates low commitment – a lack of job-related enthusiasm, motivation, or confidence.

Consider the process by which you learned to drive a car. If you're like most Americans, you began with an *orientation* of what the process involved. From there, you entered the *cognitive* (first) stage of learning (where you gained knowledge and skills in a classroom setting). Although your competence was steadily increasing, that stage of development was neither easy nor fun – so your enthusiasm, and perhaps your confidence, were most likely decreasing at the same time.

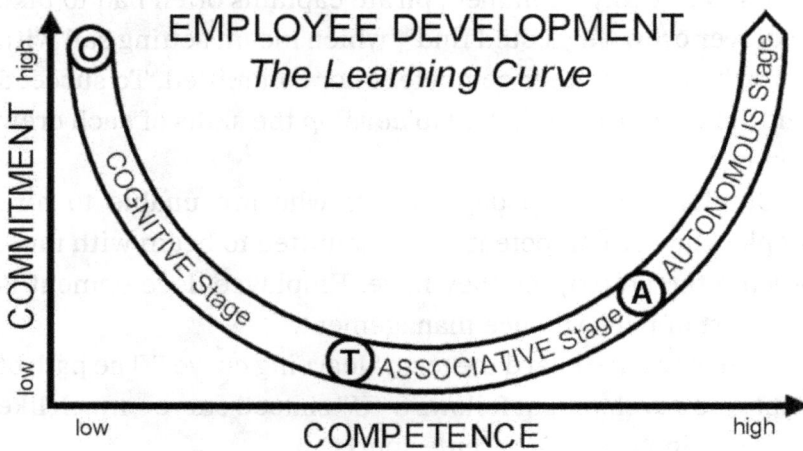

EMPLOYEE DEVELOPMENT
The Learning Curve

COMMITMENT — high / low
COMPETENCE — low / high

COGNITIVE Stage
ASSOCIATIVE Stage
AUTONOMOUS Stage

Had learning to drive been a "hobby" (like learning to play a sport or a musical instrument), you might have quit at this "low point." Yet because you really wanted your license, you made the *transition* to the next phase – you received your "learner's permit" and began the *associative* (second) stage of development. Here, you applied your knowledge and skills on the road (with an expert driver in the car to guide you). Finally, you were ready for an *appraisal*, which resulted in the receipt of your license.

Even then, the learning didn't stop. You still had to gain experience in traffic and weather situations that never arose during driver training. This was the *autonomous* (third) stage – you were driving by yourself, but continued to receive guidance from your parents or other authorities when warranted. Eventually, you became an "expert" driver (although you are still subject to appraisals of your capability).

Through each phase of the learning process, a "leader" provided you with something that you could not provide for yourself at that point. When you lacked knowledge, the leader provided instruction. When you lacked skill, the leader provided coaching. When you lacked confidence, the leader provided reinforcement. The leader didn't *manage* you, but rather *developed* you (perhaps into a better driver than he or she was).

Here's a fact that most managers never consider. The knowledge, skills, experience, and judgment required to operate a motor vehicle are more complex (and potentially far more dangerous) than those associated with 99 percent of the jobs found in a modern workplace. Even so, the average 16-year-old achieves autonomy with only 42 hours of guidance spread over a 90-day period.

Do the employees under your leadership who have 90 days or more of experience at a given job consistently achieve goals and meet standards – with minimal supervision on your part? If not, it doesn't *have* to be that way. You can apply this same development curve to the employees you manage, and to the jobs and work tasks they perform.

The remaining chapters in this section explain the specific techniques you can use to:

- *Hire intelligently* by recruiting and identifying the right person for a job to begin with (when you have the opportunity to do so);
- *Create expectations* by conducting an orientation that clearly communicates the goals, actions, and standards associated with a new job (or with a new task being assigned to a current employee);
- *Teach and train* an employee on the basics of a new job or assigned task (during the cognitive stage);
- *Inspire commitment* from an employee who has basic competence, but little or no motivation;
- *Connect* with and *coach* an employee toward "self-management" (during the associative stage);
- *Document progress* by formally assessing the employee's readiness to work (or continue working) without supervision;
- *Support and mentor* employees who are working independently (during the autonomous stage);
- *Handle performance problems* (when you have done all of the above correctly, but still have a non-performing employee).

As a leader, you will provide each employee with different things at different times in order to help the person develop fully. One size does not fit all!

Hire Intelligently

As ALREADY NOTED, performance management is not a singular event. It is a series of conversations that a leader has with a follower to help the follower develop the competence to do his or her job, and the commitment to do the job as well as possible.

If you can hire a highly competent and totally committed job candidate to start with, the performance management conversations you have with that person will usually be simple and pleasant – so intelligent hiring is the logical place to begin.

As previously noted, however, pirate captains rarely had the opportunity to "hire" highly competent and committed people. If you don't either, read this chapter anyway – because once you begin to apply the performance management techniques presented in the chapters immediately following this one, the factors that limit your current hiring situation will almost certainly change for the better.

The three most important aspects of intelligent hiring are the job description, the recruiting/application process, and the interview.

The Job Description

It will be nearly impossible to find a suitable job candidate if you don't really know what the job involves. Create a clear written description of every position you supervise or manage, including the tasks and responsibilities associated with a job, and the qualifications required to fill it.

One simple way to do this is with a question-driven job description software program. These programs are readily available and quite affordable. The software poses questions to those who know the job best (i.e., everyone who supervises or performs the job currently, plus anyone who did so in the recent past).

Each participant provides responses that define the actual job duties, physical demands, qualifications, and behaviors necessary to produce a desired result. Based on the replies (and other occupational factors), the software generates a thorough and legal job description for your review.

The Recruiting/Application Process
When you post or advertise a job opening, include the specific requirements listed in the job description to screen out unqualified individuals.

Ensure that your job application form is legal. It cannot ask for date of birth, gender, or information pertaining to U.S. citizenship, criminal arrests, or personal health.

The application may ask if the person is authorized to work in the United States, and if the person has any criminal *convictions*.

The form should include a place for the applicant's signature and date, along with a clause granting you permission to check references and background information, and a waiver of liability for doing so. If your application doesn't comply with these guidelines, create one that does.

Review every application and résumé you receive for omissions and misrepresentations. Look for gaps in employment, and be suspicious of information that is vague or incomplete. Never accept an applicant's word that he or she has a particular license, diploma, or degree. Check with the applicable school or agency.

Visit the candidate's on-line social network pages (MySpace, Facebook, etc.). Someone who brags to his friends about being a "slacker" probably is.

Find a reliable third-party to conduct background checks. In addition to cost and speed, consider how the investigating firm acquires its information, whether the information is accurate and up-to-date, and what assistance the firm provides to help you comply with federal and state privacy laws.

If an applicant has a criminal history, it should only disqualify the person in cases where the conviction is related to the work the person would be performing. For example, a conviction for sexually molesting a child is relevant to working at a day care center. A DUI conviction ten years ago may not be relevant to working as a spot welder in an assembly plant.

Refuse to hire anyone who provides false information on the job application, and be sure to document that your refusal to hire was because they gave you fraudulent or misleading information.

If an applicant is otherwise qualified, don't allow an irrelevant conviction, past termination, or one-time discipline problem to automatically eliminate the person from consideration. To find a crew, pirate captains usually had to overlook past mistakes and give people a chance to start fresh. You may have to do the same – but don't waste your time on people who begin the relationship by trying to deceive you.

Of course, these are just helpful guidelines. Always know and follow your organization's policies.

The Interview

The main reason to conduct an employment interview is to predict performance. By the end of the interview, you want to know as accurately as possible if the candidate can (and will) do the job.

Predicting future performance requires an accurate assessment of not only a person's aptitude and abilities, but also his or her behavior on the job. The interview should give you some insight into this, yet the "traditional" interview questions used by most organizations fall well short of doing so.

"What can you tell me about yourself?" is the cliché example of an interview question that gets you nothing more than a well-rehearsed monologue.

"What did you like most about your last job?" merely gives you some insights into the candidate's personal preferences – or worse, the preferences that he or she thinks you want to hear.

These, and other often-used questions like them, have no predictive value in a job interview.

Education, qualification programs, skills testing, and proficiency exams can accurately predict a person's capability to perform a specific job task, and are therefore useful selection tools. The best predictor of future behavior, however, is past behavior in a similar situation. Therefore, your interview questions should reach beyond what the candidate can do – and help you to determine what the candidate will do.22

The key to intelligent hiring is the use of interview questions that focus on past behavior. For example, suppose you are interviewing a person to staff your Customer Help Line. You know that you are looking for a good communicator who will be well-organized, exhibit a service-oriented attitude, and have the persistence to stick with a problem until it is resolved. How can you predict if the candidate you are interviewing will have what it takes? By asking questions about his or her past behavior in similar circumstances, for example:

"Tell me about a time when you had to give instructions or directions to someone over the phone who was upset or under stress."

"Give me an example of a job or assignment where you had to organize and maintain records, logs, and other paperwork."

"Good service means different things to different people. Thinking back over your experience with customers, what were some of the differences you saw in the type of service that people expected?"

"Tell me about a time at work when someone commented on the self-discipline and persistence you used to solve a problem or complete a task. Feel free to brag on yourself."

The information that comes from these questions allows the interviewer to more objectively assess an applicant's ability and willingness to do the job. It's almost as if the interviewer were watching the candidate at work.

To prepare these types of questions, consider which behaviors are the most crucial to the success of the organization. Among workers who are now performing the job, what makes them effective? What actions or conduct would you like to see more of?

Identify from three to five behaviors that you consider essential, and then develop a question for each that will invite your candidates to talk descriptively about their personal experiences in relation to the characteristics you are seeking.

Create a balance in the "tone" of the questions you prepare. The first two or three predictive questions you ask should be worded so candidates can respond by discussing positive characteristics and experiences. Later in the interview, you can introduce questions about challenges or failures.

As for the interview itself, it will usually be limited to an hour or less. The first few minutes are dedicated to putting the candidate at ease.

Begin with small talk, sticking to "safe" topics like the weather. Avoid asking questions that the candidate may not know anything about (sports and hobbies), or that may be illegal (family-related inquiries). If possible, conduct the interview over the corner of a table, rather than across a desk.

Once you are seated, give the candidate a brief background of your experience with the organization, and describe the position for which the candidate is being interviewed. Then outline your agenda for the interview (be sure the candidate knows that you are allowing ample time at the end of the meeting to answer his or her questions). Mention that you will be taking notes to help you remember each candidate.

Next, describe the nature of the questions you will be asking. For example, "Some of the questions in this interview will ask you to recall a specific event or accomplishment from your past. It may take you a few moments to remember the details of something that happened, but don't let that stress you. Relax and take your time. The more information you can offer, the more useful it will be in getting to know you better."

When you have completed this introductory portion of the interview, you may begin asking the predictive behavioral questions you have prepared. When you ask a question, allow the person at least fifteen seconds to formulate a response. This will seem like a very long silence, but be patient. Most candidates do not come to an interview prepared to talk in such detail about their past experiences – so give them the time to think and respond.

If the candidate has not said anything after fifteen seconds, or indicates that he or she simply can't think of anything to say, you will then offer a reassuring statement. "That's okay. It can be difficult to recall specific events from your past like that." Then rephrase the question.

For instance, if you initially asked the candidate to describe a time when she gave instructions over the phone to someone who was upset, you might restate the question to say, "Can you think of anyone you tried to help recently who was upset? Tell me about that."

The more recent and the more detailed the response, the more likely it is to be a predictor of good performance. Help the candidate to be specific by asking for names, dates, and other details. As a candidate responds, take enough notes to allow you to recall the details of the example.

Be wary of vague answers, such as "It happens all the time." Empathize, and then restate the question to try to get a specific example.

Also be cautious of general answers that use the word "we." Offer a reassuring statement, and then rephrase the question. For example, "It sounds like your team handled that very well. I'm most interested in hearing what *you* did, personally, to bring about the solution. Tell me more about that."

Finally, listen for "slip" answers that begin with phrases like "What I usually do is..." or "The general procedure for that would be..." These answers confirm that the candidate *knows* what actions and behaviors are expected – but not that he or she actually *performs* those actions or exhibits those behaviors. If you "get the slip," take responsibility and then rephrase the question. For example, "I'm sorry – maybe I didn't ask that clearly. I'd like for you to tell me about a *specific* customer call that you handled recently."

When you have completed the predictive behavior questions, invite the candidate to ask his or her questions about the job or organization, and provide the appropriate responses. Wrap up the interview by accurately describing what the job entails, including the challenges the candidate would face and the rewards to be gained. Thank the person for coming in and explain what happens next in terms of when the hiring decision will be made and how the applicant will be notified.

Ask every candidate the same predictive questions. When all interviews for a given position are complete, gather your notes and score the candidates' responses. Using a "1 to 5" scale, a non-answer would rate a "1." If an example lacked detail or relevance, it might rate a "2" or "3." A detailed response with names, places, and dates would rate a "4." If the names were verifiable and could serve as references, or if the experience provided a well-known or well-documented benefit, the response might rate a "5."

Tally the score for each response and divide it by the total possible points. A result of 70 percent or higher is a reliable predictor of overall success.

Of course, this predictive interview technique is meant to augment, not replace, the other guidelines provided by your organization for legal and effective hiring interviews.

Create Expectations (Orientation)

WHEN ANY NEW ACTIVITY is undertaken for the very first time, the normal starting point in the development process is high commitment and low competence. Before learning can begin, the leader must provide the employee with an *orientation* to create expectations about what lies ahead.

The Karate Kid

Although it isn't considered a pirate movie, *The Karate Kid* (Columbia Pictures, 1984) poignantly illustrates each stage of the performance development curve, beginning with the orientation.

In the film, teenager Daniel LaRusso (Ralph Macchio) is caught in a whirlpool of negativity after his father's death, his family's move from New Jersey to California, and numerous confrontations with students from a local karate dojo who bully him at school. Daniel has high commitment (he's motivated to learn karate and believes he can), but low competence (no knowledge, skill, or experience in martial arts).

Mr. Miyagi (Noriyuki "Pat" Morita, who received an Oscar nomination for the role) eventually agrees to become Daniel's *sensei* (meaning leader, teacher, coach, and mentor as the term is generally used in English). Before the training begins, Mr. Miyagi asks Daniel if he is ready. Daniel replies, "Yeah, I guess so."

Miyagi explains, "Either you karate do *yes*, or karate do *no*. You karate do *guess so*, get squished just like grape. Understand?"

When Daniel confirms that he understands and is ready, Miyagi communicates his expectations: "First make sacred pact. I promise teach karate. That my part. You promise learn. I say, you do. No question. That your part. Deal?"

An actual employee orientation involves a bit more than that, but the purpose is the same. The leader's role is to *create expectations* by clearly explaining what the job (and the process of learning the job) will entail, and by outlining the skills, actions, and behaviors that the employee will need to demonstrate.

There are three kinds of employee orientations. The first is a *new hire* orientation, normally conducted by a Human Resources professional on the first day of employment. The second is a *work area* orientation, conducted by a supervisor or manager when the new employee joins a workgroup. The third is a *situational* orientation, conducted by a leader whenever a new task or project is assigned (or when a substantially new tool or process is introduced to an existing job).

New Hire Orientation

The purpose of this orientation is to provide a new employee with an overview of the organization and an awareness of important policies and procedures that apply to everyone (for example, pay periods, holidays, parking, insurance, pension plans, and union issues). A discussion of the organization's policies regarding workplace safety, violence, and harassment are especially important – as are legal requirements such as the location of mandatory employment posters.

Required paperwork is also completed during this orientation, including forms for social security and employment eligibility verification, credential and reference checks, payroll withholding, benefits elections, identification or security card issuance, personal data, and emergency contact information.

Work Area Orientation

This orientation helps a newly hired employee understand the function of the work unit to which he or she is assigned. Topics include the general layout of the work area, the employee's specific workspace (office, cubicle, etc.), an introduction to coworkers, and an overview of the employee's basic job responsibilities (and how these fit in to the unit's overall mission). This is also the time to discuss any specific rules and regulations that apply (i.e., your "code").

Most work area orientations are conducted too quickly, and without a checklist or agenda. In some cases, the manager simply tells the first available employee to "show the new hire around" (and too often, the person chosen at random is a resentful workplace pirate who converts the enthusiastic new arrival to the dark side before lunch!). Remember, during the first few days, a new employee seeks positive confirmation that joining your organization was the right decision. Seize the chance to present your organization and department in a favorable light!

A work area orientation is best conducted by the immediate supervisor and/or manager, since much of the content will be specific to the workspace and the type of work to be performed. This orientation should begin with the most important information (basic job survival). The orientation should emphasize people as well as procedures (a new employee should be given some insight into both the social and work styles of his or her future teammates).

A new employee can't absorb everything on the first day, so don't try to rush through this orientation. Prepare an outline in advance of the things the employee needs to know, prioritize your list, and present the new information gradually (over the course of the first week, for example). Let the employee see your agenda up front so that he or she realizes when and how everything will be covered.

If you choose to delegate some of the items on your orientation checklist to another experienced employee, be sure that the designated person has the competence, commitment, and communication skills to carry out the orientation as thoroughly and effectively as you would.

During the orientation, take an opportunity to talk in terms of "how we do things around here" and "nothing is more important than..." – so the employee understands your vision and values. Be positive and emphasize the things that are truly important to you and your work unit. Also, be sure to give the employee regular opportunities to ask questions along the way. This is the first and best chance you'll have to create the attitude you want in your new worker.

Done correctly, a work area orientation will make a significant difference in how quickly a new employee becomes productive – and will set the tone for the remainder of the employment relationship.

Situational Orientation

The purpose of a situational orientation is to allow the person to "drop in" to the learning curve with a reasonable expectation of what lies ahead. Obviously, this orientation is necessary for a new hire, but it should also be provided for any employee who is given a new job, assignment, project, or task (or when a substantially new tool or procedure is introduced to an existing job). In other words, any time an employee is expected to learn or do something new, the process should be "launched" with a situational orientation.

A new job or assignment (even a desirable one) can be stressful. Change creates a sense of anxiety in most people. A situational orientation reduces this anxiety by giving the person an idea of what to expect from the job, the learning process, and the other people involved. It also lets the employee know what others expect of him (or her) relative to the assigned task.

Besides reducing anxiety, this information allows the initial learning stage to proceed at a faster pace. It also keeps the employee from sinking so low in terms of commitment once the learning process begins.

If the employee is dropped into the learning situation without an orientation, he or she may feel that: (a) the job is not important, (b) he or she is undervalued, or (c) he or she is being "set up to fail." In all three cases, commitment takes a nosedive.

This orientation is conducted personally by the immediate supervisor. It should include the following:

- Define the goal (desired outcome) of the job or assignment, and explain how it fits into the larger operational, tactical, and strategic goals of the organization.
- Outline the action steps that will be required to achieve the goal, and the responsibility the employee will have for completing those steps during each stage of development.
- Discuss the output, process, and behavior standards that apply to each action, and clarify the how each will be measured or observed.
- Identify the other people with whom the employee will be working to complete assigned tasks (not just coworkers, but all individuals with whom the employee will be expected to interact).

- Identify the resources (tools, materials, equipment, etc.) that the employee will require, and explain the process for accessing controlled or consumable items like supplies.
- Describe the development process that lies ahead of the employee, and the leadership style you will use in each stage of development (as explained in the next five chapters) to ensure that the employee is successful.
- Clarify the scope of the employee's initiative and authority (i.e., what is the employee encouraged to do on his/her own, and what actions require your awareness or advanced approval).

It may take several hours to cover these points with a new hire when you are making an initial job assignment. As with the work area orientation, don't rush the process, and don't overload the employee with too much input at once.

It may take only a few minutes to cover the above seven points when you are orienting an experienced employee on something as simple as a new procedural step that will be used to perform an existing job. Whether it's comprehensive or brief, however, an appropriate situational orientation will shorten the learning curve, increase productivity, reduce errors, facilitate compliance, promote job satisfaction, and create a solid framework for communicating with your employees about the work they do.

Teach and Train (Cognitive Stage)

WHEN THE ORIENTATION is complete, the employee enters the *cognitive* (first) stage of development. The leader's role in this stage is to *teach and train* the employee by presenting the basic knowledge, core skills, fundamental procedures, and rudimentary "mechanics" of the job. The leader also helps the employee prevent mistakes, avoid "bad habits," and attain the level competence necessary to understand and correctly perform an assigned task.

If you're teaching and training a person who has never performed any aspect of the job before, the cognitive stage may run for several weeks. If you're simply teaching a new safety procedure to a long-time employee, or explaining a company-specific process to an experienced new hire, this stage may take only a few minutes. In either case, you follow the same training steps (although the steps may be abbreviated or conducted at a faster pace when the employee is already competent at most of the related skills).

You've no doubt heard of "Rosie the Riveter," the American icon that represents women who entered the U.S. workforce for the first time during World War II. Before the war, women were considered to be capable of performing only 29 percent of the nation's jobs. In July, 1942 the government declared that 85 percent of all jobs, including many factory positions, could be filled by women *if* they were properly trained.[23]

Job Instruction Training (also called JIT) was the structured method that enabled people who had absolutely no prior knowledge, skill, or experience in a job to quickly complete the cognitive stage of development. JIT was the essential key to America's wartime production (and to Japan's post-war recovery).

Job Instruction Training is different than other forms of education in that *one* leader teaches *one* employee how to perform *one* specific task. Once the employee is able to perform the task and to consistently produce desired results under normal operating conditions, then the next related task is taught.

For the manufacturing operations that supported the war effort, three to six JIT sessions (conducted during the first two weeks of employment) were instituted to replace an arbitrary and unstructured apprentice program that often lasted four years or more. By 1944, more than 6 million American women with no prior experience were working productively in a demanding array of industrial jobs.

Although JIT was initially conceived for craft labor occupations such as welding and riveting, it has since been used effectively for almost every type of job (it is sometimes called *on-the-job training* or "OJT").

Preparation

The Job Instruction Training process begins with *preparation*. To prepare for JIT, consider the goal that the employee is to achieve, the actions that are necessary to achieve it, and the standards that apply.

With those things in mind, identify the basic *operation* (or sequence of activities) that the employee must complete in order to achieve the goal and meet the related standards. Break the operation into *key learning points* (logical "chunks"). Outline the knowledge and skills associated with each learning point, and determine the order in which the points should be introduced and accomplished. (For recurring goals, you'll likely do this only once – then simply *review* it to prepare for future JIT sessions.)

Preparation also means making a list of the equipment, tools, supplies, and other materials that are needed – and making sure they are available and ready before the JIT begins. Be sure to have the work area set up and arranged in the same way that the employee will be expected to maintain it.

In *The Karate Kid*, Mr. Miyagi uses four chores (washing/waxing cars, painting a fence, sanding a deck, and painting a house) to teach Daniel the fundamental posture, stance, breathing, and brain-muscle memory movements associated with self-defense. Each time Daniel arrives, Miyagi has everything prepared. Daniel never has to wait for his sensei to get organized. Each training activity begins immediately.

The JIT Process

As already noted, Job Instruction Training involves one leader teaching one employee how to perform one specific job task. This teaching process occurs in four simple steps:

1. Initiate the session;
2. Present the operation;
3. Allow the employee to try;
4. Observe and follow up.

1. Initiate the session.

Describe the operation that the employee will be expected to learn during the session, and explain its importance relative to the overall mission and function of the work unit and organization. Outline the key tasks, knowledge, and skills that are required to complete the operation. Ask probing questions to find out what the employee already knows about these (so you can abbreviate or accelerate the teaching process where appropriate).

Put the person at ease by outlining the next three training steps that you are about to complete together. Assure the person that others have completed the learning process successfully. The employee should be upbeat and eager to get started, not anxious or nervous.

2. Present the operation.

Explain each step of the operation verbally, covering the key learning points patiently, completely, and in proper sequence. Then demonstrate how the operation is done, emphasizing the knowledge and skills you are applying. Illustrate any common mistakes, explain why it is important to avoid them, and show the employee how to do so.

Repeat the demonstration, only this time, ask questions during each step to ensure that the employee understands what you were doing and why.

If you are supervising a job at which you are not experienced or adept, you may utilize another qualified person (who has reached the autonomous stage and is performing well) to assist you with JIT.

3. Allow the employee to try.

Ask the employee to demonstrate the operation. As he or she is doing so, ask relevant probing questions (who, what, when, where, why, how?) pertaining to the operation in order to verify that the employee fully understands the details of the job. (Be sure that during step 1, you tell the employee that you'll be doing this, so he/she doesn't become frustrated or anxious.)

As the employee performs the operation, observe carefully, offer praise when appropriate, and provide corrective feedback when necessary to address errors or mistakes. If the employee is struggling, assume that that you may have covered a key learning point too quickly in an earlier step – go back and patiently repeat a portion of the instruction if necessary. You should only move on to step 4 when both you and the employee *know* that he/she is ready.

4. Observe and follow up.

Allow the employee to practice the operation "off line" – i.e., under conditions where making a mistake won't cost the employee confidence, or cost you money. Check frequently to see that the employee is following procedures and attaining the desired result. Provide useful *corrective feedback* as needed to immediately address mistakes or problems (using the 3-step process described earlier in this book). Taper off your frequency of observation as the employee gains knowledge and skill.

Reminders

Employees learn best in context, in stages, and with practice. Be sure to communicate the reason for each step you present, and the larger context of how that step fits in to the overall job and purpose. Also divide the training experience into a series of logical lessons, and be sure the employee has grasped one lesson before moving on to the next. It isn't possible for an employee to know something too well, but it is very possible for someone to not know a critical procedure well enough. Finally, allow the employee to practice (with qualified guidance and corrective feedback) as often as he or she needs to in order to get it right.

What if the employee just can't seem to "get it right," in spite of your best efforts? Intelligent hiring should keep this from happening – but if you suspect that the employee lacks the mental or physical capacity to successfully perform the task or operation, notify your Human Resources manager. There are practical, ethical, and legal reasons for not placing a person in a job that he or she simply cannot do.

In many "pirate workplaces," workers who have reached the autonomous stage did so with little or no training or support – in fact, they may have advanced *in spite* of their boss and coworkers. As a result, they often feel that new employees should have to "pay the same dues," and they intentionally make it difficult for people to progress through the cognitive stage. Don't allow this to happen. Change the culture. The more quickly and more easily an employee can become productive, the better it is for everyone.

Because employees enter the cognitive stage of development with a high degree of commitment, they are initially eager to learn. Consequently, you want to teach them as *much* as you can as *fast* as you can before that enthusiasm fades. You need to prepare thoroughly and conduct the four JIT steps deliberately, but you also need to complete the requisite training in as brief a period as possible.

As learning progresses, the employee's level of commitment will steadily decline – that's normal and unavoidable. Before it "bottoms out" however, you need the employee to have attained a basic level of competence (fundamental knowledge and skill). From there, you can provide the inspiration necessary to transition the employee to the associative stage of development.

Inspire Commitment (Transition)

WHEN A PERSON undertakes a new activity (whether it's learning to drive, learning the skills associated with a hobby, or learning the key tasks necessary to perform a job), the person begins with a high level of commitment. Yet as fundamental knowledge and skills are gained, the person quite naturally loses some of his or her initial enthusiasm and self-assurance. Eventually, commitment "bottoms out," reaching its lowest point. This happens to every new learner, regardless of how good the teacher, trainer, or leader may be.

A skater dropping in to a half-pipe cannot build up enough speed to ascend the opposite side if he or she merely "coasts" – the forces of gravity and friction are too strong. To overcome them, the skater must "pump" the board at the bottom of the pipe to create the additional momentum necessary to shoot up the curve and "catch air" at the top.

People who have a compelling desire to achieve autonomy can "pump their own boards" – they are so motivated to self-actualize (be the best they can be) that they make the transition from the cognitive to the associative stage of development without help.

You were probably self-motivated in that way when it came to getting your driver's license – but how many other new skills were you that committed to learning in your life? Most people have started a hobby (for example, learning to play a musical instrument or taking up a new craft or sport), only to lose their momentum near the end of the cognitive stage. In some cases, the "fundamentals" were more difficult than the person imagined at the outset. In other cases, the learning process was incongruent with the person's "spirit." Often, the person discovered that he or she didn't really enjoy the activity after all – and no longer wanted to acquire the related skills.

In the case of a hobby, the person who "bottoms out" can simply quit and take up something else – no big deal. When the activity is employment-related, however, there may not be a "something else." If quitting (to seek another job) is not an option for the employee, he or she may *quit in place* (and merely "go through the motions" of doing work – forever after).

Has a portion of your workforce "quit in place?" Have you seen workplace pirates settle at the bottom of the development curve – and then show up for work with little or no commitment, and perform their jobs with no more than a basic level of competence?

To keep this from happening, the leader must apply a *transitioning* style of management as the employee nears the bottom of the learning curve. This style provides recognition, support, and inspiration to "pump the board," and gives the employee the momentum to proceed upward into the next stage of development. (For self-motivating employees who can make the transition on their own, this style provides acknowledgment and reinforcement.)

In *The Karate Kid*, Mr. Miyagi's "wax on, wax off" only went so far. By the fourth day, Daniel announced that he was quitting. Of course, Miyagi knew that Daniel would reach this low point eventually, and that the teaching and training style of leadership he had employed initially would become ineffective. He knew he'd have to change to a coaching style to develop Daniel any further – but first he'd have to convince Daniel to come back. Miyagi had to give his student what the student was incapable of giving himself – inspiration. The master was ready.

In one of the film's more dramatic sequences, Miyagi regains Daniel's respect and inspires him to return the following day by: (1) revealing a hidden power ("magically" relieving the pain in Daniel's shoulder); (2) confirming basic competence (requiring Daniel to demonstrate the brain-muscle movements he has learned); (3) linking the newly acquired knowledge and skills to a personal goal (showing Daniel that he has become adept at basic defensive moves, and actually taken a major step toward his objective); (4) providing meaningful recognition; and (5) previewing a positive future.

As a leader, you'll want to be prepared to do those same things yourself when an employee reaches the end of the cognitive learning stage and "bottoms out" in terms of commitment. For employees who have been stranded at the bottom of the curve for years, those same five actions – combined with the previously presented techniques for taking command, formulating a vision, motivating, and communicating – will often allow you to inspire and transition even the hardcore "scurvy dogs" in your workplace pirate crew.

Reveal a Hidden Power

You may not be able to heal an injury with your hands, but you do have "magical" powers from the perspective of an employee. Most leaders don't realize that. Successful pirate captains did. They always acquired, revealed, and leveraged certain "mystical" proficiencies – for example, expert navigational skills, a unique knowledge of weapons, or the ability to negotiate with a territorial governor.

Workplace pirates believe that their boss has the power to do things that would help them – but that the typical boss doesn't care and simply chooses not to. In an earlier chapter, you confirmed your sources of power. Now is the time to reveal one of those powers, and use it to benefit (and to impress) an employee who has lost his or her commitment. The point is to show the person that you're *not* a "typical" boss. It's one of the keys to the transition process.

Confirm Basic Competence

You can't move an employee into the associative stage of development if he/she doesn't have basic competence (much as you couldn't put a teenager behind the wheel in driver training if he/she couldn't pass the basic test to get a learner's permit).

Miyagi insists that Daniel demonstrate each of the movements he has learned over the previous four days. The reason is two-fold. First, Miyagi has to know that Daniel had internalized the basics – only if Daniel can do everything correctly and automatically (without thinking) will he be prepared to enter the next stage of development. Second, Miyagi needs Daniel to recognize just how much knowledge and skill he has gained in four days – so in spite of being fed up with the process and the teacher at that point, Daniel cannot help but realize that he has, in fact, *learned.*

Link Basic Competence to a Personal Goal

"Show me wax on, wax off. *Hi-yaa!*" Miyagi's fist flies toward Daniel, and Daniel handily deflects it (somewhat to his own amazement). Perhaps the most important element of the transition process is showing the employee *why* the training was valuable – and *how* the training has very quickly moved the person toward a desired goal (whatever he or she wants from the employment situation, and from life).

The best way to accomplish this is the same way Miyagi does – with a test or demonstration that requires the employee to use the basic knowledge and skills you have been developing throughout the JIT process. The more visible and dramatic the demonstration is, the more impact it will have and the more momentum it will create to propel the person up the learning curve.

A major retailer uses a series of JIT programs for entry level employees at its Internet Fulfillment Center. When the new employee has completed training and the supervisor believes the employee is ready, the employee is asked to cover the shipping floor while others on the shift attend a brief meeting. Soon, the printer runs out of labels, the dispenser runs low on packing peanuts, the conveyor jams – everything the employee has been trained to do (including safely retrieving supplies from upper shelves) is tested.[24]

Passing this "trial by fire" gives the employee pride and confidence, and shows future coworkers that the person is qualified to join the team. It also improves the overall quality of training. From the general manager's viewpoint, when an employee fails the test, it's because the leader failed to teach and train properly. Everyone has a vested interest in success.

Provide Tangible Recognition

Some form of visible recognition should be provided to acknowledge that an employee is transitioning from the cognitive stage of development to the associative stage. For example, a motor vehicle "learner's permit" provides tangible recognition for someone who has just passed a written driving exam. Employees in the previous example receive a company logo pin in a brief ceremony when they pass the "trial by fire." The pin symbolizes the end of their probationary training period and their acceptance as regular employees.

Although Miyagi gives Daniel tangible items to mark each stage of development (including an iconic head scarf, an embroidered dogi, and a 1950 Chevrolet convertible), the recognition you provide to your employee doesn't have to be fancy or expensive. It simply needs to be meaningful and representative of the employee's accomplishment. Remember, the goal is to recognize and inspire the employee to commit to the next stage of development.

Preview a Positive Future

As a leader, you can provide a final bit of momentum for the employee by offering a realistic, yet encouraging glimpse into the future. This preview should let the employee know that much work lies ahead, but that he or she is right on-track – and that the leader-to-employee relationship as it existed so far is about to change significantly. You will no longer be the teacher/trainer for this job or work process, but rather a performance coach...

Connect and Coach (Associative Stage)

AN EMPLOYEE at the *associative* (second) stage of development has some competence (basic knowledge and skill), but only a provisional degree of commitment (i.e., confidence and motivation are temporarily on the rise after a successful transition, but these factors are tentative, at best).

In *The Karate Kid*, if Mr. Miyagi had staged Daniel's transition and then, the next day, gone back to the same directive style of leadership that he used initially, it would have failed miserably. JIT can only take a person so far. Once Daniel reaches the transition point in his development, Miyagi changes his leadership approach to a more supportive and interactive style – *connecting* and *coaching*.

As a teen, when you received your learner's permit and entered the associative stage of driving, you most likely had a "driving coach" (instructor) for the behind-the-wheel portion of your development. How effective was that coach?

Some so-called coaches try to combine the first four stages – orientation, cognitive learning, transition, and associative development – into a single behind-the-wheel event. Others coaches do little more than sign a form stating that the required training is complete. Neither approach is effective at developing competence or confidence.

Hopefully, your coach was better, and guided you through a series of increasingly more challenging driving situations – situations that required you to apply the knowledge and skills you had attained in the classroom. The coach was in the passenger's seat, permitting you to make small mistakes in order to gain proficiency, yet preventing you from doing anything destructive or tragic.

At the appropriate times, your coach praised and reinforced the things you did well, answered questions, and constructively pointed out areas where you might have done better.

The coach also got you to think and talk about the various challenges and situations you encountered – and when appropriate, the coach shared meaningful tips, advice, and personal experiences.

The more driving you did, the more *competent* you became. The better you performed, the more *confident* you became. Of course, if you made a mistake or did not perform well, you may have temporarily lost some confidence – until your coach reassured you, helped you learn from the error, and gave you the opportunity to repeat the process until you were capable.

An effective leader doesn't try to develop an employee in one shot, nor does an effective leader expect the employee to figure it out alone. Effective leaders *connect* with employees through earned trust and skillful communication in order to increase commitment. Effective leaders also *coach* employees through a process of guided application, reflection, and improvement in order to increase competence.

The process of connecting and coaching is one of the most time-consuming aspects of a leader's job. It is time well-spent, however. Done properly, it moves the employee to the autonomous stage, where very little supervisory time is needed. Done poorly, it stalls the employee near the bottom of the curve – and creates a seemingly endless flow of performance, behavior, and disciplinary problems – taking up substantially more of the leader's time in the long run.

Connecting

The teaching and training that accompany JIT and cognitive development are somewhat generic and impersonal. In other words, the same knowledge and skills are taught to everyone in the same way. Because an employee begins that stage with a high level of commitment, the leader focuses on transferring as much knowledge as possible as quickly as possible (rather than "getting to know" the employee).

That's no longer the case once an employee enters the associative stage. Leadership now becomes customized and personal.

In order to eventually exit the associative stage and begin working autonomously, the employee will need both the *judgment* and the *desire* to perform to the best of his or her ability. You can teach an employee *what* to, but knowing for sure that the employee will actually *do* it (without your supervision) requires a personal "connection."

As a leader, you must utilize the motivation principles and communication techniques presented in earlier sections of this book to build a constructive relationship. Each employee is unique. It is during this stage that you gain insight into an employee's judgment – and here that you win an employee's heart, mind, and spirit.

The basic technique of praising people daily is especially crucial to connecting with an employee during the associative stage. As noted previously, praise gives the employee confidence, and creates a sort of "credit balance" to draw on. (An employee will more readily admit mistakes and commit to improve problem areas if he or she is receiving regular positive feedback. These things won't happen if your only conversations with the employee are when he or she does something wrong.)

Coaching

"Coaching" has become the catch-all term for a vaguely-defined method of supervising employees. In the context of leading workplace pirates and other employees, however, *coaching* refers to the very specific way you develop a person whenever he or she falls short of expectations during the associative stage.

Coaching is much more involved than the basic 3-step technique for offering useful *corrective feedback* that you used during the cognitive stage of development. Of course, corrective feedback may still be used early in the associative stage to reinforce a key lesson from Job Instruction Training. For example, if on your very first day behind the wheel you were following the car ahead of you too closely, your coach might have used corrective feedback to tell you what you were doing, remind you of what you should have been doing instead, and explain why it was important.

If you were following too close on the second day, the coach might have asked, "How's your distance from car up ahead right now?" This question would have prompted you to perceive, think, judge, and act (which is exactly what you'd have to be capable of doing before you reached the autonomous stage and were licensed to drive alone).

It's acceptable for the leader to offer a "real time" reminder like that if the employee is doing something risky (for example, an action that could cost the company money or result in an injury). The leader may also offer "real time" praise and encouragement when appropriate. Otherwise, the leader should keep quiet and observe – then conduct a coaching session afterward to discuss performance (unlike JIT, where corrective feedback is immediate).

For example, if on your fourth day, you were still following too closely, the effective coach would have changed drivers and conducted a coaching session with you, one-to-one, in private, as soon as possible.

A coaching session is the most effective way to handle performance issues, behavior problems, and rule violations during the associative stage.

An effective coaching session has six steps:
1. Initiate the discussion;
2. Agree on the facts;
3. Handle excuses;
4. Explore alternatives;
5. Commit to a solution;
6. Close the discussion.[25]

1. Initiate the discussion simply means stating the purpose of the conversation that you're about to have with the employee (for example, "Let's talk about your machine efficiency this morning," or "I'd like to discuss your arrival time at work today.")

2. Agree on the facts by asking open-end questions to confirm that both you and the employee have the same perception of what happened, what was supposed to happen, and why it matters.

The objective is to get the employee to start monitoring and taking responsibility for his or her performance. For example, "What was your machine throughput and error rate this morning?" or "What time did you clock in today?" obliges the employee to reflect and respond.

If your facts agree, you will then follow up with questions regarding the expectations – for example, "What's the standard for throughput and reject rate?" "How does falling short of that efficiency standard affect us?" Another example: "What time were you supposed to clock in?" "How does it impact our customers if you are not at work on time?"

If the employee's facts *disagree* with yours, don't argue – simply state what you observed, and confirm that you both agree on what is expected in the *future* and why it is important that the expectation be met. (You can't change what the employee has already done. You can only influence what he or she does next.)

3. Handle excuses by rephrasing any questions or statements that an overly-sensitive or defensive employee might perceive as accusatory. (For example, if the employee reacts to the machine efficiency issue by saying, "So you think I'm careless?" you might reply, "No, I'm just confirming all the facts so I can help you be successful.")

Handling excuses may also involve the techniques for building rapport that were presented earlier in the book, especially if the employee tries to rationalize what happened. For example, if an employee starts explaining how everything that *could* go wrong *did* go wrong (causing her to be late for work), you need to listen and *empathize*. Remember, you have to maintain a *connection* with the employee.

Once you have empathized (and the employee knows that you have understood the situation), focus on the future. Confirm that the employee is clear about what is expected, and move to the next step.

4. Explore alternatives is a process that begins with you asking the employee how he or she will correct a current performance or behavior problem, and prevent a similar occurrence in the future.

It's not enough for the employee to say, "It won't happen again." You must help the employee think through a variety of ways to avoid or handle the causes and circumstances the led up to an unsatisfactory result – so when a similar situation presents itself, he or she is prepared and able to respond.

When the unsatisfactory result is performance-related (for example, if you are coaching a machine operator whose efficiency is low), you could use a *probing* technique to ask, "How might you reduce your error rate and decrease your running scrap?" When the employee offers an option, *paraphrase* to ensure that you've understood it, and then utilize the *exploring* technique to have the employee discuss the benefits and the drawbacks of the possible solution.

Once that option has been considered, make an acknowledging statement such as, "Okay, good!" Then ask for another idea (even if you think the first option was fine), and have the employee discuss the pros and cons of it. Continue this cycle until the employee can't think of any more options.

Your objective is to have the employee explore as many alternatives as possible. There are two reasons for this. First, the process will give you insight into the employee's judgment – it will permit you to see just how much the employee really knows about the job (and how close he or she is to being ready to work autonomously). Second, the process may lead the employee to discover a way to improve performance that no one else (including you) has thought of.

If *you* think of a possible solution, benefit, or drawback that the employee doesn't mention, use the *expanding* technique to offer it as a suggestion – for example, you might say, "What about cleaning the machine more frequently?" This allows the employee to consider your input equally, rather than giving the impression that you've already decided what the employee should do. The employee will be more likely to consider your idea if it's a *choice* that he or she makes, rather than a requirement that you impose.

This fourth step is essential not only for performance-related issues, but also for unsatisfactory behaviors. For example, if an employee is late for work, offers an excuse (most do), says it won't happen again, and you let it go at that – it *will* happen again, eventually. The employee must change something about his or her routine when a problem results, or the unacceptable outcome is destined to be repeated.

With behavior issues, you must listen and empathize as the employee explains – and then focus on the future. Utilize the *probing* technique to help the employee identify things he or she will do differently, and the *exploring* technique to lead the employee through a discussion of the benefits and drawbacks of each possible option.

Many leaders try to go through this step of the coaching process too fast. They allow the employee to suggest only one or two alternatives and fail to discuss the key benefits and drawbacks of each option. They don't take the time to discover what the employee really thinks, feels, or knows about the situation – and as a consequence, seldom succeed in bringing about a permanent solution.

5. *Commit to a solution* should involve a choice on the part of the employee. As the leader, you may prompt the choice by saying, "You've discussed a lot of good options. What will you do differently from now on to get your error rate down to the standard?" (or "What will you do differently in the future to ensure you get to work on time?").

When the employee chooses an option, ask a closed question (requiring a "yes" or "no" answer) to confirm. For example, in the case of a performance issue, you might ask, "So, you've decided that you'll clean your machine before lunch and breaks, and pay closer attention when you crimp a product piece, right? Will that bring your error rate down to the standard?"

If the employee states that it will, lock-in the employee's commitment. "By what date will those actions enable you to start meeting the standard?" Allow the employee to choose, but be sure the date is realistic, yet challenging. You want to stretch the employee's abilities, but you don't want an overly optimistic worker to set himself up for failure.

In the case of behavior issues, it may be more appropriate to lock-in commitment with a duration-based question. For instance, "So, I have your commitment that you'll arrive at work on time every day for the next month?"

Whether it's a performance or behavior issue, be alert for answers such as, "I'll try" or "I think so" or the inclusion of a new condition ("Sure I can get my error rate down to standard, but my throughput might suffer"). These are not statements of commitment, but rather the employee's way of telling you that he or she is already planning to fail.

Workplace pirates are experts at *sounding* as though they have committed to a desired course of action, but at the same time, using words that will come back to haunt you when the problem happens again. Many long-term performance and behavior problems are born at this critical moment – when the leader allows the coaching session to end without a firm commitment on the part of the employee.

If the employee offers a conditional response rather than a firm commitment, go all the way back to step 2 – asking open-end questions about what is supposed to happen and why it matters – and repeat the entire coaching session if necessary. The workplace pirate has to realize that the issue you are discussing is important enough that you are going to take however long it takes to get performance or behavior on track.

6. *Close the discussion* by briefly summarizing what was discussed, and then thank the employee for his or her input and participation in finding a solution. Express your confidence that the solution the employee has chosen to implement will solve the problem and result in all expectations being met in the future. Finally, set a date and time for a brief follow-up meeting to confirm that the solution is working as envisioned.

After the session ends, make an effort to "catch" the employee doing what he or she committed to do, and then praise the person for the action.

Conclusion

Connecting and coaching should always result in a specific performance or behavior change. As an employee progresses through the associative stage, he or she should become more competent at the job, more dedicated to doing it well, and more appreciative of the leader. Take the time to connect and coach – and then document progress…

Document Progress (Appraisal)

THERE ARE TWO OCCASIONS when a leader should formally appraise an employee's performance. The first is the annual performance review or evaluation that is required by most organizations. The second is when an employee reaches the end of the associative development stage, and is about to be given responsibility for performing a job, task, or activity without direct supervision (a job, task, or activity for which the employee has been fully trained and recently coached, of course).

Documentation

The purpose of a performance appraisal, in either of the cases above, is the same – to document progress. You must establish a written record of the employee's development, and all the steps you took to assist in that development – orientation; teaching and training; transition; connecting and coaching. This written record is essential for three reasons.

First (and most obvious), it provides legal evidence. If a performance or behavior problem eventually results in disciplinary action or the termination of an employee, a lawsuit may follow. In almost every case, the real question that attorneys, judges, and juries will ask is, "Was this employee treated fairly?" If the legal discovery process reveals a document that shows when and how you guided the employee through each of the development stages outlined in this section (and how you applied the motivation and communication techniques presented earlier in this book), you'll have nothing to worry about.

Second, systematically using a written appraisal to assess an employee's progress is a valuable tool to keep you on track. The life of a leader is a busy one, and it's fairly easy to allow a few days to slip by without praising your employees or checking on someone's progress. Knowing that you'll have to create a formal written document each time an employee reaches the appraisal point for a given job, task, or activity will prompt you to be more organized (and keep better informal notes) as you complete the orientation, JIT, and coaching sessions that lead up to that point.

Third, a formal appraisal provides an evaluation and acknowledgement of the employee's competence (much like your final driving test and the receipt of that coveted driver's license). It also sets very specific performance and behavior targets for the employee (something your parents may have done when they handed you the car keys for the first time).

In many ways, appraisal is like graduation – it marks the transition of the employee from "pupil" to "practitioner." The appraisal document serves as a diploma in this case, and the related performance appraisal discussion is the commencement ceremony. It's an event through which the leader launches the employee into the autonomous stage to achieve full potential. (*Annual* appraisals are regular checkpoints that occur during the autonomous stage, like a driver's license renewal.)

The appraisal document may be a form that your organization provides, or it may be one that you adapt from another source. In any case, it should contain spaces or sections that allow you to:

1. Describe the specific job duties, tasks, and activities that the employee performs;

2. Rate the performance of those duties, tasks, and activities relative to established goals, actions, and standards;

3. List the occasions on which you praised, offered feedback, or provided training, coaching, and other assistance to the employee;

4. Evaluate work habits and behaviors demonstrated by the employee that either enabled or inhibited unit effectiveness and efficiency;

5. Summarize any major accomplishments that contributed to unit success;

6. Identify specific plans for future development that will enhance unit performance or increase job satisfaction;

7. Set new performance targets for the employee.

The first five elements should be self-explanatory at this point. Because it can be difficult to recall and write up all of those things when you reach the appraisal point, make it a weekly habit to update this information for each employee in a blank journal, an appraisal file, or a worksheet. It will only take you a couple of minutes, and it will make the process of preparing the formal appraisal document relatively quick and easy. Don't worry about spelling, grammar, or complete sentences – just make brief notes that will allow you to recall and reconstruct key performance details at a later time.

The sixth item (identifying specific plans for future development) refers to any new job, duty, task, or activity for which you intend to provide the necessary orientation, training, transition, and coaching before the next scheduled appraisal. The future development may be necessary for many reasons, including the need to provide cross-training or coverage of a critical function. It may also be a chance to delegate a portion of your job and/or to provide the employee with an opportunity to advance.

The seventh element (set new performance targets) is one of the most critical aspects of performance management. As already noted, the *standards* associated with any job, goal, or action task are applicable to every employee (once training is complete) – yet each employee may have different performance *targets* based on experience.

Targets

If the standard throughput for a machine operation is 110 units per hour with a 1.8 percent reject rate, that same standard would apply to *all* machine operators – from one who is just entering the autonomous stage of development to one who has been operating the machine for twenty years. However, the experienced operator would naturally be expected to perform better, and might have a performance target of 130 units with a reject rate of 1.6 percent, while the "rookie" might have a target of 114 units at 1.8 percent.

A target should obviously be set to meet or exceed a standard. Like a standard, a target may be define outputs, processes, or behaviors – and like a standard, it should fully consider the issues of application, congruence, and primacy as they relate to the employee's job overall. A new target should always be mutually *agreed upon* by the leader and the employee during the appraisal meeting.

There are some graduate school professors who give everyone an "A" at the beginning of a course, and then require each student to submit a written outline of what he or she will do during the semester to earn that grade. Most students define (and commit to) a far more stringent set of study behaviors than they would have otherwise, and often excel as a result. Although this technique may not be adaptable to every workplace, it's something to consider when you and your employees discuss performance targets and appraisal ratings.

In general, as an employee becomes more experienced, the targets should become more ambitious. There is a practical limit to any employee's performance, however, and setting an unreachable target is both demoralizing and unfair to the employee. If the employee's performance level is in the top 20 percent relative to his or her peers, it may be unwise to "raise the bar" any further. Instead, expand the employee's duties or responsibilities.

Targets, though documented in writing, are not set in stone. If external factors (beyond the employee's control) should impact performance, the target may be adjusted (but again, the new target should be mutually agreed upon by the leader and the employee).

The Dreaded Appraisal

The performance appraisal meeting is a dreaded activity for most managers in most organizations (and if truth be told, their employees aren't too crazy about it, either!).

One reason is because too many organizations use performance appraisals as a tool to manipulate and manage compensation. In some cases, managers are required to give less favorable evaluations than deserved so an organization can justify smaller raises. In other cases where compensation is based on a performance rating system, managers are compelled to give higher ratings than deserved to "look out for" their group of employees.

Ideally, the total focus of an appraisal meeting should be on performance, not pay – but if your organization links the two into one process and you are unable to change that, you can still use the appraisal meeting steps outlined in this chapter to increase your effectiveness. You can also conduct interim appraisals that focus only on performance.

A second reason that traditional appraisal meetings are so disliked is the judgmental framework within which most such meetings are conducted. The leader "grades" the employee, and in most instances, focuses on what the employee did wrong or needs to improve.

Say the word "appraisal" aloud. The accent is on "praise," and that's where the accent should be during the appraisal meeting, as well. The appraisal process launches the employee into the autonomous stage of development – the steepest part of the curve. If a skater at this point on the half-pipe hesitates or tries to "bail" on the trick, the only way to go is down – hard. Skill and confidence are essential – to the skater, and to an employee at this stage of development.

The appraisal meeting must be a skill-enhancing and confidence-building event. That's not to say problem areas aren't addressed and documented – they are, but in a positive way.

Conducting the Appraisal Meeting

When appraisal meetings are scheduled on an annual basis only, there is often too much to discuss in the time available – especially if the employee has any problems or concerns. Consequently, it's a good idea to conduct appraisal meetings and to document progress on a more frequent basis for most employees.

To create the desired outcome, an effective appraisal meeting will follow these six steps:

1. Open the meeting;
2. Explore accomplishments and concerns;
3. Overcome defensiveness;
4. Set targets;
5. Rate performance (if required);
6. Close the meeting.[26]

1. *Open the meeting* by putting the person at ease. Create a comfortable, unhurried atmosphere. Outline an agenda for the meeting to describe how the discussion will be conducted.

2. *Explore accomplishments and concerns* by inviting self-appraisal. Pose a broad opening question such as, "How would you assess your production throughput as a machine operator?" or "How would you assess your promptness at getting to work on time?" Begin with areas where the employee is doing well, so you can build on those strengths later when introducing areas of concern. As with coaching, encourage discussion using open-end questions, and confirm details with closed (yes/no) questions. Use praise to build confidence and motivation.

Be certain that you have coached the employee previously on any problem areas that you discuss or document during the appraisal (i.e., avoid surprises – an appraisal meeting should never be the first time an employee hears about a performance or behavior problem). When introducing an area of concern, continue to use probing questions – the employee should do most of the talking. If he or she is unwilling to acknowledge a problem, however, be factual and specific when you bring it up.

3. *Overcome defensiveness* by sticking to the agenda and keeping the meeting on track (don't get drawn into

arguments or irrelevant discussions). If the employee brings up complaints or makes excuses, control your reaction – respond empathetically, and ask for (or provide) relevant facts and examples. Focus on the future, and get the employee to take responsibility for suggesting solutions and taking action steps that will resolve his or her grievance. If there is a problem or issue that you (or the employee) simply can't get past, cut off the discussion and schedule a separate meeting to explore the issue at a later time – then move to the next item on the agenda.

4. *Set targets* by prompting the employee to suggest an appropriate measurable or observable objective. Use probing questions to help the employee consider and discuss the benefits and risks associated with any new target under consideration. Build on strengths – be positive and solution-focused if reaching the target will require the employee to overcome a problem discussed in step 2. If it's necessary to suggest a target yourself, use the expanding technique (for example, "What if we build on your excellent operator efficiency and set your throughput target at 120 units with an error rate of 1.7 percent? Do you think you could hit that?") Agree on the target, and the date by which (or duration for which) it will be achieved. Confirm the employee's commitment to each established target and document the details.

5. *Rate performance* (only if your appraisal form requires a numeric rating on specific elements) by taking personal responsibility for the rating you assign. State each rating as *your* rating, for instance, "I rated this as a 4" – and then provide a valid rationale for the number. Don't blame the "system," your boss, or Human Resources for the ratings you give (it makes you appear powerless). If there's

something wrong with the system, then it's your job as a leader to step up and work to change it.

If the employee disagrees with a rating, recycle the discussion back to step 2, and explore the employee's assessment more carefully (using open-end questions). If the issue is still unresolved, determine whether you have different facts, or a different conclusion regarding the same facts. If it's the former, set aside the rating for now, and schedule a follow-up meeting to resolve the factual discrepancies. If it's the latter, advise the employee of his or her options to dispute the rating or to attach comments to the appraisal form.

6. *Close the meeting* by summarizing the employee's past performance, and the targets that the two of you have agreed upon for the future. Express your confidence in the employee's ability and dedication to achieve those targets.

If the appraisal is being conducted to mark the end of the associative stage and the beginning of the autonomous stage for the employee, provide some type of formal acknowledgment or tangible award to reinforce the significance of the milestone (there are literally thousands of low-cost employee recognition items that are satisfactory for this).

The employee must enter the autonomous stage feeling positive and excited about the future, not frustrated and demoralized. Even if there are areas in which the employee still needs to gain experience and improve his or her performance, the appraisal meeting should propel the employee up the remainder of the development curve, not send him or her crashing to the bottom. (Metaphorically, you want employees to leave the appraisal meeting feeling as though you handed over an unrestricted license and a set of car keys – not as though you just flunked them on the driver's test!)

Conclusion

Your coaching role concludes (at least, for a given job, skill, or activity) once the performance is documented, an appraisal meeting is held, and new targets are set. Your role then shifts once again – as you support and mentor the autonomous employee...

Support and Mentor (Autonomous Stage)

EVEN WHEN YOU *finally* received your license, your development as a driver was not totally complete. You were competent and committed, but you lacked the one critical characteristic that separates *capable* drivers from *expert* drivers – experience.

There is no substitute for experience. In order to reach your fullest potential as a driver, you had to venture out on your own and gain experience. Even so, your parents didn't just hand you the car keys and hope for the best. They continued to offer guidance – when they felt it was necessary, and when you requested it.

For instance, if your formal training didn't include driving on icy roads, you most likely consulted those who had actual experience when you faced that challenge for the first time. If you ran into difficulty (got stuck or had an accident), you probably sought assistance from the same people.

In *The Karate Kid*, Daniel eventually has to fight in the tournament. All the same, Mr. Miyagi doesn't drop him at the door and go home. He guides Daniel by (once again) providing what Daniel cannot provide for himself – in this case, the wisdom of experience.

As a leader, your role with an employee who has reached the autonomous (third) stage of development is to support and mentor. *Supporting* an employee involves creating a workplace climate of achievement, encouraging the employee to excel within that climate, and being there to help the employee recover when he or she falls. *Mentoring* an employee involves sharing your wisdom and experience (successful and not so successful) to help the employee achieve expertise.

Support

The climate you create for employee performance is critical to individual success, especially in a pirate workplace. Consider the public education system in America. In schools that are rated academically superior, students not only encourage each other to excel, they respect and honor those outstanding achievements. Parents and teachers don't just acknowledge or reward exceptional performance and behavior on the part of students – they *require* it.

The atmosphere is much different in the nation's academically inferior schools. Students who attempt to excel are "punished" by other students. The majority of parents are uninvolved, allowing the remaining few to undermine discipline and prevent policies that would hold students accountable for a higher standard of performance and behavior. Teachers who try to break this cycle are discouraged – even threatened.[27]

As a leader, you must serve as a "support system" for the third-stage (autonomous) employees you initially develop – because in a world of pirates, their efforts to excel are unlikely to be appreciated by friends or coworkers. Once you develop a few winners, you can apply the team building techniques outlined in the next section of this book – and the group as a whole will begin to cultivate an atmosphere of achievement. At the beginning, however, it's up to you, the leader.

Another element of support is encouragement. In spite of being a little cocky throughout the training and coaching process, Daniel suffers a moment of panic once he arrives at the karate tournament. Employees often experience a similar sense of fear or hesitation when they realize that they are really on their own and solely accountable for the outcome they achieve. They wonder, "Am I really ready for this?"

The leader must assure nervous employees that they are, in fact, ready to fly. If you have done your job properly – to orient, teach, train, transition, connect, coach, and appraise – then its time to push the employee out of the metaphorical nest.

Even as you do so, you must also *reassure* the employee that should anything unexpected happen, you'll be close by to assist. In other words, even though you're giving the employee the freedom to work without direct or constant supervision – and even though you're holding the employee accountable for achieving agreed upon targets – you won't abandon the employee if he or she needs assistance. You will be there to mentor.

Mentor

According to Homer's epic poem *The Odyssey*, Odysseus entrusted Mentor to teach and develop his son during a long absence. Over the years, the word "mentor" has been used as a noun to describe an experienced person who develops a less experienced person, and as a verb to describe the development process itself. Here, it refers specifically to the employee development technique that is used when the employee is in the autonomous stage.

Mentoring is always a joint venture, and there are prerequisites for both the leader and the employee.

First, the employee must have a high level of underlying skill and knowledge about the specific job or activity (i.e., the only aspect of competence that should be lacking – and therefore in need of development – is experience). Second, the employee must have a desire to master the job. Finally, the employee must be willing to ask for help from the leader when needed, and be receptive to the leader's input and advice.

The leader, of course, must have experience at the job or activity (the experience that the employee does not possess). The leader must also be willing to share with the employee all the wisdom gained from that experience (this includes the leader's successes *and* failures, because both contain valuable lessons).

The process of mentoring may be either predictive or reflective. With *predictive* mentoring, the leader and employee meet to discuss an upcoming task or activity that may present a set of challenges or circumstances the employee has never encountered. With *reflective* mentoring, the discussion centers on a task or activity that the employee has already completed, but one in which an unexpected problem or undesirable outcome occurred. In the first case, the leader's experience enables the employee to analyze and plan – in the second, to assess and correct. Either party can request or initiate a mentoring session.

The basic steps you will use as a leader to conduct either type of mentoring session are the same:

1. Clarify the objective;
2. Promote discovery;
3. Agree on parameters;
4. Authorize and empower;
5. Schedule a follow-up.[28]

1. *Clarify the objective* by asking the employee to describe the specific outcome he or she wants from the session and from the action that will be taken following the session.

2. *Promote discovery* by asking open-end questions and sharing your experiences in a way that allows the

employee to discover what he or she should do (or should have done) to deal with the challenge or problem, and to achieve the desired outcome. This step can be thought of as "super coaching" (instead of the leader guiding the employee, the two are pooling their knowledge, skill, experience, and judgment – and the employee uses that to guide him/herself).

3. *Agree on parameters* means that you and the employee have a mutual understanding of what the employee will do to address the upcoming challenge (or in the case of reflective mentoring, to deal with a similar challenge the next time, and to mitigate or repair any damage done in this instance).

4. *Authorize and empower* requires you to notify other people that the employee is acting with your approval and on your behalf. (There is nothing more frustrating to an autonomous employee than being told that he or she doesn't have the "authority" to carry out a course of action that the two of you agreed upon.)

5. *Schedule a follow-up* date to meet and verify that the employee's stated objective was achieved – and to determine what (if anything) would make future mentoring sessions more effective.

Mentoring (in this context) is effective only when the employee has a high level of knowledge and skill. If an employee at the autonomous stage suddenly develops a problem, it may not be always be due to a lack of experience. For instance, if the knowledge or skills required for a job had changed, you would address that with an abbreviated orientation, training, transition, or coaching session – rather than mentoring.

What if you lack the relevant experience and expertise to truly mentor a highly competent employee? All pirate captains faced this problem (it's impossible to be experienced at *every* job or task). When it was clear that one man possessed more capability and experience in a given area than the captain or any of the crew did, that fact was formally acknowledged – the man was made a ship's officer and received a larger share of the treasure for mentoring other crew members in that specialty. Becoming a mentor to others encouraged the crew member to hone his skills even further, and allowed his expertise to "cascade" down through the entire crew.

The success of this methodology on pirate ships was one factor that influenced the United States to depart from the British, French, and Prussian practice of choosing military leaders from the aristocracy only. Instead, the newly-formed Continental Army created the role of the non-commissioned officer (NCO) – which came to be known as the "backbone" of America's military. NCOs are still relied upon for the bulk of the practical first line operational and support experience in every branch of the armed forces.[29]

Consider the creation of a non-management "NCO" position within your work unit (call it a "crew chief," "team captain," "lead person," whatever), and then train and coach an experienced person on how to be a mentor to the less experienced. When the person is ready to accept and fill the new role, provide the appropriate acknowledgement and compensation.

Handle Performance Problems

PERFORMANCE PROBLEMS are basically any repeated actions or behaviors on the part of an employee that interfere with – or fail to contribute to – an organization's ability to achieve its mission.

Performance problems must be confronted immediately. If you and the employee have discussed an issue once already (e.g., within the context of a coaching or appraisal session), and if the employee (during that discussion) committed to correct the problem – but didn't – you must be proactive. Do not "let it slide" in hopes that the situation will gradually improve (it won't).

By taking action immediately, you keep the problem from getting worse. You also keep employees from feeling "entitled" (after all, if you didn't address it, then it must be okay). Finally, you let other employees know that you are aware of what's going on (which reduces the resentment they feel if a coworker appears to be getting away with not doing his or her job).

Never try to resolve a performance or behavior problem with a "global solution" that punishes everyone. Address issues individually, one-to-one.

When Problems Occur

When an employee falls short of expectations during the cognitive (first) stage, the reason is usually a lack of knowledge or basic skill – so the effective leader uses training and corrective feedback to get the employee back on track. If the same problem continues to occur, the leader may conclude that employee lacks the aptitude to learn the job – or is perhaps battling a personal problem outside of work. Whatever the case, you'll want to consider releasing the employee while he or she is still in a "probationary" status.

When an employee falls short of expectations during the autonomous (third) stage of development, the reason is usually lack of experience – so the leader offers wisdom and mentoring to help the employee explore what happened and why. Autonomous employees rarely make the same mistake twice.

Consequently, most performance problems arise during the associative (second) stage of development. In many cases, the problems that arise during this stage are due to a lack of functional skill and applied judgment – so the effective leader uses coaching to increase competence. In almost as many cases, the problems are caused by a lack of commitment (the employee doesn't have the confidence or the desire to apply the necessary skills) – so the leader uses positive feedback (praise) and "transition" techniques to inspire commitment. Ninety percent of the time, the employee responds and the problems are resolved.[30]

In ten percent of the cases, the same issue comes up again… and again. At some point, the leader must decide that the "developmental" approach isn't working and handle the situation as a performance problem.

Examine Yourself

The first step in addressing any potential performance problem is to examine *your* performance. Be honest. Did you really do your part in providing the employee with the proper orientation, teaching, training, transition, connection, coaching, assessment, support, and mentoring during every stage of development? If not, then you must accept partial responsibility for the problem that exists – and provide the employee with the developmental elements you missed previously (in order to correct the situation).

In addition to skipping over or rushing through the development process, other common leadership mistakes that impact employee performance are:

- Inadequate feedback (the employee didn't know what was he or she was doing wrong – or right);

- Ineffective communication (the employee didn't understand the goal, actions, or standards);

- Sending mixed messages (for instance, the leader preaches "safety first," but rewards other employees who shortcut safety to increase production);

- Ignoring workplace issues (the employee is being sexually harassed or threatened by a coworker).

Any of these may legitimately impact an employee's ability to do his or her job, and all are the responsibility of the leader to investigate and resolve.

Examine the System

If you have done everything "right" relatively to the developing the employee, you will next examine the "system" within which the employee was working each time the problem occurred. Did other people do their jobs properly, or did someone else make a mistake that impacted this employee's results? Did something about the facility, equipment, and materials (availability, quality, working conditions, etc.) affect the outcome? Were the processes or methodologies flawed, inefficient, or ineffective in some way?

If a systemic problem impacted an employee's performance, it is the leader's responsibility to diagnose it and work out a solution. Be careful not to blame the "system" for every problem, however (or use mitigating circumstances as an excuse to avoid confronting non-performers). Just as a dedicated golfer will play when weather and course conditions are far less than ideal, a committed employee should be able to overcome routine systemic problems and meet expectations. A helpful guideline in this instance is to examine how *other* employees performed. Systemic problems usually affect everyone involved, not just one employee.

Categorize the Problem

If the problem cannot be linked to actions (or inactions) on the part of the leader, nor to any serious shortcomings in the working environment or "system," the next step is to determine what type of recurring problem you are dealing with. There are three general categories: (a) missed targets, (b) "code" violations, and (c) objectionable behaviors.

Missed Targets

A missed target is the easiest type of problem to isolate and categorize. It usually involves an employee who has not performed or not completed a job, task, or activity in the manner that was previously agreed upon. Not meeting a production objective, not following an approved plan of action, or not using the proper tool for a given task would be examples of a missed target.

Because targets always involve measurable or observable processes and outcomes, the facts are generally indisputable when an employee falls short of one. If examination reveals that a target is repeatedly being missed due to a lack of competence on the part of the employee (i.e., the employee doesn't know what to do or how to do it), then the burden falls back on you (the leader) to provide the employee with the necessary remediation. However, if a target is repeatedly being missed due to lack of commitment (the employees knows what to do, but simply isn't doing it), then it is time to "cross the line" and begin the process of *progressive discipline* (more about that later).

"Code" Violations

A "code" violation is also easy to identify. It usually involves an employee who has not adhered to a written regulation, policy, or procedure. There are two classes of "code" violations – serious and minor.

Serious violations refer to actions and behaviors that defy or abuse a specific condition of employment (as stated in the organization's policy and/or employee manuals). Physically assaulting a coworker, or testing positive for a controlled substance, would be examples of a serious violation in many workplaces.

Serious violations, while troubling, are not usually that difficult for a leader to address. In most cases, the organization's policy on the subject will spell out exactly how you are required to handle first-time or repeat offenses – and that's precisely what you do (usually with extra support and guidance from an HR specialist and an employment attorney).

Minor violations refer to less severe breaches that do not have a pre-defined disciplinary action associated with them. Arriving at work ten minutes late, or not wearing protective gear when briefly passing through a construction area, would be examples of minor violations in most settings.

Minor violations are generally left to discretion of managers (who independently determine when and how to handle the offense). The best thing to do is to think proactively and build any relevant rules or procedures into the performance targets that you and the employee agree upon. For example, if an employee is repeatedly late for work, it will be much more effective to set a performance target that can't be achieved unless the employee starts on time.

If it is impossible to directly link the rule or procedure to a target, you will use the *corrective feedback* technique presented previously – with two additional steps – to address minor violations:

1. Tell the person what he or she did;

2. Tell the person what he or she might have done instead to be more effective;

3. Explain why the action you are suggesting would be better in the future;

4. Get the employee's commitment that he or she will take that action in the future (remember that "I'll do my best" or "I'll try" are not statements of commitment – the employee must say something like, "Yes, I will do that.");

5. Set a follow-up date.

If the employee solves the problem by the agreed-upon date, praise the effort and outcome. If the same violation occurs before then, however, begin progressive discipline (more about that shortly).

When setting the follow-up date (step 5), keep in mind that most minor rule violations are the result of bad habits. For example, people who are *chronically* late for work have often been chronically late for everything their whole lives. It's inconceivable for them to commit to being on time *forever* – so you must help them gradually replace their bad habits with good habits. Allow them to take "baby steps." Have them commit to being on time (or wearing protective gear, or whatever) *tomorrow* – then follow-up with praise. Then have them commit to the rest of the week – and follow-up with praise. (Then a full week, and so on, until the new habit takes hold.)

You might think that you shouldn't have to go to all this trouble with a grown-up – but you do. Leaders have to provide this type of employee with the discipline that the employee can't provide for himself.

A final point to consider on minor violations is whether or not you can provide a legitimate reason or benefit for what you're asking the employee to do (step 3 in corrective feedback). If so, great – but the larger and more bureaucratic your organization, the more likely it is that you (as a leader) are expected to enforce certain rules that are, well – stupid.

You cannot simply choose to *ignore* the stupid rules and allow your employees to violate them. You must have the courage to take your concerns up the organization and lobby for a sensible amendment. In the meantime, insist that employees follow the "questionable" rule to the letter – and update them regularly on your progress to change it. This will earn you respect from both up and down your organization.

Objectionable Behavior

Objectionable behavior is a tricky category. One extreme example might be the repeated use of a word or phrase (not specifically covered by the organization's "code") that almost everyone finds insulting or offensive. At the other end of the spectrum might be something an employee does that simply "drives the boss crazy" (like socializing on the job, procrastinating on projects, having a disorganized or "messy" work area, dressing inappropriately, etc.). Objectionable behavior might also include statements or actions that are uncooperative in general (the so-called "bad attitude") – for example, an employee who only grudgingly participates in a coaching discussion and refuses to commit to solving a problem.

It's easier to deal with objectionable behavior if you can identify a target that was missed or a rule that was violated (you can then use the techniques already mentioned to address the problem). The next section of this book (*Teambuilding*) presents additional guidance on how to elicit more cooperative and collaborative behaviors from employees working in groups.

If it's not possible to link an objectionable behavior to a missed target or code violation, then carefully consider the *real* impact of the behavior. If the employee is doing something that you don't like or don't approve of – yet it isn't affecting the achievement of target objectives, and it's not violating any written rules – consider the possibility that it's *your* problem, rather than a performance problem.

After considering that possibility, if you conclude that the behavior *is* genuinely offensive or disruptive, provide corrective feedback using the same five steps that were outlined for minor violations. If the employee commits to improve and does so, praise – but if the same behavior is repeated before the follow-up date, begin progressive discipline.

Keep in mind that some people are, by nature, difficult to get along with – and that you cannot change a person's nature in one conversation. Your goal is to influence the employee's behavior, not to effect a total personality makeover. All the same, "bad attitudes" are often rooted in the motivational causes presented in an earlier section (*Part IV*) of this book. Re-examine the "spirit factor" that drives a difficult employee.

It's often the secret to understanding why people who are "hard to get along with" behave as they do.

Finally, understand that if an employee refuses to follow (or willfully disregards) the safe, lawful, and ethical directions given by a leader who has the authority to give such directions, then that behavior constitutes insubordination. Insubordination is a form of misconduct that starts small, and then quickly gets out of control. Don't let that happen. Be firm and clear is stating your expectations, and if the employee refuses to comply, begin progressive discipline.

Progressive Discipline

Progressive discipline is a four-step process for handling a recurring missed target, minor code violation, or behavior problem (any previously discussed issue that an employee has failed to correct).

The conversations you have with employees for developmental purposes (training, coaching, mentoring, etc.) are intended to help them become successful. Employees must know that mistakes are an acceptable part of the learning process, and that (short of "zero tolerance" rule violations like assaulting a coworker) doing something wrong will not cost them their jobs. In other words, they must understand that there are no "consequences" associated with falling short of expectations on occasion. (Employees *will* sometimes fall short of expectations until fully developed.)

When a problem becomes *chronic* and is not corrected, however, the situation changes. Progressive discipline *does* have employment consequences (i.e., the employee can potentially lose his or her job if the problem continues). Everyone needs to understand that distinction. In fact, the employee must be told (when the leader decides to cross the "consequence line") that the conversation is disciplinary in nature, rather than developmental. That *verbal warning* is the first step in the four-step process.

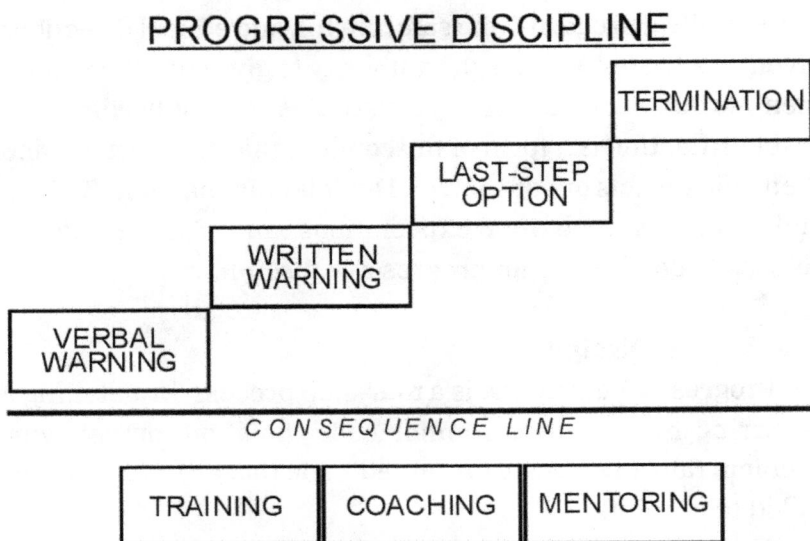

PROGRESSIVE DISCIPLINE

```
                                              ┌──────────────┐
                                              │ TERMINATION  │
                                    ┌─────────┤              │
                                    │LAST-STEP│
                                    │ OPTION  │
                          ┌─────────┤         │
                          │WRITTEN  │
                          │WARNING  │
                ┌─────────┤         │
                │VERBAL   │
                │WARNING  │
                └─────────┘
```

_____

CONSEQUENCE LINE

| TRAINING | COACHING | MENTORING |

Progressive discipline (like corrective feedback, coaching, and mentoring) is always done in private with the employee – never in front of his or her coworkers. There may be occasions, however, when it is acceptable or advisable for you to ask another manager sit in on the discussion (for example, if you are a male supervisor discussing inappropriate dress with a female employee).

When giving an employee a verbal warning, begin by stating that the discussion constitutes a verbal warning. Outline the *facts* that led up to your decision to cross the consequence line (with dates and details, including the most recent occurrence). Next, clearly state the *objective* (the specific outcome or improvement the employee must achieve in the future, including the time by which the outcome must be reached and/or the duration for which it must be maintained).

Then ask the employee for his or her *resolution* or pledge to achieve the stated objective (use open-end questions to identify what the employee intends to do to prevent another occurrence). Finally, explain the *consequences* of not achieving the promised objective (the standard phrase is, "You will be subject to disciplinary action up to and including termination.")

Document the discussion afterward (either in a written memo or on a form specifically designed for the purpose). Be sure to capture the facts, objective, resolution, and consequences you covered with the employee. This is also the place and time to formally document any "extra" training, coaching, or mentoring you provided (prior to initiating discipline). Should you eventually have to terminate the employee, your documentation should make it clear that you first gave the employee ample support and multiple opportunities to succeed. Remember, in a lawsuit, if it wasn't written down at the time, it never happened!

If the employee fails to keep his or her resolution and meet the stated objective, then you will move to the next step – a *written warning*.

A written warning is handled the same as a verbal warning, except you advise the employee that it is a written warning, and you provide a copy of the written warning memo or form (updated to include the latest occurrence) to the employee for signature. If the employee refuses to sign it, simply note the date and time, and ask another manager confirm that the employee read and received a copy of the document, but refused to sign.

If the employee again falls short of expectations, you implement the *last-step option*. It is handled like a written warning, except you advise the employee that it is her or her last chance. Many organizations send the employee home for the remainder of the day to seriously consider their employment future and come up with a permanent solution to the problem.

If the problem occurs again, update all of your documentation (the relevant facts, the objective, the resolutions, the consequences, and extras you've provided), then move to the last step – *termination*. (Note: Certain organizations require an additional step such as an EAP referral or union arbitration hearing prior to termination.)

Termination

Most employees will correct the problem after receiving a verbal or written warning – and that's the preferred goal. Employees who continue to fall short of expectations will often quit before you reach the termination stage. Consequently, when employee development is done properly – and when progressive discipline is initiated in cases where training, coaching, and mentoring fail – terminations are extremely rare.

If you ultimately need to fire someone, seek out the advice of a qualified employment attorney or HR professional. The actual termination process itself can be a tense and tricky one. The steps you have taken up to this point (supported by your documentation) will provide these professionals with everything they need to help you navigate both the emotional and legal minefields – and in most cases, get the person off of your ship with as little risk and "ugliness" as possible.

Part VII.
"Ready All Hands"

Teambuilding

Understand Team Development

THE PREVIOUS SECTION of this book provided tools for developing your workplace pirates into peak performers. Now the challenge is to get those peak performing individuals to work together as a team.

Pirate ships had very diverse workforces. A brigantine (a two-masted vessel favored by many pirate captains) was about the size of a single-wide mobile home. Aboard it was a crew of 100 or more men (and in rare cases, a few women) of all ages, skill levels, and backgrounds.

Living and working in such close quarters, a captain placed great emphasis on creating and preserving *esprit de corps* – a condition where each individual valued the group and the mission more than himself. In a time when personal freedom was a lofty ideal, rather than a human right or expectation, this was perhaps an area where the pirate captain had it easier than you do today.

American culture seems to steadily reinforce the importance of the individual, while downplaying the significance of the team. U.S. companies and government entities sustain a variety of programs to recognize and reward *individual* performance, yet comparatively few to salute *team* accomplishments. School sports and other extra-curricular activities (which were originally intended to unify students and teach them to work together) are now focusing on individual "stars" and their personal statistics, records, and achievements.

Teamwork has become little more than a buzzword. Consequently, many employees in today's workforce have no concept of how a "team" should function – and virtually no skills or practical experience at being a contributing member of a productive work unit.

A team is a group of people working together toward a common goal. As such, a team is a living entity in its own right. Just as an individual follows a development path or "learning curve" to become competent and committed at a job task, a group of individuals must be developed into a functional team. It doesn't happen automatically. The leader has to guide the process.

In the first stage of team development, the leader must make every team member aware of the collaborative skills required to be effective as a group. The leader must also clarify the roles and relationships of each person on the team.

In the second stage, the leader applies the collaborative force of the group to complete specific work assignments. The leader must identify and leverage the strengths of each person, and facilitate everyone's participation and involvement.

The third stage involves issues that are dealt with perpetually by any team leader. These issues include interpersonal conflicts, workplace safety and security, complaints, gossip, group decisions, and change. Handling such issues as they arise is an ongoing and normal part of team leadership. After all, there are no perfect teams – and even if you did manage to develop one, it would be temporary (since conditions and goals eventually change, existing team members depart, and new members join).

Generate Collaboration

IN TERMS OF personal background and motivational "spirit," it might be said that the majority of workplace pirates are not natural "team players." Employees must be *taught* to work together.

Most managers can readily identify behaviors that destroy or interfere with teamwork. Simply telling an employee to "stop" doing something isn't enough, however. The leader has to (a) prompt the employee to do something else instead, and (b) provide an explanation for why the preferred behavior is better.

The problem for many managers is that they don't really know what they want instead. In their experience, collaborative skills have not been clearly defined or actively developed. So nothing improves.

Seven basic skills are necessary for an individual to be a productive contributor to a team. Team leaders can use these as development, coaching, and appraisal points – so instead of saying that an employee "is not a team player" or "doesn't work well with others," the leader can offer explicit suggestions for improvement.[31]

Collaborative Skill #1 – Taking Responsibility

On a great team, everyone feels personally responsible for the team's mission or purpose. Every statement, behavior, and action moves the group closer to the objective. That's not to say that dissenting viewpoints are not encouraged, heard, and respected – they are, so long as the rationale behind the dissention is to benefit the team.

When an employee says or does something that suggests he or she is not putting the team first (e.g., pursuing a private agenda, playing politics, being sarcastic, or arguing just for the sake of argument), don't let it slide – skillfully bring it into the open. State what you saw or heard, indicate the impression it created, and ask for an explanation.

For example, "When you said [whatever the employee said], it gave the impression that you were just criticizing other people on the team. Was that the case? Because, given that our goal is to [whatever your goal is], I need to understand how that comment helps us get there."

Asking the employee to explain or defend behaviors that inhibit teamwork will help to break the person of a bad habit. If the employee has a valid explanation, you may still be able to suggest a more effective way of expressing it the next time.

Collaborative Skill #2 – Listening to Understand

The success of a team depends on how quickly team members can reach a common understanding. Actively *listening* to one's teammates (as opposed to merely waiting for one's turn to talk) is essential to understanding all the issues that affect a team or situation. It is also a sign of mutual respect – when team members really listen to one another, many of the "typical" interpersonal conflicts that occur in team settings begin to disappear.

When you observe an employee not listening (e.g., not giving other team members his or her full attention, interrupting the person who is talking, or losing track of discussions and decisions), offer feedback in private as soon as possible. State what you observed, describe the specific behavior or action that would have been more effective in the situation, and explain how that suggested behavior or action would benefit the team. Then ask the person to commit to that alternate behavior in the future (and offer praise the next time he or she does so).

Collaborative Skill #3 – Presenting a Message Clearly

Employees must be able to express themselves in a manner that others can understand. It's the only way that knowledge, experience, and viewpoints can be exchanged by members of the group.

There may be cases when the problem is not with the listeners, but rather with something a speaker is doing that inhibits understanding. Examples of this might include: rambling (rather than focusing on key points); being too indirect (or "wishy-washy"); presenting opinions without evidence; not making eye contact; speaking too softly; overusing buzzwords or jargon; using complex descriptions (when a simple picture, model, or story would be more effective).

As with listening problems, timely corrective feedback (delivered in private by the leader), plus on-going coaching and support, can be used to make an employee aware of a habit that may be undermining his or her communications.

Collaborative Skill #4 – Following Through

In a team setting, everyone's work is interrelated. When one person fails to complete an assigned action item by the agreed-upon deadline, everyone else (whose work depends on that action) falls behind – momentum is halted, and the entire crew is exposed to a giant whirlpool of negativity.

When deadlines are being missed, confirm that the employee isn't overloaded (or prioritizing his or her work improperly).

If the employee's workload is reasonable, the problem may be a lack of confidence. Some people have a fear of making mistakes, especially in front of other team members – so they avoid completing their work on time in order to deflect the focus and provide a built-in excuse ("I needed more time") for any work they complete that is not up to standards. The transition and coaching techniques covered in the previous section can help you build an employee's confidence. In addition to that, the concepts presented in subsequent chapters of this section will help you ensure that everyone finds his or her place on the team.

If you determine that deadlines are being missed due to a lack of competence (the employee didn't have the knowledge, skill, or experience to perform the assigned task) or a lack of motivation (the employee didn't *want* to perform the assigned task), then you can handle it using the developmental and disciplinary techniques explained in the previous section (*Part VI*).

Collaborative Skill #5 – Giving Corrective Feedback

The leader should not be the only one on the team providing corrective feedback. Team members should coach each other, and everyone should help everyone else improve. For that to occur, the leader must teach employees the three-step collaborative process for giving a coworker corrective feedback.

The steps are: (1) Tell the person what he or she said or did; (2) Tell the person what you think would have been more effective; (3) Tell the person why you think the suggested action would be better.

When a team member criticizes someone in an ineffective manner – or clearly exhibits disagreement in a non-verbal way – you can ask questions to prompt and guide the person through the use of the three-step process. You can also praise team members who give useful corrective feedback on their own, without prompting. Eventually, the technique will become second-nature for most of your group.

Collaborative Skill #6 – Accepting Feedback

Team members must also be taught to listen to the feedback they receive, acknowledge it (with a "thank you," for example), and consider it carefully.

If an employee reacts with unwarranted defensiveness or aggression when a coworker offers effective feedback, you can use probing questions to help the employee calm down, listen, paraphrase what was offered, and consider the validity of the suggestion. If you have people who are especially sensitive to criticism, you may have to coach them to simply acknowledge the feedback, and take time to sort it out (or even meet later with the person who offered it to ask for clarification and examples).

Encourage team members to acknowledge that their coworkers' suggestions are valid and that feedback is appreciated – even when they disagree with another person's observation or interpretation. This builds trust, and creates an atmosphere where obstacles can be quickly identified and overcome.

Collaborative Skill #7 – Cheering Each Other On

Encouraging one's teammates is an essential collaborative skill. As with corrective feedback, the leader shouldn't the only one cheering people on.

$E=MC^2$ is a formula where E represents energy – but in this case, M is money and C is congratulations. Just as the caffeine and sugar in an "energy drink" provide a temporary boost, *money* (bonuses and rewards) can temporarily raise a team's enthusiasm. The effect, however, wears off (plus there's a limit to how much money you can inject). *Congratulations* (praise) is exponentially more powerful – plus (unlike money) it can be supplied endlessly if everyone on the team is willing to offer it.

Teach your team members the three steps for praising a coworker: (1) Tell the person what he or she did; (2) Explain why the action was beneficial or important; (3) If appropriate, ask the person how he or she completed the action or achieved the result (to allow the person to talk about it and feel proud).

Encourage everyone to "catch" other people doing things they liked or appreciated – and to "cheer on" their teammates with praise.

Summary

Just as you teach an employee the functional aspects of a job during the cognitive stage of development, you must teach your team members these seven collaborative skills. When a new employee becomes a regular member of the team, observe and document how effectively the employee demonstrates each of the seven skills. If the employee fails to meet expectations, handle it as you would any other job performance or behavior issue.

Map the Team's Relationships

No, THIS HAS NOTHING TO DO with the dating habits of your employees. However, there are two categories of relationships that *are* important in a team setting – work-assigning relationships and work-initiating relationships.

A *work-assigning* relationship exists between two people when one is legitimately authorized to assign work to the other. For example, you (the leader) have the authority to assign work to your employees – you therefore have a work-assigning relationship with each of them.

A *work-initiating* relationship exists between two people when neither is authorized to assign work to the other, yet one is in a position to *cause* work to be done. For example, suppose an employee asks a teammate to "give me a hand" (a common and desirable occurrence in a team setting). The employee is not *assigning* work to that teammate, but if the teammate helps, then the two have a work-initiating relationship.

For any team you lead, it is recommended that you map the work-assigning and work-initiating relationships that exist for every team member.[32]

Work-Assigning Relationships

As the sample organization chart (indicated by blocks and solid lines) on the following page illustrates, Employee 2 reports to Supervisor C (in Division II of Department X). Because Supervisor C (as Employee 2's boss) has the authority to assign work to Employee 2, they have a work-assigning relationship (indicated by the dotted line from Supervisor C to Employee 2)

WORK-ASSIGNING RELATIONSHIPS

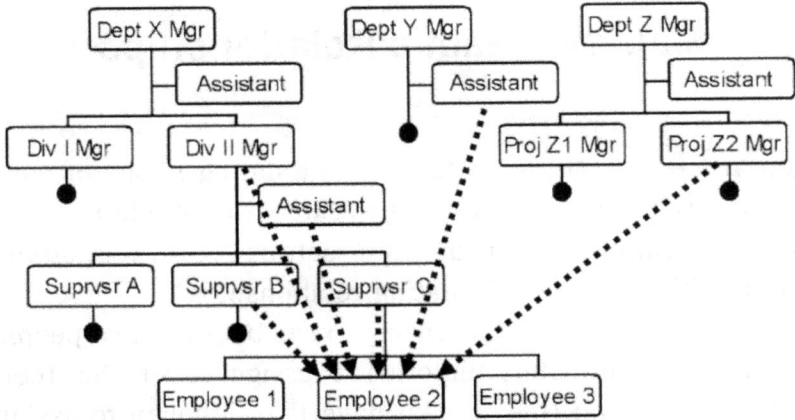

Because Division II utilizes "matrix management" (where employees may be sent to assist another crew or team as workload demands), Employee 2 sometimes reports to Supervisor B. Consequently, Employee 2 has a work-assigning relationship with Supervisor B, as well (as shown by the dotted line from Supervisor B to Employee 2).

The Manager of Division II has work-assigning authority over everyone in the division (and while the supervisors would prefer that the manager go through them when assigning work to their employees, the manager doesn't always do that). In this case, the Manager of Division II has a habit of directly assigning unofficial "pet projects" to Employee 2. Further, the manager has delegated his work-assigning authority (relative to those projects) to his assistant – so both the manager and the assistant have a work-assigning relationship with Employee 2 (as illustrated by the dotted lines).

This organization has a Safety Committee that is chaired by the Assistant to the Manager of Department Y. Employee 2 is Department X's representative on that working committee, so the Assistant (as chairperson) has work-assigning authority over Employee 2 in that context (as mapped with a dotted line).

Z2 is an information technology project being managed in Department Z, and Employee 2 is Department X's user representative on that project. So the Z2 Project Manager has work-assigning authority over Employee 2 there (dotted line).

In this example, Employee 2 has six work-assigning relationships – and therefore, six "bosses." This is very common in an organization that emphasizes teamwork. All six bosses understand that Employee 2 will be available to them for a certain percentage of time. The problem is, the six percentages usually add up to more than 100!

Work-Initiating Relationships

Employee 2 (who may be feeling a bit overloaded and under-appreciated by now) doesn't just work when work is assigned by a "boss." The employee is also compelled to respond to other people – inside and outside the organization – even though those people have no authority to *assign* anything. Those people are work initiators.

The most common work initiator is an employee who asks another coworker for help or assistance. For example, if Employee 3 requests assistance from Employee 2 (and Employee 2 responds), then they have a *collaborative* relationship (illustrated by the dotted line on the organization chart on the following page).

A similar work initiator is a coworker who offers advice or guidance. If Employee 1 sees Employee 2 struggling with a work task and offers to help or assist (and Employee 2 accepts), then an *advisory* type of work-initiating relationship is created.

WORK- INITIATING RELATIONSHIPS

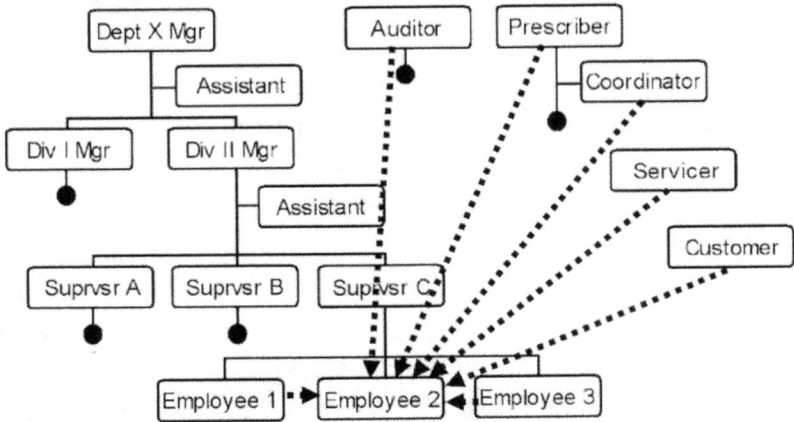

Up to five additional types of work-initiating relationships may be present. The initiators can be people within or from outside the organization.

If Employee 2 deals with customers or clients (internal or external), then the employee has a *customer* relationship with each of them. In many organizations, customers are the most demanding work-initiators, and the ones employees are taught to respond to first. This is no problem when the employee's job is, by definition, to serve customers. When it isn't, however, responding to a customer and preserving those relationships can be a hidden demand that many leaders overlook.

Very few organizations allow vendors, repair personnel, technicians, or other official visitors to wander around a workplace unsupervised. If Employee 2 is asked to escort such a person while a related task is being performed, then the employee and that person have a servicer relationship. Servicers often take the employee out of his or her normal work setting, and require the employee's undivided attention. It's another time-consuming relationship that leaders often overlook.

A *prescriber* relationship exists when someone has the authority dictate *how* an employee will do something. For example, an organization's Waste Management Officer could have the authority to mandate new site-wide procedures for the disposal of batteries, aerosols, plastic containers, and aluminum cans. The officer would not have the authority to *assign* work to Employee 2, but implementing the prescribed procedures would *cause* the employee to do work that wasn't being done before. Again, leaders often overlook the impact that new procedures have on their employees and work goals.

A *coordinator* relationship exists when someone is accountable for collecting data or information from an employee, and then combining it with other input to produce a proposal or report. The output may be critical to winning new business or complying with the law, yet (because the coordinator is just one of many people demanding time from Employee 2) the employee may not realize the strategic importance of the task.

An *auditor* relationship is created when an inspector, auditor, or other regulatory official is present (or scheduled to be present) in the workplace. Again, an auditor cannot *assign* work to Employee 2, but a current or upcoming examination of tasks that are within the auditor's realm of oversight (and within the employee's scope of responsibility) will certainly *cause* work to be done that might not have been otherwise.

Conclusion

Mapping the relationships that exist within your team is relatively easy (begin by asking each employee, "Who assigns work to you, and who initiates work on your part?"). This offers three significant benefits. First, it allows you to identify and correct situations where some employees are being stretched too thin, and others are being under-utilized. Second, it allows everyone to plan more realistically (reducing both the frustration and fallout associated with missed targets). Third, it provides evidence of when and why additional personnel are necessary (every team leader wants more people, but a relationship map can help you illustrate why you really need them).

As noted in the previous chapter, collaboration is a core requirement for effective teamwork – but it does take time for team members to learn to provide help, give feedback, and cheer each other on. The more work-assigning and work-initiating lines an employee has on the map, the less time that employee will have available (as an individual team member) to respond to any one boss or demand. It's a critical resource planning "fact of life" that is often forgotten (or at least, severely underestimated) in team and multiple project work settings. Mapping your team's relationships is a relatively fast and easy way to address the issue.

Explore Team Member Roles

YOU'VE HEARD THE ACRONYM for TEAM – *together everyone achieves more*. That's only true when everyone on the team knows his or her role, as well as the roles of all the other team members.

A team member's role is determined by the individual's *competencies* (knowledge, skills, and experience) and by his or her *strengths* (outstanding personal qualities and characteristics).

Imagine a pirate ship sailing into battle without anyone on board (including the captain) knowing anything about his fellow crew member's competencies and strengths. Imagine a football team taking the field without any of the players knowing who among them could pass the ball, catch, block, tackle, or run. Could either of those groups work efficiently or be successful?

You know the answer, of course – yet business, government, and volunteer teams "sail into battle" or "take the field" every day with team members who really have no idea what the person working next to them has to offer.

Consider the frustration of a customer who contacts a business or government agency with a question, only to be passed from person to person. Employee 1 truly doesn't know the answer – and says so, then passes the call to Employee 2. Employee 2 knows how to *find* the answer, but didn't want to bother – so he also says that he doesn't know, and then passes the call to Employee 3. Employee 3 wants to help, but it's not her area of expertise – so after careful deliberation, she tells the caller, "Well, I sort of maybe think the answer might possibly be..." At best the caller's time is wasted, and so is the time of the three other people. But worse, the caller may be given information that is inaccurate, or that results in costly legal or safety issues.

What if all three employees had known that Employee 4 is an expert on the caller's question (so much so that he is helping to train Employee 5 on the subject)?. If the leader had taken the necessary steps to explore team member roles, that would be the case.

Exploring team member roles in your organization is a simple, three-stage process that involves (1) a short survey, (2) a series of brief one-to-one interviews, and (3) a group meeting.

Team Roles Survey

A Team Roles Survey prompts team members to think about their competencies and strengths. Prepare a one-page survey with three questions:

- What knowledge, skills, and experience do you possess (i.e., what proficiencies and expertise do you bring to this team)?

- What personal strengths do you possess (i.e., what special qualities or characteristics do you bring to this team)?

- How does your role relate to those of the other people on this team (i.e. what would this team be missing without you)?

With the second question, you may wish to include a list of personal strengths so employees can mark the ones that apply to them.

Use the pirate ship or football team analogy to explain the purpose of the survey, and then distribute it to each team member for completion. Emphasize that you will *not* collect the surveys – that the survey form is simply a tool to help each member think about his or her role on the team.

Team Roles Interview

A Team Roles Interview allows each team member to interview one other team member, and to be interviewed by a different team member, regarding his or her role on the team.

Set up the interviews by preparing and distributing an interview match-up sheet that shows who will interview who (allow employees to decide the time and place to conduct each interview). When matching up employees, try to select an interviewer who doesn't normally work with the interviewee, if possible. Each person will participate in two different interviews – one as the interviewer, and one as the interviewee.

During the interview, the interviewer will ask the same three questions that were asked on the survey. The interviewee will respond, but must not give or show his or her survey to the interviewer. It is the interviewer's job to listen and take notes. Limit the interviews to five minutes each.

Team Roles Meeting

The Team Roles Meeting allows every team member to learn about the competencies, strengths and roles of everyone else.

Schedule the meeting so everyone on the team can attend, if possible. At the meeting, post the names of each team member – from the newest member, to the person who has been with the team the longest. As you come to each name on the posted list, ask the person who interviewed that team member to "introduce" the member to the rest of the team by giving a three minute synopsis of the team member's competencies (knowledge, skills, and experience) and personal strengths (special qualities or characteristics). The introduction should conclude by highlighting how that team member's role relates to the rest of group, and what the team would be missing if that member was not a part of the group.

As leader, you will facilitate the process by prompting the speaker/interviewer with open-end questions when necessary. When the speaker is finished, give the team member who was being introduced an opportunity to clarify or add any competencies, strengths, or role functions that were not mentioned by his or her interviewer. Then move to the next name on the list and repeat the process.

You can complete such a meeting in under an hour for a team with ten members. The gains in productivity, efficiency, and trust will more than offset the investment.

Conclusion

Exploring team member roles can be even more valuable for ad-hoc groups, project teams, and working committees. When everyone learns about the competencies, strengths, and benefits that other team members bring to the group (especially in a cross-functional setting), an atmosphere of mutual cooperation emerges – and teamwork thrives.

From this point, the team now enters the second stage of development, where the leader leverages strengths and facilitates involvement...

Leverage Strengths

EIGHT OUT OF EVERY TEN EMPLOYEES feel that they have been "miscast" in the workplace – that the roles they are required to play as part of a team are not utilizing their greatest strengths. This feeling impacts the spirit and commitment they bring to group work, and in turn, reduces the team's effectiveness.[33]

It isn't possible, of course, for everyone to be the quarterback or wide receiver on a football team. The team needs players who are wholly committed to the other positions, or it won't matter how good the quarterback is. The same is true in the workplace. Some jobs simply need to be done, even though they are not particularly visible or glamorous.

Consider the goals of your team (as goals are defined in the previous section of this book). Do those goals involve operational level results that are primarily for the purpose of maintaining an existing capability? Are those goals also recurring, and set in a top-down manner? If so, you may not have the opportunity (at present) to "recast" your team members into different roles that better utilize their strengths.

If, on the other hand, your team is working on goals that produce *strategic* or *tactical* results – or if your team is working on *achievement* or *elimination* goals – there is a good chance that you *do* have that opportunity. If your team is working on *project* or *ad-hoc* goals, you almost certainly have that opportunity.

Take those opportunities. Leverage the strengths of your team members. Here's how.

Individual Strengths

When working with others to achieve a specific goal, every individual attempts to draw upon his or her perceived strengths. As the team encounters problems or challenges, strengths dictate the approach that a person will naturally take to solve the problem or deal with the challenge.

Problem-solving strengths can be visualized in two dimensions. On the horizontal axis is the person's natural preference for thinking about problems in either a conceptual manner or a normative manner.

The personal strengths of *conceptual* thinkers are their abilities to: look at the "big picture," come up with new ideas; discuss theories; imagine the future; explore alternatives; outline a master plan.

The personal strengths of *normative* thinkers are their abilities to: examine details; put ideas into a familiar context; discuss norms and expectations; relate past experiences; explore consequences; fill in the missing facts and information.

On the vertical axis is the person's preference for taking either a spontaneous approach or a methodical approach to working on problems.

The personal strengths of *spontaneous* workers are: non-conformance; freedom from constraints; the ability to multitask and to easily move from one thing to another; a sense of urgency and bias for action; reliable intuition.

The personal strengths of *methodical* workers are: a desire to make things fit together; a preference for order and structure; the ability to focus on one thing and to complete it step-by-step; a bias for thorough examination; precision and accuracy; attention to detail.[34]

You and your team members gained an insight into everyone's personal strengths by completing the team roles process described in the previous chapter. Now you want to review and categorize those individual strengths.

INDIVIDUAL STRENGTHS & TEAM ROLES

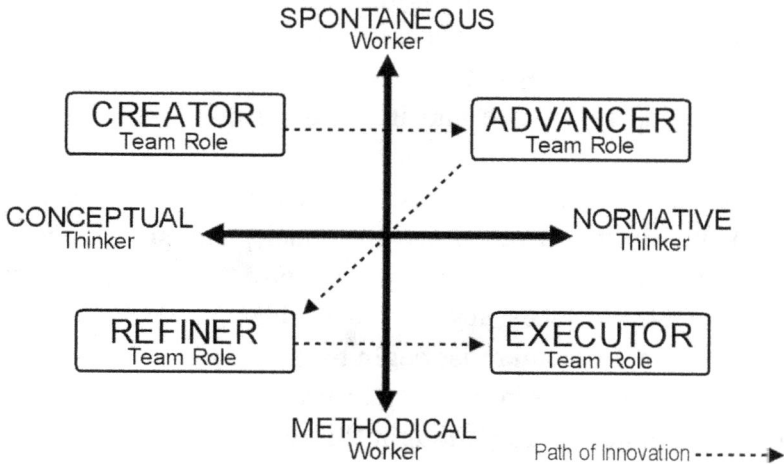

Team Roles

Team members whose strengths lie in the conceptual thinker and spontaneous worker quadrant may be categorized as Creators. On a team where innovative solutions are needed, their role is to examine challenges, explore concepts, and generate ideas. They "play" with the problems involved, create fresh approaches, and search for unusual alternatives. They're not constrained by fear of failure or traditional boundaries.

When Creators are "cast" in the proper team role, they have the ability to take the team in exciting new directions. However, once a viable conceptual solution is identified, the Advancers on the team must begin to take over – otherwise the Creators will work to solve "the problems within the problem" and lose sight of the overall mission.

Team members whose strengths lie in the spontaneous worker and normative thinker quadrant may be categorized as *Advancers*. Their role on the team is to recognize promising ideas in the early stages and develop ways to promote them. They use insightful planning, past experience, and solid evidence to frame new ideas into a familiar context that others can understand. They use energy, determination, and optimism to overcome resistance and instill a sense of purpose in the team.

When Advancers are cast in the proper team role, they have the ability to recognize the most promising ideas and convince other people to pursue them. Once a conceptual solution has the necessary structure and support, however, the Refiners on the team must begin to take over – otherwise, the Advancers may jump directly to implementing an idea that hasn't been adequately thought through.

Team members whose strengths lie in the conceptual thinker and methodical worker quadrant may be categorized as *Refiners*. On a team where innovative solutions are needed, their initial role is to challenge any new concept or idea that is being advanced. They play "devil's advocate," and then use an orderly, procedural approach to review and test the proposed solution in an effort to identify the flaws that would keep it from being successful in practice.

When Refiners are cast in the proper team role, they ensure that everything is examined thoroughly and improved as much as possible. They may modify an idea themselves, or pass it back to the Creators and Advancers with suggestions. If they are allowed to control the innovation process, however, they may steer the team toward low-risk ideas, and filter out the higher risk (but bigger "payoff" solutions) – so there must be a balance. Once a preferred solution is ready for implementation, the Executors begin to take over.

Team members whose strengths lie in the methodical worker and normative thinker quadrant may be categorized as *Executors*. Their role on the team is to implement the solution by completing each task with a focus on quality and attention to detail. They stick to the plan of action, finish what they start, and "do things right."

When cast in the proper team role, Executors get the job done. They are also good at recognizing potential errors and inefficiencies before a solution is implemented. They prefer proven processes, and are therefore not as comfortable with the ad-hoc approaches that may be necessary to formulate new ideas initially, or to troubleshoot a total breakdown – so if major obstacles appear during an implementation process, progress may stall unless the issue is handed back to the Refiners (who may in turn pass it back to the Advancers or Creators, depending on its magnitude and nature).

It is not unusual for a team member to have strengths in two quadrants – for example to be a conceptual thinker who can work both spontaneously and methodically. Obviously, this gives you (as the team leader) more options in determining how to fill every team role for the various projects and work tasks your team may be pursuing.

Innovative solutions flow from Creator to Advancer to Refiner to Executor. When there is a void on the team (i.e., no available member possesses the personal strengths required to fill a specific role), the leader must be ready to step in and demonstrate those strengths – otherwise, innovation ceases and nothing ever changes.

If a team becomes stagnant and "stuck" in the status quo, team members with strengths other than those necessary for an Executor role will become frustrated. They may try to apply their strengths inappropriately (as pirates are sometimes prone to do), or lose their commitment and drop back to the bottom of the development curve. Of course, your most talented team members (the ones who have the highest competence and strongest commitment) will be the ones most likely to seek (and find) employment elsewhere.

Conclusion

Leveraging the strengths of your employees can help you discover and implement highly innovative solutions to difficult problems. It can also increase employee collaboration, job commitment, and overall satisfaction. Failing to utilize the strengths of your team members can leave your ship dead in the water – and make it far more difficult to build, retain, and motivate the workforce you need to achieve your objectives.

With roles clearly defined and team members working from their areas of strength, the leader becomes less like a "boss" and more like a coordinator or *facilitator* of the group. At this stage, the main focus of a leader's job will shift yet again – to helping the group resolve issues or problems that interfere with good teamwork.

Resolve Conflicts

IT IS THE LEADER'S JOB to create a work environment that allows people to thrive. When a feud, disagreement or difference of opinion escalates into interpersonal conflict, many leaders want to leave it alone – hoping the situation will blow over. It won't.

Conflicts between team members may erupt for a variety of reasons. Most often, the core issue is that both parties involved in a conflict feel that the other person doesn't respect them, and/or is trying to take advantage of them in some way. In that context, even the smallest disagreement can boil up into a major controversy. When it does, everyone on the team is affected. At best, team members feel as though they are walking on egg shells when they are in the presence of the antagonists. At worst, team members take sides and the entire group becomes polarized.

The impact is even more serious if a team is isolated, or if members spend virtually all of their working hours together. The reality television series *Survivor* creates this effect by sequestering contestants and presenting them with a series of challenges that are often designed to provoke conflict. It may be entertaining to watch on TV, but it's no fun for anyone in an actual workplace.

Given the relative isolation of a crew aboard a ship at sea, a pirate captain often faced this same leadership challenge – except the parties involved in those disputes were armed! A captain could hardly afford to let a conflict get out of hand.

A pirate captain used four tools to keep potential conflicts in check, and those same four tools are available to you in the workplace. Three of them have already been discussed in this book.

The first tool is your "code." Your policies and procedures must strictly prohibit physical and verbal assaults in the workplace. People on a team will disagree with one another sometimes. That's unavoidable. In fact, it's *healthy* on a collaborative team. Yet team members must disagree within the boundaries of the code. When an interpersonal conflict turns to personal insults or violence, there must be decisive action and serious consequences.

The second tool is the behavioral "spirit factor" (DISC) model that was introduced in the section on motivation. When team members begin to recognize that most conflicts are the result of "pace" and "focus" differences (two people using different approaches to get what they want), disagreements become less "personal," and both parties become more flexible in their communications.

The third tool is the set of seven collaborative skills described earlier in this section. Team members will be better able to resolve disagreements and avoid conflict (without your assistance) once they learn to take responsibility, listen to one another, communicate clearly, give feedback, accept the feedback offered, and cheer each other on.

Until team members are developed to the point of being able to apply these collaborative skills by themselves in everyday situations, you will need to use the fourth tool when interpersonal conflicts between your employees emerge. You will need to *intervene and mediate*.

Mediating a Conflict

Conflicts rarely appear out of nowhere – they brew for awhile. So anticipate the situations where a potential for conflict exists. Be prepared to act. If a conflict surfaces and begins to disrupt the team's effectiveness or progress, schedule a mediation meeting immediately with the parties involved.

Open the meeting by explaining its purpose and objective (i.e., that the parties reach a mutually agreed upon solution to the issue, and each commit to keeping their differences from negatively impacting the team's mission). Next, describe the process you will use to facilitate the meeting, and outline the ground rules that the participants will be required to follow. Get the agreement of both parties to utilize the process and abide by the ground rules as stated.

Begin the process by asking each party to briefly summarize the issue or situation from his or her point of view – first one person, then the next. The ground rules for this are: (a) the other party must listen without comment or interruption; (b) neither party may insult or attack the other.

As each party relates his or her viewpoint, listen and paraphrase. Reframe statements to help identify and verify the relevant facts (as opposed to opinions, gossip, or hearsay). Attempt to pinpoint the main issues or obstacles that are at the heart of the conflict, and get each party to confirm that his or her core concerns have been heard and understood.

When the main issues are clear to you and to each party, verify that both parties are in agreement with the team's mission, goals, plans, standards, and operating guidelines. Clarify any team roles or accountabilities that may be relevant.

Then ask each party, in turn, to suggest one possible option for resolving the conflict. Guide the parties to calmly discuss the pros and cons of each option. Manage their interactions according to the ground rules. Do not comment on or attempt to influence their conclusions. Listen and emphasize the key points on which the parties agree.

When one option has been explored, discuss the next one. Get each party to generate and discuss as many options as they can think of. Ensure that both parties are respectful and fair, and that they confront the issues, not each other.

When all the possible options are on the table, ask the parties to choose the best collaborative (win-win) solution. When they do, outline their specific individual responsibilities for making the solution work. Determine how and when the agreed-upon solution will be implemented, and set a date to follow-up and confirm that the solution was effective.

Emphasize that you expect both parties to fulfill their commitment to resolve the conflict. State what you intend to do (including disciplinary action, if appropriate) should they be unwilling or unable to work it out as agreed. Close the meeting by assuring both parties that you have faith in their ability to resolve their differences and work cooperatively to accomplish the team's objectives.

Helping team members resolve conflict in this way is challenging, but it is part of your role as a leader. Your willingness to intervene when appropriate will set the stage for success. Your ability to mediate a conflict effectively will allow you to craft a team environment that nurtures the success of every employee.

Promote Safety and Security

ASK ANYONE to name three actual pirates and Edward Teach ("Blackbeard") is almost sure to be mentioned. He was well known for putting his men at risk. He was even accused of inventing unnecessarily dangerous tasks as a way to "downsize" the crew and increase his own share of the treasure!

Although Teach went to sea at an early age and served aboard pirate ships for about five years, his career as a captain was brief – less than eleven months. When he was caught and killed by Lt. Robert Maynard for a £100 reward (about $11,000 in today's money), he was on the run with a crew of only nineteen.

To a great pirate captain, it made no sense to build a well-functioning team, and then put its members (not to mention all the other resources that everyone had worked so hard to obtain) needlessly at risk. And yet it happened on the average pirate ship, and it happens in the average workplace.

Thousands of workplace regulations are enforced by the Occupational Safety and Health Administration (OSHA). One of these is known as the General Duty Clause, and it is contained in Section 5(a)1 of the Occupational Safety and Health Act.

The General Duty Clause states that each employer *shall furnish a place of employment that is free from recognized hazards which cause, or are likely to cause, death or serious physical harm to employees*. The OSHA website provides an A-to-Z list of "recognized hazards" (from *aerosols* to *Zika virus*). OSHA further explains that if an employer knows or should have known that a hazard exists in the workplace, yet fails to take action to protect workers, then the employer is in violation of federal law.[35]

Here's the kicker that a lot of managers are surprised to learn. When serious safety-related incidents occur, OSHA (and in most cases, state and federal courts) tend to rule that if *any* person in a formal position of leadership (i.e., someone who supervises employees) was aware of the hazard, then the *employer* knew about it and may be liable. It's important to recognize that a key responsibility for any leader is to keep his or her team members safe.

There are certain occupations that require employees to walk boldly into inherently dangerous situations in order to protect the lives and property of others. If you lead the folks who perform those kinds of jobs (soldiers, police officers, firefighters, etc.), feel free to skip this chapter – you're probably already doing your utmost to ensure that team members go home safe at the end of the shift.

For everyone else: A *recordable injury* is defined as one requiring medical treatment beyond first aid. Annually, there are about 3 million recordable on-the-job injuries in the U.S. in private industry – that doesn't even include public service or government jobs. According to the Bureau of Labor Statistics, 42 of every one thousand workers in private industry are seriously hurt on the job each year.

The cost is enormous. An American Medical Association study found that more health care dollars are spent in the United States treating workplace injuries than are spent treating any other problem. (Yes, more money is spent treating workplace injuries than cancer, heart disease, or AIDS.) Who pays the bill? Businesses do – with lower productivity and morale, plus higher health care coverage, injury compensation, and worker compensation costs.[36]

Job-related injury statistics are available for virtually every type of business and occupation in the U.S. Compare those companies that rank among the top twenty percent of "safest" places to work (in terms of recordable injuries) with the "average" companies in the same industry. The safest companies often have *less than half* the number of injuries. In most cases, they are also happier and more productive places to work, plus their health care and insurance costs are significantly lower.

The difference between a safe workplace and an average workplace is very often *leadership*. In an average workplace, managers often handle mandatory walkthrough inspections and monthly safety meetings as a chore. The attitude flows through the workforce, and employees soon learn that "working safely" really means "working unsafely without getting caught."

There are ten steps you can take (or initiate) as a leader to create a safer workplace:

1. Set a safety goal for your team that is measurable and realistic, and manage it as you would any other performance objective.

2. Examine your workplace and work processes to identify any known hazards that may exist.

3. Determine the prevention and control measures that are available to eliminate or reduce the impact of known hazards.

4. Prioritize the proposed prevention and control measures.

5. Implement the highest priority prevention and control measures (i.e., fund and support those that address the highest risk hazards, but ensure that

any no-cost or low-cost solutions on the list are also implemented).

6. Provide employee training on the specific measures being implemented.

7. Praise employees who work safely, and ensure that there is an effective process for employees to report potential hazards and suggest improvements.

8. Stop unsafe work practices immediately, when observed. Investigate all incidents and occurrences, and follow-up with appropriate actions.

9. Maintain thorough records of the actions taken and results achieved – both as evidence of your responsibility and as financial justification for additional investments in worker safety.

10. Keep score – provide regular feedback to employees regarding your team's safety goals.

Your organization should also have a Crisis Management Team (and a Crisis Management Plan) for addressing serious incidents. The plan should cover the details of how your organization will work with emergency responders, attend to the needs of affected individuals, communicate with employees, families, and the media – plus any other steps necessary to minimize the operational, financial, and legal impacts.

There is a wealth of free information available from OSHA to guide you through all the steps above. A variety of affordable tools and training aids are also offered by third party vendors. The important thing is that you care enough about your team to do what everyone expects a leader to do – keep them safe.

Investigate Complaints

NO MATTER HOW GREAT your team or how terrific your workplace, employees will sometimes have complaints. An effective leader can resolve most complaints on the spot with active listening and other interaction skills.

When an employee's complaint pertains to illegal conduct (such as thefts, violence, harassment, and discrimination), or when it relates to a problem that affects workplace safety or security, you should follow your organization's formal procedures for reporting and handling the issue. If the complaint is of a less threatening nature, or if your organization has no official process for addressing employee complaints, then it is up to you to investigate.

In the vast majority of cases, employees complain to their supervisors long before they decide to retain an attorney or contact an outside agency such as the EEOC for help (that is, unless the supervisor is the offender). Most employees simply want a solution, not a lawsuit. They tend to escalate grievances only when the manager does not respond promptly, fairly, or seriously to the initial complaint. Of course, complaints that escalate are costly to the organization and devastating to good teamwork.

The main goals of an investigation are to determine what happened, decide what remedies are required (if any), and implement those remedies as appropriate. While this may seem straightforward, leaders sometimes make mistakes that damage the effectiveness of an investigation. The following guidelines will help you avoid those mistakes and deal with complaints properly.

Set a Positive, Proactive Tone

The manner in which you initially react when hearing a complaint will set the tone for the entire investigation (at least in the mind of the employee). If you trivialize or dismiss a complaint as "whining," or if you appear to be "glossing over" a problem you'd rather not deal with, the employee will be frustrated and you will lose the only opportunity you have to address a potentially damaging situation early on. Granted, some complaints are silly, and you are not required to remedy each one – but you are obliged to make the person feel heard, understood, appreciated, and respected.

Keep in mind that seemingly minor complaints can often be traced to an employee's behavioral "spirit factor" as discussed previously in this book. For instance, a high "D" spirit who seeks control in most circumstances is more likely to have complaints in a situation where he or she feels that control is being taken away. Rather than dismissing these types of complaints, use the communication skills you've developed to allow both you and the employee to identify the real underlying issues.

Decide What You Are Investigating

When a complaint is brought to you, ask questions to determine what transpired, the context in which it occurred, and who else witnessed it. Also, determine if people and/or property are immediately at risk – or if something unlawful or in violation of regulations or procedures is taking place. If so, you may need to take appropriate short-term responsive action (without accusing anyone of anything) before you begin your investigation.

Employee complaints may begin with a general statement such as, "Joe has been drinking." When such a complaint is made, don't jump to conclusions. Clarify the circumstances in question so you can identify the "scope" and urgency of your investigation. For example, if Joe the forklift operator was intoxicated and driving dangerously, the scope and urgency of your investigation would be different than if Joe the janitor appeared to be hung over and the employee making the complaint was primarily expressing his disapproval.

When you and the employee have agreed on exactly what the complaint consists of, write it down. Taking the time to document a complaint is another way of saying it is worth your time to resolve. Allow the employee to read the complaint document to ensure that nothing important is omitted.

Create an Expectation of Action

Once you have gathered enough information to know the scope and urgency of your investigation, give the employee an idea of how you will proceed and the timeline involved. The employee must believe that you will investigate and take the appropriate action. Otherwise, he or she may rush to bring in a third party.

If an employee is the potential victim of sexual or other harassment, you must act immediately (even if it's a temporary measure) to take the person "out of harm's way" while you conduct your investigation.

The investigation of an employee complaint should never take more than two weeks to complete. Promise to keep the employee informed of your *progress* (but not your *findings*) on a regular basis.

Do not guarantee anonymity to the employee (or to anyone else associated with the investigation). You can only promise that the investigation will be conducted on a *need to know* basis, and that anyone contacted during the course of the investigation will be instructed not to discuss it.

Plan the Investigation

Inexperienced investigators tend to "dive in" and follow their instincts from witness to witness. Instead, plan ahead. List the individuals you will want to speak with and the information you believe they will be able to provide. Create a list of facts to confirm, and a list of questions to be asked -- then determine the sequence in which these must to be addressed in order to complete the investigation. Consider logistical or scheduling issues that might interfere with your investigation. Make sure that the right people are properly notified in advance, especially if you need to interview individuals from outside your team.

Interview the Witnesses and Respondents

When meeting with witnesses or a respondent (i.e., a person "accused" in the complaint), open the interview by briefly explaining the purpose of your investigation. Provide the interviewee with only as much background information as he or she will need in order to answer the questions you intend to ask. Advise the interviewee that the investigation is "need to know" – and that if he or she is asked about the content of the interview, the response should be, "I have been asked not to discuss it."

During the interview, work from the list of questions you prepared in advance. Use whatever method you find suitable to take notes. (After the interview, you should be able to accurately reconstruct what was said.) Keep in mind that your notes will be *discoverable* if the issue escalates into a lawsuit – i.e., a court could subpoena your notes and made them public record – so do not write subjective comments (such as "she's a liar"). Document the facts only.

Let your interviewees do most of the talking. Ask the planned questions, and clarify or confirm the responses. Do not reveal your opinions or any of the facts you obtained from other witnesses. Also, avoid "fishing" for unrelated information.

If there is a respondent or accused, be sure to let that person tell his or her side of the story. Some of the additional questions you might ask include: *Were you aware of the employee's concern? Did that person discuss the concern with you? How would you describe your relationship? Are the allegations true, and if not, what are the inaccuracies? Is there a reason why that person might falsely accuse you?*

Throughout the interview process, remember that you are investigating the *events* that occurred, not the people. Focus on finding out what happened.

Prepare Your Report

When you have completed your interviews, assemble all the facts you've gathered into one document. Next, analyze those facts, including any relevant policies or procedures. Then, write a report summarizing what happened. Be sure to reference the specific facts and analysis that led to your conclusions, and explain how you resolved any inconsistent or conflicting details. Finally, state what has already been done (if a short-term solution was implemented prior to the investigation), and what permanent actions or remedies will be taken or recommended.

If your investigation "opened a can of worms" (i.e., revealed a broader set of ethical or criminal issues), alert your manager, or seek help from an attorney or an outside investigative service.

When you consider possible remedies, be sure to involve the employee who initiated the complaint. Most employees simply want the problem corrected. They are usually eager to move forward once they are certain that it will be – so the remedies they request are often much easier to put in place than you might have anticipated.

Follow Through and Follow Up

Meet with the employee who filed the complaint and discuss the *actions* that will result (but not the details or findings of the investigation itself). If you determined that the complaint was unfounded, explain your reasoning in a patient and empathetic manner. If you are seeking, implementing, or recommending specific remedies, outline them. Check with the employee 30 days and 90 days later to ensure that no retaliation has taken place, and that your action has been effective. (Be sure to document those meetings.)

Summary

A complaint provides you with the opportunity to address a potentially serious problem early on. The investigation you conduct as a result will not only help you solve the problem quickly, it may improve morale, enhance teamwork, and prevent costly litigation.

Discourage Gossip

GOSSIP GETS IN THE WAY of teamwork. Most leaders are aware of that, but they don't realize just how much trouble gossip can cause. In many states, employers can be held liable for damages when gossip creates a negative or hostile environment for an employee – especially if conversations stray too far into an employee's personal and private life.

Define "Gossip"

Draw clear lines to distinguish the differences in "rumors," "gripes," and "gossip."

Rumors generally center on emerging issues that directly affect team members (for example, a pending policy change). The best way to deal with rumors is to keep your team informed about the key issues that affect them – and to keep everyone's "eyes on the prize" (the goals and targets you are pursuing).

Gripes are reactions to work-related issues that irritate employees, yet do not warrant a formal complaint (an unpopular decision, for example). The best ways to deal with gripes are to: (a) explain the rationale behind any unpopular, yet legitimate policy that is implemented, (b) listen and explore options to remove any *real* obstacles that are getting between your team and their targets, and (c) manage employee performance (many gripes are about things that bosses or coworkers do – or don't do – that impact everyone).

Gossip deals with topics that don't directly affect the people who are discussing them (unlike rumors or gripes). Gossip is always about what *other* people said or did, and how they were affected. The best (and only) way to deal with gossip is to stop it when it happens.

Proactively Intervene

When you hear team members gossiping, don't simply try to change the subject or offer input that challenges the story. Instead, provide immediate corrective feedback, in private, to the offender(s). Treat gossip like any other performance problem.

When discussing the incident, state what you overheard, and confirm that the employee agrees that it meets the definition of gossip. Next, identify the behavior you want instead (i.e., for the employee to stop gossiping) and explain why it is important. Emphasize that gossiping is an understandable human behavior, yet one that must be avoided on a productive team due to the potential damage it can cause. Ask for the employee's commitment to avoid gossiping in the future, and thank the employee for making the extra effort to address the issue. After the meeting, casually monitor the situation. If the gossip decreases, be sure to praise the employee.

Remember, it will be difficult for some people to stop the habit of gossiping – it's their connection to others, and they perceive it to be a harmless form of entertainment rather than a potentially damaging force. Be understanding, yet persistent. If your repeated attempts at corrective feedback fail to have the desired effect, don't be afraid to initiate progressive discipline. You simply can't afford to allow "gossip" to become "gospel" on your team.

Finally, *never* participate in gossip yourself, no matter where you are or who you are with.

Make Rational Decisions

THERE ARE TWO WAYS a leader can make a decision: (1) unilaterally (on his or her own), or (2) with the active involvement of team members.

There are some decisions that a leader can and should make alone. For example, a leader may make decisions without involving the team when:

- The situation was anticipated in advance, and a policy already exists that dictates the leader's course of action.

- The decision can be "programmed" – i.e., there is a recognized objective methodology for deciding (such as a financial analysis), and anyone who applied the same methodology would reach the same decision.

- The outcome of the decision (whether it is ultimately a "good" decision or a "bad" one) is a factor of logic alone (i.e., it will not be significantly influenced by whether your team members like or dislike the decision).

- The situation is private or personally sensitive, and cannot be discussed openly with team members.

- The situation is an emergency, and there is no time to involve the team.

- The leader has subject matter expertise (no one on the team has any relevant information or insight to add), and the leader has complete authority (there's no question that it's the leader's decision to make).

Although that list is neither complete nor absolute, it does provide a guideline. When you have a decision to make unilaterally, apply the following steps to ensure that you decide rationally:

1. Specify the desired outcome of the situation, and clearly define the problems or issues (about which a decision must be made) in order to achieve that outcome.

2. Gather the information you need to make the decision, including any operating constraints, past experiences, and stakeholder expectations.

3. Determine if the decision can be programmed. If so, apply the appropriate methodology. If not:

4. Determine if the decision is discretionary (strictly up to you). If not, adhere to whatever action is dictated by the applicable policies. If so:

5. Determine if the situation requires a decision that is congruent or consistent with past decisions. If so, apply the *de facto* standard that has already been established. If not:

6. Determine if you are authorized and qualified to make the decision. If not, analyze the situation and provide a recommendation to your manager. If so:

7. Make the decision, and then monitor the outcome and follow-up as needed.

Misinformation, mistaken assumptions, poor judgment, time pressure, and ego can all contribute to "bad" unilateral decisions. Consequently, when the nature of the decision permits the involvement of team members, it is best to involve them and facilitate the process...

Facilitate the Group

MANY LEADERS AVOID involving their team members in the decision-making process for two simple reasons: (1) it's inefficient (it involves too many people and takes too much time), and (2) it's ineffective (the decisions made by a group are often no better than the ones that leaders would have made on their own).

A leader can't know *everything*, however – so unilateral decisions often turn out to be much *worse* decisions in the long run. There may be a time savings up front, but far more time may be required later to resolve misunderstandings, overcome resistance (or apathy), handle conflicts, and address complications that arise once the decision is implemented.

Involving team members in the decisions that affect them can increase your knowledge base (after all, two heads are better than one, and seven may be better still). Involving others can also build collaboration, ensure commitment to the action decided upon, and produce better results in the end.

Group decisions are an essential element of team success. So, as a leader, you need a process that will allow you and your team to make group decisions *faster* and *better*.

This book has already presented two useful aids. The team decision-making process is a type of meeting, so the keys for conducting more efficient and effective meetings will also apply to group decision-making. In addition, many team decisions are directly associated with a team problem or dilemma, so the steps presented earlier for dealing with a crisis situation can also improve the decision-making process.

Even with those guidelines, it can still be a challenge to facilitate group decisions when the issue is complex or controversial, or when open discussion brings forth contradictory or emotional responses. In such cases, you must take yourself out of the role of ultimate decision-maker (at least temporarily) and become a group facilitator.

Consider the role of a judge. In a municipal traffic court, the judge hears the case and makes the critical decision of guilt or innocence – and if guilty, another decision regarding punishment. In a capital trial, however, a jury makes those decisions, while the judge serves as a facilitator of the process.

For a group to make an effective decision (whether it's a jury or a work team), the facilitator must actively manage three distinct elements – the content, the process, and the interactions.

Managing the Content

The *content* includes all the facts, data, and evidence that pertain to the decision. Just as a judge preserves the integrity of the evidence, and decides what testimony is admitted or excluded, prejudicial or fair, valid or unsubstantiated – you will ensure that all of the information on which your team is basing its discussions and decisions is complete and well-organized.

Studies have shown that the average person can maintain between four and seven "chunks" of related information in short-term memory. When soliciting input or gathering information (such as alternatives, criteria, pros, cons, data points, etc.) for a team decision, you should strive for at least four chunks (such as four options, and four advantages associated with each option) – but no more than seven. Fewer than four may be a warning that you're rushing to a solution and overlooking something important. More than seven makes it significantly harder for people to mentally keep track of everything – plus the items of critical value will almost certainly have been introduced by that point in a group discussion.[37]

Of course, this is not an absolute rule, so another technique for managing the content is to use "group memory" such as flipcharts or marker boards. The process will flow more smoothly, and the interactions will be more constructive, when everyone is seeing the same content in the same way at the same time.

Managing the Process

The *process* encompasses the methodology by which the team will reach its decision. That decision cannot be based on who shouts the loudest. It cannot be based on a vote where the majority rules. It must be a consensus. Just as a judge in court case is accountable for ensuring that a strict set of procedures are followed from start to end, and that the jury reaches a unanimous verdict – you will guide the process by which your team reaches its conclusions.

Team decision-making sessions are often inefficient and ineffective because they begin with the leader stating a problem, and then asking, "Any ideas?" People immediately jump in with solutions to the problem as they perceive it. In most cases, both the solutions and perceptions are off the mark.

To avoid this error, the first stage of team decision-making should be to clarify the question about which a decision must be reached. What is the desired outcome (i.e., what should a "good" decision cause to happen)? What constraints or limitations could impact the way in which any final decision is implemented? Focus the team on those issues and invite discussion. Take the time necessary to surface all key points, and formulate a good "decision question" up front.

For example, a broad opening question like, "What kind of holiday office party should we have?" is sure to inspire a long and fruitless debate. Begin instead by asking people to define criteria that would be characteristic of an enjoyable workplace holiday celebration. Use group memory to capture and discuss those criteria. That will lead to a much better decision question (such as, "What type of after-hours event would encourage the highest percentage of participation by employees and their spouses or guests, and also be feasible with a budget of...?").

Next, help the team generate alternative answers to the decision question you have formulated. Solicit lots of ideas initially, and encourage an open discussion of the strengths and weaknesses of each option. Allow all team members to contribute. You may *eventually* reject some ideas, but not at this early stage.

When an array of options has been identified, assess the risks and opportunities associated with each. Ask "what-if" questions about the future. Use probing questions to draw out the concerns associated with each option on the table. Discover what your team members think before you offer your opinions.

Finally, review each alternative and all the facts collected. When appropriate, utilize a tool or methodology (agreed upon in advance) for evaluating the probable success of each option. (The Delphi method, nominal group technique, criteria rating, and paired-choice scoring are four examples of these). Whatever method is chosen should allow the team to weigh the risks against the rewards, and collectively choose the preferred option.

Consensus means everyone agrees that a specific decision or solution is acceptable (it may not be every person's idea of the *best* course of action, but it is *acceptable* to every person). Consensus also means that everyone is committed to making the chosen solution work. When a decision is made, poll the team to verify that the decision is a true consensus and that the team's commitment to make it work is universal and genuine.

Managing the Interactions

The *interactions* are, of course, the discussions that occur among team members. Again, just as a judge enforces courtroom etiquette and maintains order, you will ensure that your group's participants adhere to the process and ground rules you've established.

The techniques for uniting, focusing, and mobilizing meeting participants (as covered in *Part V*) can be applied to team decision-making, too. It is especially important that you have an agenda, and that you open the meeting by showing your team that you have a reliable process planned. Review the ground rules for how the group will interact with one another, offer ideas, display issues, and reach consensus.

Make sure that every team member is participating. Maintain a balance – don't allow one person or clique to dominate, and encourage people who are less demonstrative to get involved. Never insult or embarrass anyone in front of the group. Maintain or enhance the self-esteem of every participant.

Provoke controversy (in a constructive way). This means guiding the team to consider all sides of an issue. You cannot allow *group think*, "it's always been that way," or "let's just decide and move on" to drive the acceptance of a lesser option. The leader must ensure that the group is tough on the problem and issues – without being tough on each other.

Distinguish between useful and wasteful contributions. *Bad* ideas are often the building blocks to a good solution. *Irrelevant* ideas rarely are. So welcome any input that is relevant, no matter how unworkable it may seem. However, if you feel that a team member's input is irrelevant, ask that person to help the group understand how the comment relates to the issue under discussion. Usually, the participant will admit that it doesn't (which will allow you to get the discussion back on track). On the other hand, if you were overlooking a key connection, your question will give the participant a chance to contribute something valuable to the process.

Finally, always keep participants focused on the ultimate goal. The goal is not to simply make a decision and get the meeting over with – it's to produce a specific desired outcome in the future. Never let the team lose sight of that primary objective.

Guide Change

THE LIFE OF A CARIBBEAN PIRATE, as portrayed in Hollywood movies, is entertaining – but mostly fictitious. At least one aspect is represented with some accuracy, however – the pirate captain's need to be ready for anything.

Change was a constant in the life of a pirate captain, just as it is for leaders today. Business customers, non-profit beneficiaries, and government taxpayers all want *M.B.C.F.* – they want *MORE*, they want it *BETTER*, they want it *CHEAPER*, and they want it *FASTER*. No matter what type of team you lead, the pressure to adapt and deliver has never been as intense as it is now.

Change includes any alteration, transformation, conversion, or variation of an existing process that is undertaken for the purpose of improvement (or in some cases, survival). It may be as minor as a modification to an operating procedure, or as major as a corporate merger. Regardless of the magnitude, however, change means that at least one thing has to be done differently than it was done before (and often, *lots* of things).

The initial effect of change on team members is almost always negative in the sense that it pushes an employee backward and down the development curve. (If an employee is highly competent at a job task – and something about that task changes – then the person can't help but be less competent at it, at least initially.) If the employee feels threatened by that loss of competence, then commitment may also decline – and the employee will slide even further backward and down the curve. Considering that even a very simple change can have that effect on every member of a team at once, it becomes apparent that guiding your employees through change is critical.

Leading a team through a period of change can be a colossal challenge. Only about one in fifty managers is truly proficient at it. Consequently, the more effective you become at managing change, the more you ensure not only your team's success and survival, but your own. Leaders who are competent at guiding change have nearly unlimited career potential in a world where change is a constant.

Steps for Leading Change

The process for guiding a team through change (whether the change is minor or major, and whether your "team" is an entire agency or single work unit) involves nine fundamental steps.

Step 1 – Accept that Change has Happened

You may recall that this was the first step in taking care of crisis situations (in *Part II*), as well. Acceptance is the opposite of rejection and resistance. Acceptance keeps your mind calm and positive, and allows you to more clearly see both the opportunities and obstacles that lie ahead.

If you find acceptance difficult, diagnose the reason. Ask yourself, "Exactly what am I worried about?" and "What is the very worst that could happen?" Write down the answers. Simply defining your concerns on paper will very often resolve them. When it doesn't, it will at least allow you to prepare for the worst – and move forward.

Step 2 – Share the Facts Immediately

As soon as someone mentions that a potential change is under consideration, rumors are born. In a pirate culture, rumors travel fast and are almost always inaccurate in some way. As a result, team members are loaded with misinformation before they ever receive any official explanation of what might be happening. In such cases, resistance and negativity get a giant "head start."

What if you are a supervisor or manager, and see this happening? Go to the source, gets the facts about what is really going on, and share them as soon as possible with your employees and team members. Factual information is to rumors what water is to fire.

If you are a senior executive (or anyone empowered to initiate change), you must have a sense of urgency about sharing facts – maybe not *all* the facts, but share as much as you can as quickly as you can. Any meeting in which a potential change is discussed and considered must also include a decision regarding what to tell employees and other stakeholders about that pending change. The absence of information breeds misinformation to fill the void.

Taking days or weeks to draft and disseminate the "official word" is too long. Unless there are legal or security reasons for maintaining confidentiality, the facts should be released within minutes or a few hours. The longer the delay, the more difficult it will be to effect the change.

Step 3 – Communicate with your team

It is critical for the leader to communicate continually with his or her team about the change. The three things the leader must emphasize are (1) the vision of the future (once the change is implemented), (2) the plan for getting there, and (3) the consequences of not getting there.

You are already aware of the importance of a vision. There must be a compelling and desirable reason for people to stop doing something that they are familiar with and start doing something different. They can't supply themselves with that reason – you must provide it for them.

You must also help people understand how to get from "here" to "there." For a major change, it isn't necessary that they know the *entire* plan in detail – but they must know that there *is* a plan, and they must know the details of what they're expected to do *next* as part of the plan's execution.

What happens if the change stalls? Are there regulatory or market consequences? How would those affect team members? Could people lose their jobs? Just as you use the vision to present a positive view of the future, you must paint an equally vivid picture of the consequences of *not* implementing the change.

As you can see, communicating with your team about change is not a singular activity where you hold a meeting or send out an e-mail, and presto – you're done. It is an on-going process, and you must use every communication medium available (e-mail, memos, presentations, meetings, one-to-one conversations, etc.) throughout the life-cycle of the change.

Step 4 – Enroll Everyone in the Process

Change is not an event that happens all at once, it's a process. That process evolves depending on how people interpret and react to whatever is occurring at the moment. When people believe that they are "victims" – that an undesirable element of change is being forced on them – they naturally resist.

As a leader, you must ensure that every member of your team perceives the change as something that he or she is personally involved in. It is not something that's happening *to* them, but rather something they are actively bringing about. This concept has been called "respect for followers" and focuses on winning their hearts and minds through inclusion and participation.

This approach allows you to share not only information, but *power*. Sharing power enhances your team members' self-worth and gets them excited about the plan of action. Even more important, it puts those who are best acquainted with the grassroots operation in a position to solve problems quickly as the change is implemented.

Step 5 – Model the Change

To guide change, leaders must set the example. No one follows the leader to a place the leader isn't willing to go. Leaders must "walk the talk" to develop trust and to build credibility for the change. In organizations that have a history of initiating and then abandoning new ideas, modeling the change provides evidence that *this* change is for real (and not just another "test" or passing fad).

Schedule one or more visible actions that relate to the change into your daily routine. In other words, think about how you can personally demonstrate your commitment each day in a way that your team members and others will be able to observe – and put those actions on daily to-do list.

Audit your past actions. If you had a reputation for fighting change and preserving the status quo *before* you were in a leadership role, own up to it and correct yourself (even if it's after the fact). Acknowledging your past mistakes can send a potent message about your commitment to the current effort.

Think before you act. Enlist a "shadow" if necessary – someone on the team to monitor your words and actions, and give you feedback if you say or do something that contradicts the example you need to set. Again, if this occurs, acknowledge it and correct yourself.

Change (especially a change where technology is involved) often requires people to do "double duty" for a period of time – they must perform certain activities both the old way and the new way (in parallel) while the change is being implemented. When you are the first to make visible sacrifices and model the change, it's easier to ask your team members to take on extra work when necessary.

Step 6 – Create a Supportive Environment

It is virtually impossible for people to change without learning something new. Learning and change go hand in hand. For many people, learning is difficult under the best of circumstances. Add in the time pressure and the consequences of failure that are associated with change, and an even more stressful situation is created.

As leader, you can help team members in several ways. First, acknowledge that they are in a learning mode, and that you know there will be trial-and-error involved. When problems occur, avoid the temptation to affix blame – focus instead on how the problem occurred, how it can be corrected, and how it can be prevented in the future.

Encourage the early discovery of problems. Create opportunities to practice new skills without the threat of embarrassment or reprisal. Challenge people to "shoot holes" in the proposed change, and then "bulletproof" the points of weakness.

Remember that in the absence of support, people will revert back to what they know best. To avoid this, reinforce the idea that it's acceptable for team members to admit when they hit an obstacle or are uncertain of how to proceed. When they do, remove the barriers that impede their progress (if you can), or provide them with the necessary time and resources to figure out the answers for themselves.

Step 7 – Focus on Interim Successes

Most organizations make the mistake of establishing only one milestone that means anything: the point at which the change is fully implemented. That's very much like asking an athlete who just had knee surgery to run a marathon. Running a marathon may be the *ultimate* objective, but it can only be achieved if a series of interim goals are set, attained, and celebrated. Change works the same way.

Identify interim milestones to serve as indicators of progress toward the full implementation of any change effort you are leading. The more milestones you create, the better it is (especially early in the implementation process). Celebrate each of those "small victories" as a way to build team confidence and momentum (there are more tips about celebrating in a later chapter).

Celebrate the failures, too. In a supportive environment, learning that something *won't work* can be an important breakthrough – but even when it isn't, a celebration will re-energize your team and keep them from feeling defeated by the experience.

Step 8 – Help People Break from the Past

When people hold on to the old way of doing something, milestones are missed and the pace of change slows dramatically. When people begin to let go of the past, the pace accelerates and resistance becomes the exception rather than the norm.

Communicating about the vision, plan, and consequences will go a long way in helping people break from the past. In addition to that, you'll want to make it a habit to openly question the status quo. This is particularly true when people claim that something can't be done because of a regulation or policy (yet they can't cite the specific source or rule). Track it down. More often than not, the obstacle will turn out to be something non-existent or totally irrelevant.

Raise the bar. Most change initiatives are designed to *improve* something. If people could achieve the improvement doing a job the "old" way, then the change would not have been necessary in the first place. So don't wait for the change to be fully implemented – start modifying team standards and individual targets as soon as a related interim milestone is realized. People are more likely to let go of the past when they *have to* in order to maintain satisfactory performance.

Step 9 – Institutionalize (Lock-in) the Change

Monitor and measure the benefits that are realized after each milestone is achieved. Actively promote those benefits as they relate to stakeholders (both internal and external) and to the organization's overall mission.

When you advertise the fact that positive results are being achieved with a new process, it will help that new process become the new "way things are done" and therefore permanently "locked in."

Finally, have an exit strategy in mind for those who cannot or will not change. During the implementation process, individuals who continue to strongly oppose a change initiative can be used constructively to test and troubleshoot the problems (since they think it's a bad idea anyway, you can give them the chance to prove it – and use their findings to improve the solution). Eventually, however, you must direct them to get on board – and you must be prepared to use progressive discipline if they refuse.

Overcoming Negativity

Negativity is a virus. It begins with a few "carriers," but can quickly infect an entire team. Soon, the change effort is pulled into a vortex like flotsam into a whirlpool. You can't "vaccinate" the entire team against negativity, but you can attempt to quarantine and treat the carriers.

Over 85 percent of people who are described by coworkers as being "negative," "pessimistic," and "uncooperative" do not see themselves that way. No one ever tells them! In fact, three out of four managers say that they routinely avoid dealing with negative employees, rather than providing feedback. No wonder there's a problem.[38]

When you encounter negativity, address it. The following tips should help.

First, do not become defensive. It may sound as though negative people are criticizing you personally, but they are actually attacking themselves in a way. If you "defend" yourself or fight back, they will only become more negative.

Instead, focus on solutions. Negative people constantly think about reasons *not* to do things. So don't ask them why a change should not be implemented (they'll have a good answer), but rather what they would do *differently* to make it work. If they can't provide suggestions, praise their abilities, past actions, and accomplishments. Then ask them to use those strengths to develop possible solutions to the problems or obstacles they perceive – and then set a meeting to discuss their findings.

In extreme cases, you might schedule this as an overtime activity. Yes, it will cost you a little money if the employees involved are eligible for overtime pay, but it's unlikely that you'll ever have to do it more than twice. Negative people may resist change on *company* time, but not when it is inconvenient and means giving up some of their *own* time.

Once people realize that it's taking more effort to oppose the change than it would take to implement it – and that "resistance is futile" (i.e., you're not going to give in, but instead will continue to involve them even deeper in finding solutions) -- they'll stop spreading the virus and get on board. Of course, if their concern is a legitimate one, they may actually find an innovative solution (given the opportunity) – making it time and money well-spent!

Finally, be attentive when a person who is *not* normally negative suddenly becomes outspoken about a pending change. This behavior is most likely related to the person's "spirit factor," specifically a fear that the proposed change will take away an aspect of the job that the employee finds enjoyable and motivating. You may need to reassure and "win the spirit" of this team member once again.

Capitalize on Diversity

AS NOTED AT THE START of this book, an 18th-century pirate ship was a highly diverse workplace, even by today's standard (except for being a predominantly-male environment).

Diversity means differences – not just in race, but in age, gender, religion, background, behavior, physical ability – in everything. America's workforce is becoming increasingly more diverse – and that diversity is a source of strength when leaders capitalize on it. *Capitalizing* on diversity means making the most of those differences, rather than merely tolerating them (or worse yet, trying to eliminate them).

The two greatest obstacles to capitalizing on diversity are prejudice and belligerence. *Prejudice* is a preconceived and irrational judgment about someone who is different. *Belligerence* is an eagerness to be offended or create a confrontation. Both are stimulated by things that may not be very "pretty," yet are a natural part of the human make-up. *Everyone* is prejudiced regarding some differences, and almost *everyone* has sensitivities that can make them behave belligerently. As a leader, you can't change that.

You *can*, however, influence your team member's actions and behaviors. What people *think* and *feel* is their own business – but what they *say* and *do* at work affects everybody. It isn't necessary for everyone on your team to *like* each other, or to *be* like each other – it *is* necessary for them to work together productively toward a common goal.

Prejudiced employees are often insensitive. Belligerent employees are often overly sensitive. Put the two behaviors together and you have a problem.

You can't generate collaboration, leverage strengths, and achieve your team's objectives if your employees are continually "acting out" on the basis of either prejudice or belligerence. Four ingredients are necessary to overcome those negative behaviors, and each must be distinctly developed in order to capitalize on diversity. The four ingredients are knowledge, understanding, acceptance, and respect.

Knowledge

Your team members must actually *know* each other to collaborate constructively. When age, language, culture, or other differences create cliques or factions within a team, an invisible wall goes up – and keeps team members from learning anything personally significant about their coworkers. As a result, people make broad assumptions about those on the "other side" – which merely reinforces all the misinformation and stereotypes that already exist.

As a leader, you have to knock down this invisible wall and not only *help* people get to know each other – *require* them to learn at least the basic facts about the other people on the team (such as their names, backgrounds, families, interests, and what they hope to gain from the job).

Some people won't *care* (they'll refuse to learn anything about anyone who is different). Some people won't *share* (they'll refuse to let anyone who is different learn anything about them). Both are blatant demonstrations of prejudice and belligerence. Handle them as performance or behavior issues.

Understanding

It's one thing to *know* your coworker, and another thing altogether to *understand* him. Understanding goes beyond merely speaking the same language. For example, in spite of the number of single mothers and foreign nationals in today's workplace, individuals in both groups have felt (very strongly at times) that some of their teammates just don't "get it."

The results of not understanding are rigid perceptions and a lack of empathy. A person cannot excel in a team environment when his or her coworkers believe that *their* perception of reality is the *only* perception of reality – or when they don't have the emotional or intellectual capacity to put themselves in a teammate's shoes. At the same time, most people do not intend to hurt or offend anyone – they simply lack knowledge and understanding (which they'll never gain if a teammate reacts with belligerence, rather than calmly explaining his or her perspective on the issue).

As a leader, you help your team learn to share *facts* in stage 1. You must help them do the same with their *feelings* and *perceptions* in this stage.

Acceptance

Acceptance is a willingness to include and be included. It happens when team members begin to voluntarily invite each other to their respective "sides" of the invisible wall. This requires everyone involved to modify their behaviors (at least somewhat) in order to accommodate and collaborate with others.

People make these adjustments with friends and family all the time (it's called "common courtesy"). Once team members know and understand each other, all you have to do to bring this third stage of acceptance into your workplace is give it an occasional "nudge" with praise, feedback, and support.

Respect

The fourth and final stage of maximizing a diverse workforce occurs when employees go beyond accommodating or "tolerating" differences – and begin to see *value* in them.

Respect for other people means granting them full regard, without compromise, for the capabilities and contributions they bring to the team. In an environment of respect, team members seek out opportunities to get involved, interact, and work with those who are different.

A facilitated diversity training workshop may help your team reach this level of respect (especially once they achieve knowledge, understanding, and acceptance). Respect allows a team to "work it out" for themselves when a problematic difference arises, rather than having to rely on official policies to cover every diversity challenge or situation.

Conclusion

A well-developed team is like a well-prepared meal. Award-winning chefs don't just throw things together – they ensure that each ingredient enhances the flavor and effectiveness of the others. The final product is better than the sum of its parts. The same can be true for your team.

Your job as a leader is to help your employees learn about their differences – and to keep learning until those differences no longer make any difference. Only then can you capitalize on the diversity that's required for a team to be competitive in today's world.

Celebrate Success

CAN YOU IMAGINE a professional football season in which none of the players, coaches, or fans celebrated *anything* until after the Super Bowl – and even then, it was the only the winning team that rejoiced? Far too many business teams operate in just that manner.

In fact, a winning season is made up of game victories – all of which are celebrated. Games are made up of touchdowns, first downs, interceptions, and turnovers – all of which are celebrated. Even individual plays like blocks, tackles, sacks, and receptions are celebrated. Granted, not every play justifies the degree of celebration it receives (on the field, in the stadium, or in front of big screen TVs across America), but that's not the point.

The point is, celebrations make people feel good. The effect is not just psychologically, either. The process of celebrating impacts the body's chemistry to create a sense of well-being and to relieve stress. Celebrating also reminds everyone on the team of what's important. It unifies and energizes the group to pursue the next target.

There are three basic types of celebrations – spontaneous, formulated, and planned.

Spontaneous celebrations occur naturally in a healthy team environment. Like the celebrations that take place on a football field after a game-changing play, they should be instantaneous, brief, and neither insulting nor offensive to others.

Formulated celebrations were popular with pirate crews, and remain so with all kinds of teams. These basically involve team members gathering together after a milestone event to discuss and "replay" the highlights of the achievement. Leaders can help stimulate these discussions by providing a time and place, and by prompting team members to talk about the things that went well or the challenges that they successfully overcame.

Planned celebrations are usually reserved for major victories. Go "all out" for these celebrations to the degree that your budget will allow. Whether it's a team dinner at a great restaurant or a cookout in your backyard, consider what everyone will enjoy and find relaxing – yet be sure the celebration is different enough to suitably mark the special event.

Strive to include everyone who was a part of the team's success, even if they are not actual members of your team. This may include senior managers, employees from other departments, customers, and suppliers (if appropriate).

When it comes time to "say a few words" about the success, be sure to thank the team and talk about how they have developed – as individuals and as a group. Also, highlight the benefits that have been realized as a result of the success you are celebrating. Finally, personalize your thanks by giving each team member a card or note that specifically mentions his or her contributions to the success.

Don't forget employees who worked behind-the-scenes or "covered" routine tasks for the team members who had a more visible or active role. Recognize *everyone* who was a part of the success.

Part VIII.
"Drink Up, Me Hearties!"

Enrichment

Remove the Barnacles

BARNACLES ARE CRUSTACEANS, about the size of a quarter, that attach themselves to the hull of a ship. They are hidden below the waterline, so you'd never know that they are there – except their presence creates drag as the ship moves through the water. They can eventually build up to such a point that speed may be cut by 30 percent (and on a power craft, fuel consumption may double!).[39]

These organisms excrete a form of cement that is strong enough to hold the weight of a car, so it takes serious effort to remove them. The traditional method is to place the ship in dry dock, manually scrape or sandblast the creatures off the hull, and then apply an "anti-fouling" paint to inhibit future growth.

The earlier of sections of this book provided useful tips and techniques for dealing with the obvious (above the waterline) factors that can create drag on you and your organization. This chapter emphasizes things that often hide below the surface.

These issues may seem minor in comparison to the employee motivation, communication, performance management, and teamwork problems you've already faced – yet, like barnacles, once these tiny freeloaders start grabbing on, they have a way of getting out of control. They can slow your progress and sap your energy.

So this final section of the book might be considered your "dry dock" – the place where you examine the harder-to-see aspects of yourself and your leadership – and remove the barnacles. The remaining chapters focus on some of the most common leadership barnacles, and offer guidelines to help you detect them, blast them away, and keep them from reappearing.

Be aware that barnacles can also take the form of "emotional baggage." Your emotional baggage is how you *feel* about all the experiences you've had in your personal and professional life – successes, failures, smart moves, dumb moves, moments you are proud of, and moments you'd rather forget.

Effective leadership – the process of developing people, building teamwork, and producing results – will earn you a loyal following. It will also create some resentment. Resentful people (many of whom claim to be your friends) may try to offset your achievements by continually reminding you (and anyone else who will listen) of the worst things you ever did. For instance, when you and your team are celebrating a new success, a resentful coworker may bring up an old failure.

Don't let past feelings of inadequacy, guilt, embarrassment, or regret (especially those that are triggered by a resentful associate) attach themselves to you and impede your progress. Don't let "ancient history" – or mistakes that you've already corrected and learned from – slow you down. If that's easier said than done, seek out a compassionate and responsive supporter with whom you can discuss the situation and lighten your load.

Scrape the barnacles – and allow your leadership to move forward efficiently!

Eliminate Time Robbers

A TIME ROBBER is anything that "steals" minutes from your day and keeps you from effectively performing your role as a leader.

Time is a precious resource. Imagine that you had $1,440 in one dollar bills. How many bills would you let other people take away from you before you stopped them? How many bills would you be willing to just *throw* away? There are 1,440 minutes in a day, and you should manage them at least as carefully as you would manage your money.

Most people don't watch where their time goes because they are confident they'll get another 1,440 minutes tomorrow, and the next day, and well into the foreseeable future. Of course, we never know that for certain – plus unlike the people who wander through life aimlessly, *you* have a purpose to fulfill, a mission to accomplish, and a *treasure* to find!

The typical manager loses nearly three hours a day to time robbers. Reducing that by just one hour (to two "lost" hours a day) would make you one of the most efficient people in your organization. If the techniques in this section can save you just an hour each workday, you'll gain more than 200 hours of time over the course of a year – in effect, you'll get five "extra" workweeks to do with as you wish!

Two of the time robbers that impact managers the most are dealt with in earlier sections of the book: (1) unproductive meetings (you now know how to plan and run a productive meeting), and (2) recurring performance or behavior problems (you now know how to resolve these problems the *first* time, rather than dealing with them over and over).

While you can save considerable time by leading productive meetings and dealing with problems properly, those are not usually an every day occurrence. To recapture an hour or more each day, you'll also want to address the six *daily* time robbers that most directly and consistently impact supervisors, managers, and executives:

- Interruptions – unplanned interactions that take you away from a productive activity;

- "Fire Fighting" – having to get personally involved in routine problems that employees should have taken the initiative to prevent or resolve on their own;

- Ineffective scheduling – not having enough time for the important tasks (usually because too much time is spent on trivial or routine matters);

- Disorganization – not being able to quickly find the items or information you need to complete a task;

- Fatigue – working well below peak efficiency due to stress or exhaustion;

- Reinventing the wheel – ignoring (or being unaware of) information and solutions that are more readily available than the ones you are pursuing.[40]

The chapters that follow will present simple, yet highly effective techniques for regaining the precious time you may have been losing – as well as powerful ways to leverage that newly found time to your greatest advantage. All of this will help you reap the greatest possible enjoyment and benefit from the 1,440 minutes you have each day.

Control Interruptions

UNPLANNED INTERACTIONS (phone calls and "drop in" visitors) account for nearly one-third of a typical leader's day. Supervisors and managers complain that "too many interruptions" are the main reason they don't get as much done as they'd like.[41]

Obviously, leaders cannot isolate themselves. They need to be available. Leaders who are not available can cause delays and steal time from others who need to see them. Consequently, you cannot *eliminate* interruptions. You can *manage* them, however, and reduce the impact they have.

Begin by *scheduling* time for unplanned interactions. Set aside large blocks of time for focused work and "protect" that time – do not receive visitors, answer the phone, and or check e-mail during those periods unless it's an emergency. Allow adequate *scheduled* time between each of those blocks to deal with unplanned calls and visits (and let people know that those scheduled times are when you're available).

When an interruption occurs during your "protected" time, take a few seconds to write yourself a "recovery note" – a reminder to help you get back on track once you've dealt with the unplanned issue.

Use the "Plus, Plus, Dash" technique to confirm the urgency of the interruption. This consists of two positive statements ("I'm glad you stopped by. I really want to visit with you about that.") followed by a "dash" to get back to what you were doing ("I need to get this report to the Director by 10:30. Can I stop by to see you at 10:45?"). If the matter can't wait, the person will say so and you can handle it appropriately. If it *can* wait however, you will have successfully protected your "focus" time by scheduling the visit for later.

An egg timer is a great tool for shortening the duration of interruptions. When someone asks, "Do you have a second?" you can say, "I have three minutes right now. If you need longer, I'll have to schedule a time to see you later." Then covertly press the button on the digital egg timer you have in your pocket or in the top drawer of your desk. After three minutes, the timer will beep like an alarm clock or pager, and you'll have a legitimate excuse to either wrap up the call/visit, or to reschedule.

When one person has an emergency and interrupts you, others may take it as cue that you are now available and start "lining up" outside the door. To prevent this, use the "walk with me" technique. Invite the person to go with you (and discuss the issue) as you do something you needed or intended to do anyway (such as stretching your legs, getting a bottle of water, or making copies).

If casual visitors (people who stop to "chat") are a problem, don't give them a place to sit down (remove the extra chairs from your office or fill them with other items). With chronic complainers, don't commiserate or offer assistance. Instead, empathize (e.g., "I can see that you're upset"), and then force them to confront the issue by asking, "So how are you going to resolve that?" When people realize that complaining to you means working on a *solution*, they'll seek out someone else.

Finally, don't allow interruptions to result in you having more work to do. Demand initiative from your employees...

Demand Initiative

EVERY SUPERVISOR AND MANAGER has heard it from an employee at one time or another: "Boss, we have a problem."

Three conditions are usually present – (1) the boss is focused on something else important when the interaction occurs, (2) the boss knows enough about the problem to get involved, but (3) the boss doesn't know enough about the problem (at that moment) to make an on-the-spot decision. So what happens?

In most cases, the boss either gives up "protected" time to deal with the issue immediately, or promises to deal with it later ("Let me look into it and get back with you."). Both are time robbers.

Workplace pirates often learn to "manage the manager" by using problems in this way. To avoid that situation, leaders must recognize that there are five levels of employee initiative. When a problem exists, an employee can choose to:

1. *Ignore* it (zero initiative).

2. *Report* it – "Boss, we have a problem."

3. *Investigate* it (and recommend a solution) – "Boss, we have a problem. Here are the details, and here's what I think we should do and why."

4. *Resolve* it (and report the outcome) – "Boss, we had a problem. Here's what I did to take care of it."

5. *Own* it (the highest initiative) – The employee resolves the problem, monitors the outcome, and consults the boss only if something unexpected evolves.

Leaders must *outlaw* the first two levels. At no time should it be acceptable for an employee to ignore a problem, or merely report the problem to the boss. Every employee should understand that he or she is expected, at a minimum, to take at least the third level of initiative when a problem arises.

When employees are required to present the leader with a recommendation, they will most likely gather enough information (before interrupting the leader) that the leader can make a decision then, rather than postponing action until later. If the employee makes a sound recommendation, the leader can authorize the person to carry it out.

If the employee fails to adequately investigate the problem, or makes a flawed recommendation, the leader will have to get involved in formulating a solution – but both the leader and the employee will have learned something important in the process. They will both know in what area the employee lacks competence and/or commitment – and where further development is needed.

Of course, once an employee demonstrates his or her competence and commitment at initiative level 3, the leader will empower that person to take action first and then report (level 4). The leader's goal is to make every employee capable of taking ownership of the problems that they can resolve (level 5) – i.e., the employee sees the problem, investigates, takes action, monitors the outcome, and provides only routine reports to the leader about the incident (unless the leader's help or assistance is needed).

Prioritize Your Work

WHICH DO YOU RUN OUT OF FIRST – work that needs to be done, or the time to do it? If you're running out of time, you may have too much to do.

If that's the case, you can talk to your manager about reducing your responsibilities – or you can consider the possibility that you're making one or more of these mistakes: (1) not creating or maintaining a weekly *to-do* list, (2) spending too much time on tasks that you enjoy, and (3) doing all the unpleasant chores and trivial tasks first (perhaps to "get them out of the way" so you can concentrate).

To avoid these mistakes, make a list (at the end of the week) of all the things you need to do in the coming week. Write down each item as you think of it (it doesn't matter what order they're in).

Next, *prioritize* the items so you can plan the week ahead. Priority refers to two things: the amount of time you need spend on an activity (its *importance*), and how soon you have to get it done (its *urgency*).

As for *importance*, the Pareto Principle (or "80-20 Rule") states that for most events, the majority of an outcome is created by a minority of the elements involved. In the context of leadership, approximately 80 percent of the results you attain (and 80 percent of their value) will typically come from about 20 percent of the tasks on your to-do list.

For example, if there are 20 tasks on your to-do list for next week, it's likely that four of them are extremely important to you and your organization. They are *high value*. The other sixteen are just things that have to get done (some of which you enjoy, some you despise, and some that evoke general apathy).

When you plan your week, schedule your regular meetings on your calendar first. Next, allocate large blocks of time during each day to focus (uninterrupted) on the 20 percent of your tasks (four, in this example) that are most important – i.e., high value. Then allow shorter periods of time between each of those large blocks to deal with the inevitable interruptions that will occur – and to work on the less important 80 percent of your tasks (sixteen, in this example).

In essence, you "protect" the time you need to complete critical tasks, and allow everything else to fall into place during the periods between. Less important tasks still get done, but since they contribute less value, they receive less of your time and dedicated attention (and therefore burn up less of your day).

The *urgency* of the tasks on your list (regardless of their importance) will allow you to determine in which order you schedule them. The sooner a task needs to be done, the earlier in the day or week you schedule time to work on it. It's not difficult.

This process will allow you to begin the week with your work properly prioritized. Once the week begins, new tasks will start to pop up (naturally). As they do, resist the temptation to "crisis manage." Instead, assess each new task in terms of its importance and urgency, and then adjust your calendar to accommodate it.

Finally, don't expect to "control" every minute. If you can keep six hours of an eight-hour day well organized, you'll be among the most effective leaders around (even if the other two hours are total chaos!).

Organize Your Space

CLUTTER – wherever you have it (in your closet, your garage, your office, or on your computer's hard drive) – can be a major time robber.

There are three main causes of clutter: (1) not having a simple system for storing and managing the information and other items ("assets") you possess, (2) not having a workable procedure for handling the new assets you receive each day, and (3) holding on to old assets after you no longer need them.

If your world is relatively clutter-free, stick with what you're doing. It apparently works well for you. However, if you waste time and energy searching for things that "could be anywhere," try these methods.

A Simple "20 Percent" System

The mistake most people make when they try to "get organized" is that they try to get *100 percent* organized. They spend more time setting up a new system than they ever save, and (unless they are mildly obsessive/compulsive) the system doesn't work for them anyway – it eventually gives way to clutter once again.

Keep in mind that the Pareto Principle applies to your assets, just as it does to your time. For example, you use about 20 percent of your assets to complete 80 percent of your work tasks. If you're like most people, 80 percent of your "worldly possessions" are rarely (if ever) used. So a simple system for organizing your workspace only demands that it be *20 percent* organized – which is far more realistic for most people!

To set up a "20 percent system," start by emptying the most convenient and readily accessible 20 percent of the space you control. If you have a five-drawer desk, empty the top drawer. If you have a five-shelf bookcase, empty the easiest shelf to reach. If you have a closet, empty the front 20 percent. Temporarily place all the things you removed in a handy (yet safe) location such as a cardboard storage box in the corner.

Then, go about your normal business for a few weeks. When you need an asset to complete a work task, retrieve it, use it, and determine if it is something that you utilize routinely. If so, find a permanent place for it in the empty space you created and put it there.

When you use the item from then on, put it back in its proper place. (This is the reason you allocate the most convenient and readily accessible space – so it will be just as easy to put something back as it is to toss it aside and create clutter.)

If any part of the 20 percent you initially emptied (i.e., that top drawer or easy-to-reach shelf) fills up, empty a second one and continue as before. Most people never fill up the second 20 percent of available space with any regularly used items.

What about all the stuff you're *not* using? Yes, it could be sitting around in boxes for a year. Make sure it doesn't become a safety hazard – but beyond that, don't worry about it (you'll get to it soon enough).

The "neat freaks" around you will hate this, and you won't *look* very organized – but "neat" and "organized" are not the same thing. The assets you use 80 percent of the time will be right where they belong. You (and your staff members) will be able to find them immediately, put them back easily, and keep the system working.

A Workable Procedure

One challenge associated with the "20 percent system" is that new assets keep arriving everyday. While the tools, equipment, and supplies that arrive for you or your team's use are not usually a burden to handle, the sheer volume of informational assets (e-mail, letters, reports, periodicals, etc.) can be.

To maintain your simple system, you need a workable procedure for integrating newly-arrived informational assets. "Workable" means *easy* – not just for you, but for anyone on your staff. After all, when you have to be away for a week, you don't want everything to pile up until you return!

Set aside specific times during the day to go through your new assets (the items in your inbox, for example). Do not let these incoming items (physical or electronic) divert your attention at any other time (stay focused on high value tasks during "protected" time).

A workable procedure requires you to follow one basic rule – if you pick it up, don't set it down unless or until you have made the "3D" decision – that is, a decision to: (1) *Discard* it (throw it away), (2) *Delegate* it (give it to someone else for information or action), or (3) *Direct* it into your simple "20 percent" system.

At least 50 percent of the information (paper-based and electronic) that you receive contains nothing of value to you or your organization. It can be discarded immediately – provided you take the time to glance at it and make the decision then.

Approximately 30 percent of your incoming information has value, but it may be hard to tell at a glance whether it is important and relevant to you or your organization. Instead of setting it aside for later (and letting it become clutter), delegate it to an employee who has reached the autonomous stage of development in that subject area. Have the employee examine the piece, and then provide a briefing to you (or even the whole group) on its content.

The remaining 20 percent of your incoming information may be important and relevant to your role as a leader. If so, place those items in one of five folders, as appropriate: (1) for action today, (2) for action later this week, (3) for action in a future week, (4) for reading/reference, and (5) for record purposes.

The five folders will each be given a readily accessible place in your system, of course. When you write your to-do lists and plan your schedule, you will allocate time for the actions they require.

Letting Go

Another challenge associated with the "20 percent system" is the clutter that will still exist a year from now (given that 60 to 80 percent of the assets in your workspace will probably not be needed for anything during that time – and will therefore not have a "proper place" in your system yet). What about all that stuff?

That's the beauty of this particular method for getting organized – if you haven't needed those things for a year, you probably never will. You can sell them, give them away, or throw them out without taking the time to look at every single item (as you would if you had tried to get 100 percent organized initially).

Sure, you'll probably dig out and keep some files that you are legally obligated to retain – and you may save a few items that have sentimental value. Even so, unless you're a huge "packrat," you'll eliminate at least half of your existing clutter with almost no effort.

Protect Your Health

ON AVERAGE, individuals who hold supervisory or management positions at American companies spend more hours per week at work than business leaders in any other developed nation. American managers also get the least amount of vacation time among all countries in the industrialized world.[42]

Leadership is a demanding role, and especially so in a competitive industry or environment. These daily demands create the potential for stress.

Stress is an emotional and physical reaction to an event or situation. Stress can be positive when it helps the leader feel focused, energized, and alert to possibilities. However, when stress creates negative emotions (e.g., fear, anxiety, or frustration), the related physiological impacts can be profound.

In stressful situations, the human body reacts as though it is in mortal danger (even when it isn't), and prepares to either confront the foe or run from it. This "fight or flight" reaction releases high levels of cortisol, adrenaline, and other hormones.[43]

Since most of your daily stresses are not "life or death" scenarios, a hormone imbalance is created. This imbalance causes fatigue, "moodiness," and digestive problems. If the stress is ongoing, more severe complications may arise, including tissue degeneration, blood vessel constriction (associated with high blood pressure, sexual dysfunction, and other circulatory ailments), and even suppression of the body's immune system.

To reduce the dangerous effects of stress (and to fulfill your role as a leader), you must ensure that you get enough sleep, exercise regularly, maintain a reasonably healthy diet, and adopt a positive life perspective.

Adequate Sleep

The human body follows a 24-hour Circadian Cycle that governs sleep, heart rate, body temperature, and waste elimination. 98 percent of adults need somewhere between 6.5 and 9 hours of sleep each night.

68 percent of the American workforce does not get enough sleep, and one in four managers is considered seriously "sleep-deprived." Sleep deprivation has the same impairing effect on judgment, reasoning, concentration, coordination, reaction time, and memory as going to work with a blood alcohol content in the 0.07 to 0.15 range (a BAC of 0.08 percent is legally intoxicated in most jurisdictions).[44]

Leaders with long daily commutes or night shift schedules often have difficulty getting adequate rest. Eliminating other time robbers and adding naps may be helpful in these cases. Establishing and maintaining a regular bedtime, adopting a pre-sleep relaxation routine, and not going to bed on a full stomach can also help you fall asleep more quickly.

Getting just a half-hour more of sleep each 24 hour period (even in the form of a 30 minute nap) can make you up to 15 percent more productive and efficient. Sleep improves digestion, protects your heart, strengthens your immune system, and allows your body to repair cell damage (so you actually look and feel younger!).[45]

Regular Exercise

Exercise allows the body to react to the "fight or flight" mechanism by "burning" the hormones that are released as a result of stress. Exercise also produces beta-endorphins (naturally-occurring morphine-like chemicals that create a sense of well-being).

There are hundreds of ways to exercise. The important thing is to (a) choose something you enjoy doing, and/or (b) people with whom you enjoy doing it – so you will stick with it. Any aerobic activity that you can do for 30 to 40 minutes at least three times a week is a suitable candidate (an aerobic workout should raise your heart rate to between 132 and 176 beats per minute, depending on your age – be sure to consult your physician before starting a new exercise routine). Allow time to stretch and warm up (to prevent injury) and time to cool down (to avoid circulation problems).

Don't overdo it. If the exercise itself is too stressful, it may simply trigger the production of more cortisol in the body. Start slowly, and increase your activity gradually.

Healthy Diet

While a new "perfect" diet seems to come along every week, most experts agree that a *healthy* diet includes (a) the recommended daily amount of vitamins and other nutrients, (b) smart choices from every food group (grains, vegetables, fruits, oils, dairy, and meat/beans), and (c) a balance between food (or caloric intake) and physical activity.

Smart choices can be a major challenge. The conditions that surround a stressful situation will often cause people to consume more caffeine, alcohol, deep fried foods, and sweets. These negatively affect the central nervous system, inhibit digestion, and deplete the body of vital nutrients. When the pressure is on, it is better to decrease your intake of these "discretionary foods" – and increase your intake of lean meats, low fat milk, whole grains, and fresh fruits and vegetables – to help your body cope.

Increase the amount of water you drink (not products made with water like coffee or tea, but plain water). 64 to 96 ounces a day is suggested. Stress causes dehydration, and dehydration impacts every major system in the body. Water is a crucial "stress-fighter." Don't take it for granted.[46]

Positive Perspective

In times of stress, it's impossible to just "think happy thoughts." You can think rationally, however, and apply the lessons presented in earlier chapters.

Remember to radiate possibilities (rather than being pulled into the whirlpool of negativity). Take care of crisis situations promptly and appropriately. Understand the behaviors that motivate people to do the things they do, and adjust your communication style to influence those behaviors (rather than becoming frustrated by them). Accept that *change* is the only constant in the world of a leader (so embrace it, and create the future you desire).

Finally, measure your success by the quantity and quality of the *contributions* you make to the development of your people and teams, and to the results they produce. Don't compare the size of your paycheck, office, or anything else to what your peers may have. Success in leadership (and in life) is not about "beating" everyone else – it's about making positive contributions.

Keep Learning

THIS BOOK PROVIDES the essential knowledge and skills required to achieve a high level of competence as a leader. Most of these skills will serve you for a lifetime, but a few will have to be augmented or "refreshed" at some point.

Your technical and administrative skills may also need to be updated. New products, tools, and technologies emerge daily. Organizations change, policies change, and people change – there is always a new challenge. Leaders who fail to keep learning will shut themselves off from fresh information and future possibilities. They will be trapped in a whirlpool.

In spite of this reality, one study indicates that 70 percent of adults have not read a book relating to their business field or profession since graduation. Americans spend $2.3 billion a year on educational books and materials (and most of that is for children). If it sounds like a lot, contrast it with the $37 billion spent on tobacco products.[47]

Granted, books are not the only source for new information. Seminars, periodicals, television, and the Internet can all provide learning opportunities. Modern technology makes it possible to learn almost anywhere at anytime. The key is to take full advantage of the resources you have available.

There is a legend of a pirate crew that was shipwrecked on a deserted island. With food and water in short supply, the decision was made to build a raft of bamboo and make an escape.

The captain, hoping to speed up the process, used a "schoolyard pick" to divide the crew into two groups with 15 men each. He then proposed a friendly competition. Whichever group cut the most bamboo by the end of the day would receive an extra ration of rum that night. The crew accepted.

The first group worked feverishly all morning, swinging their cutlasses, and building up a sizable pile of bamboo. Of course, the men cutting couldn't help but glance toward their competitors working at the opposite end of the island. Remarkably, the other group seemed to be taking breaks about every thirty minutes. Upon seeing that, the first group felt confident that they would win easily – but decided to work even harder during the afternoon in an effort to soundly drub their shipmates.

At the end of the day, exhausted (but certain of their victory), the first group hauled their load of bamboo to the beach. They were shocked to discover that they, in fact, had the lesser amount.

"How can that be?" asked the strongest man from the first group. "We worked almost non-stop. The other group took a break every half hour!"

"Aye," replied a man from the second group with a sly smile. "But every time we took a break, we sharpened our cutlasses."

To remain viable and effective as a leader in this ever-changing world, you have to keep a sharp edge. Seek out and learn something new and relevant to your career each week. People who commit to a lifelong learning philosophy actually live longer, experience better health, and have a measurably higher quality of life. So make it point to "sharpen your cutlass" and keep learning![48]

Expand Your Network

IN A BUSINESS COMMUNICATION CONTEXT, "networking" is the process of interacting with others to share and maximize the expertise of everyone involved. A leader without a good network is at a severe disadvantage in most workplaces today.

A network of professional contacts allows you to extend your problem-solving resources to include people with different backgrounds, experiences, and perspectives than you or your staff. By "tapping in" to the knowledge of others, you avoid mistakes and capitalize on the opportunities they've already found.

While some leaders seem to be "naturals" at networking, many find it difficult to start the process of building a viable group of contacts with whom to exchange information. The first obstacle to overcome is the idea that networking is either a waste of time or "cheating."

One manager summed up a common viewpoint on networking this way: "Why bother? If people had any information that was useful to me, they certainly wouldn't give it away for free."

Another manager (who saw the value in the information that others possessed) had a different hang-up: "It's like stealing gas from your neighbor's car. You're trying to take something for nothing."

In truth, networking is more like the concept of a renewable energy cooperative, where every house in the neighborhood has a wind-powered or solar-powered generator, and all of their stored energy is linked together in a grid. When one house has a higher demand for electricity, another has energy to spare.

Every leader runs low on "energy" at times, and can benefit by being part of a cooperative group that supplies supplemental "power" when necessary. Of course, this means the leader must contribute information, opportunities, and referrals to the network in return. It can't be "all take and no give."

Almost any business or social event provides an opportunity to expand your network. Remember, your primary goal at these events is to connect with new people. Regardless of the group or setting, introduce yourself to people you don't know, and briefly provide some basic information so they can get a feel for who you are and what you have to offer.

When you identify someone with whom you'd like to initiate a networking relationship, create value for that person first. Offer to take the person to lunch, or send the person a relevant article (along with your request for a scheduled call or appointment).

When you connect, ask probing questions, and listen carefully to the answers. Take notes, if desired. Be positive (don't be a complainer). Also, don't be a "know it all," and don't get caught in "one-upmanship" (where each person has to tell a bigger, better story). Finally, don't try to change the other person's mind or force your opinions on him or her.

After the meeting, keep in contact. Be alert for chances to offer assistance. If you need the other person's help at some point, ask wisely (as outlined previously in this book).

Follow these tips – and make it a point to expand your network by at least one new person each month. The resulting benefits will amaze you.

Have Fun

IN THE GOLDEN AGE OF PIRACY, the factor that may have most distinguished the crew of a pirate ship from the crew of a naval ship was FUN.

As already discussed, pirates were deadly serious about the pursuit of treasure, the code they followed, and their bond as a crew. Serious, however, did not mean solemn. Pirate captains made time for fun. In contrast, most naval officers of the era equated a crew's laughter to insubordination or "slacking off."

In recent years, much of the fun has been driven out of the American workplace as U.S. companies struggle to remain competitive in a global market, and to comply with an ever-increasing number of laws and regulations. When economic times are tough and employees are worried about their financial security, the work climate can become even more dismal.

Part of your job, as a leader (especially if you lead pirates), is to make your workplace *fun*. Ensure that the "fun factor" is part of your success formula.

When something "good" happens in a workplace, it is *multiplied* by the fun factor (the amount of fun people are having). When something "bad" happens, it is *divided* by the fun factor. In workplaces that are considered "fun" by employees, positive events have a greater impact, and negative events matter less. Fun increases productivity and improves morale. Fun relieves stress and dissolves resistance. Perhaps best of all, fun reduces employee turnover, absenteeism, and health problems.

Make fun a budget item – allocate time and money for it. For example, a large office initiated a series of "hump day" events. A special activity was scheduled each Wednesday that brought everyone together for a brief period of time.

One Wednesday, it was a video game tournament. The following week it was a dominoes tournament. The next week, caricature artists were hired to draw team members, and the images were hung in the break room. The week after, team members with musical talent performed "unplugged."[49]

Whatever you do, someone won't like it – so do a variety of different things. Encourage everyone to join in (but don't force them), and continually emphasize the goal of laughing and having a new experience over any "competitive" element that may exist.

It's important to understand that fun makes a good workplace better – it doesn't make a bad workplace acceptable. Many organizations have tried (and failed) to "program" fun into their organizational cultures. If your people are eating dirt, it doesn't matter how much honey you pour on it – they're still eating dirt. So for the "fun factor" to be effective, you must also keep to the code, embrace achievement, radiate possibilities, manage performance... i.e., all of the things covered in previous sections of this book.

Finally, as a leader, you need to be sure that *you* are having fun. If you aren't having fun, you're probably doing something wrong – and hopefully, you've found a "right" way to do it within these pages.

Leadership in any setting is one of the most important roles a person can fill. Take it seriously. Take *yourself* a lot less seriously. Find things to laugh about. Remember, people are always watching, and following your lead.

Say Yes

WHEN SOMEONE ASKS YOU for something (in your official capacity as a leader), you basically have two possible response choices. You can say "yes" – or you can say "no."

Consider the consequences of saying "no." First, the person's self-esteem is bruised (no matter how nicely you say it, you are still rejecting the person's proposal – and therefore the person himself to some degree). Second, you risk being drawn into an argument (an argument that the other person can control just by being obstinate and relentless). Third, if you shut off the argument or any potential explanation by giving your firmest "this is not open for discussion" response, then you close the door to *possibilities* (i.e., whatever future benefits or solutions might have been linked to person's request are now lost). Fourth, nothing changes (you maintain the *status quo*).

Sometimes, that's the outcome you want. When it is, by all means, reply decisively. "No."

If that's *not* the result you want, or if you are uncertain, consider the opportunities associated with saying "yes." First, you maintain the person's self-esteem (the person feels accepted because you are willing to at least *consider* the request.) Second, you avoid an argument – because what you are going to say is this: "Yes, *provided...*" and then you'll explain the set of conditions under which you can and will grant the request. (This puts *you* in control, because the other person is now the one who must accept or reject *your* proposal.) Third, it opens the door to possibilities. (The ensuing discussion may reveal options and benefits that neither of you conceived when the question was initially posed.) Finally, it potentially changes things for the better. You may both get something you want. It's a win-win.

Consider this hypothetical scenario: A homeless person or panhandler asks you for spare change outside your workplace. You could say "no" and walk on – or you could smile warmly and say, "Yes, *provided* you pick up the litter in front of the building here." If the person walks off muttering obscenities, you can go about your business guilt-free. If he takes you up on the deal, he gets what he wants and you make the world a cleaner and happier place in exchange for a moment of your time and few cents out of your pocket.

Of course, this technique would not always be practical (or safe) with a total stranger as in the example above. But it can be extremely potent with customers, suppliers, friends, and family – and it is certainly effective with workplace pirates. After all, a lot of "typical" managers are simply trying to maintain the status quo, and having seen this, workplace pirates tend to believe that *every* manager goes through the day looking for chances to say "No!"

When you look for a chance to say "yes," you set yourself apart as one of the few people who is sincerely interested in what the *other* person wants, and in trying to find a way that he or she can have it. That quality of leadership has changed the course of history on more than one occasion. It can definitely increase your power as a boss – plus, it will enrich both your life and the lives of everyone around you.

Sometimes a leader needs to say, "No" – clearly and decisively. When possible, however, say "Yes!"

Lead the Way

THE PIRATE'S WORLD was a world of *scarcity* – one where there was never enough to go around. Sadly, a similar condition often exists in the modern workplace.

In a world of scarcity, people are unfulfilled. They have far less than they want (or feel that they deserve), so they "look out for #1" (themselves). They *demand* to be respected. Conflicts arise. Trust breaks down. Teamwork disintegrates. Things get worse.

Great pirate captains created a world of *abundance* for their followers. They unified their crew members, gave them hope, and moved visibly closer each day to a shared vision. As an effective leader in today's workplace, you must do the same.

Who were those "great pirate captains" anyway? Most remain nameless – and that's how it should be. After all, your job as a leader is to make your team successful, not to make yourself famous.

There were some great pirate captains whose names you'd recognize – but only for the things they did *later* in life. For them, leading a crew of pirates was a "means to an end" at a time in history where other options were fairly limited. Is it all that different for you, today? Do you want to be in your current job, doing the same thing, ten years from now – or is this a path to something better? Where's your horizon?

Regardless of what you have now, everything you need and want is out there somewhere. Everything your employees need and want is out there somewhere. There's a treasure – waiting to be found. Lead the way!

In the end, everything will be okay.
If it's not okay, it's not the end.

"Yarrr!"

Annotations

Endnotes

1. U.S. Marine Corps, *Recruit Training Information* (Marine Corps Recruit Depot, San Diego CA, 2008).

2. DVD, *American History is Full of Pirates!* (Bicycling Through History, Washington DC, 2002) and Ramsay, Jack C. Jr., *Jean Lafitte, Prince of Pirates* (Eakin Press, Waco TX, 1996) provide numerous examples including James Bowie (once a partner with Lafitte) for whom more than 1,400 places in Texas are named (among them, 38 schools, many with "Pirates" as the mascot).

3. Consulted Survey, *The State of Working America* (Peter D. Hart Research Associates, Washington DC, 2005) and Consulted Survey, *Gallop/CNN/USA Today Poll* (Peter D. Hart Research Associates, Washington DC, 2003).

4. Zander, Rosamund Stone & Zander, Benjamin, *The Art of Possibility* (Penguin Group, New York NY, 2000) inspired the term "radiating possibilities." Ms. Zander is a practicing psychotherapist. Mr. Zander is the conductor of the Boston Philharmonic Orchestra.

5. Shea, Eugene B., *The Immortal "I", A Unified Theory of Psychology, Neurology, and the Perennial Philosophy* (University Press of America, Lanham MD, 2002).

6. Yokoyama, John & Michelli, Joseph, *When Fish Fly* (Hyperion, New York NY, 2004).

7. Sheehan, Michael, *The International Politics of Space* (Routledge, New York NY, 2007).

8. This example refers to a privately owned company and reflects personal experiences or observations by the author.

9. Ibid.

10. Maslow, A.H., *Motivation and Personality* (Harper, New York NY, 1954) and *A Theory of Human Motivation* (Psychological Review 50, Washington DC, 1943).

11. Herzberg, F., *One More Time: How Do You Motivate Employees?* (Harvard Business Review, Boston MA, 1968).

12. Marston, William Moulton, *Emotions of Normal People* (Harcourt, Brace and Company, Orlando FL, 1928). Dr. Marston also created the systolic blood-pressure test, a prototype of the polygraph, and

the character *Wonder Woman* (under the pseudonym Charles Moulton).

13. Lipski, John M., *A History of Afro-Hispanic Language* (Pennsylvania State University, State College PA, 2005).

14. Learning Module, *Straight Talking: The Art of Assertiveness* (Video Arts, London UK, 1991) provided the foundation steps for the assertiveness guidelines presented in "Respond Assertively."

15. Robbins, Anthony, *Unlimited Power: The New Science of Personal Achievement* (Free Press, a division of Simon & Schuster, Inc., New York NY, 1986) provided the framework for asking for help as presented in "Ask Wisely."

16. DVD, *Powerful Ways to Persuade People* (Briefings Publishing Group, Alexandria VA, 1998) provided the framework for persuasive communication as presented in "Persuade Convincingly."

17. Moncrief, Gene, *Meetings: Time Wasted or Well Spent?* (The Ayers Group, New York NY, 2005).

18. Wetmore, Donald E., *Time Management Facts and Figures* (Productivity Institute, Stratford CT, 1999) and Data and Statistics, *World Development Report* (The World Bank, Washington DC, 2007).

19. Mehrabian, A., *Silent Messages* (Wadsworth, Florence KY, 1971).

20. Commissioned Survey, *Clothes Make the Manager* (Sun Media Research, Toronto ON, 2008) cited in *Appearance Still Matters* (CXO Media, Framingham MA, 2008).

21. Consulted Survey, *Leadership 2000 Panel on Diversity and Performance* (American Achievement Network, Las Vegas NV, 2000).

22. Janz, Tom & Mooney, Greg, *Behavior Description Interviewing* (HRD Press, Amherst MA, 1991) provided the framework for interviewing techniques presented in "Hire Intelligently."

23. Porter, Glenn, *Encyclopedia of American Economic History: Studies of the Principal Movements and Ideas* (Charles Scribners Sons/Reference, Woodbridge CT, 1980) and Ad Council, *Women in War Jobs – Rosie the Riverter* (sponsors: Office of War Information & War Manpower Commission, Washington DC, 1942-1945).

24. This example refers to a privately owned company and reflects personal experiences or observations by the author.

25. Phillips, Kenneth R., *Coaching Skills Inventory* (HRDQ, King of Prussia PA, 1990, 1992) provided the framework for the coaching discussion presented in "Connect and Coach."

26. Phillips, Kenneth R. *Performance Appraisal Skills Inventory* (HRDQ, King of Prussia PA, 1990, 1992) provided the framework for the appraisal meeting presented in "Document Progress."

27. Commissioned Study, *CNN Report on Education* (Public Agenda, New York NY, 2003).

28. Learning Module, *The Helping Hand* (Video Arts, London UK, 1990) provided the framework for conducting a mentoring session as presented in "Support and Mentor."

29. Arms, L.R., *A Short History of the US Army Noncommissioned Officer* (NCO Museum, Fort Bliss TX, 1991).

30. Consulted Survey, *Annual Survey of Leadership Skills Certificate Holders* (Humaneering, Inc., Las Vegas NV, 1999-2005)

31. GOAL QPC & Oriel Inc., *The TEAM Memory Jogger* (GOAL QPC + Oriel Inc., Salem NH, 1995) provided the framework for the collaborative skills presented in "Generate Collaboration."

32. Jaques, Elliott & Clement, Stephen D., *Executive Leadership* (Cason Hall & Co., Fleming Island FL, 1991) provided the basis for the Work-Assigning Relationship and Work-Initiating Relationship concepts presented in "Map the Team's Relationships."

33. Buckingham, Marcus & Clifton, Donald O., *Discover Your Strengths* (Free Press, a division of Simon & Schuster, Inc., New York NY, 2001).

34. Fahden, Allen & Namakkal, Srinivasan, *Innovate with C.A.R.E. Profile* (Inscape Publishing, Minneapolis MN, 1995) provided the basis for the Individual Strengths and Team Roles model presented in "Leverage Strengths."

35. *Occupational Safety and Health Act of 1970* (Occupational Safety and Health Administration, Washington DC, 1970) and Janisch, Troy, *General Duty Clause* (Toolkit Media Group, Madison WI, 2008).

36. *Nonfatal Injuries and Illnesses, Private Industry* (Bureau of Labor Statistics, 2006) and *The High Cost of Workplace Injuries* (Archives of Internal Medicine, American Medical Association, 1998).

37. Rouder, J.N., Morey, R.D., Cowan, N., Zwilling, C.E., Morey, C.C., & Pratte, M.S., *An Assessment of Fixed-capacity Models of Visual Working Memory* (Proceedings of the National Academy of Sciences, Washington DC, 2008).

38. Patrick, Richard, *Attacking Negativity* (TeamAmerica Training, Plano TX, 1993).

39. Thomason, J.C., Hills, J.M., Clare, A.S., Neville, A., & Richardson, M., *Hydrodynamic Consequences of Barnacle Colonization* (Springer, Netherlands, 1998).

40. Baker, Larry Dr. & Douglass, Merrill Dr., *Time Mastery Profile* (Inscape Publishing, Minneapolis MN, 1992), and Wetmore, Donald E., *Beat the Clock!* (National Institute for Productivity Development, Stratford CT, 1995).

41. Ibid.

42. Commissioned Study, *Vacation Deprivation* (Expedia.com®, Alan Price, and HRM Guide Network, 2002).

43. Mayo Clinic Staff, *Stress: Unhealthy Response to the Pressures of Life* (Mayo Foundation for Medical Education and Research, 2006).

44. Hassen, Farrah, *Sleep Deprivation: Effects on Safety, Health, and Quality of Life* (National Sleep Foundation, Washington DC, 2001) and U.S. Centers for Disease Control and Prevention (CDC), *National Health Interview Study* (Morbidity and Mortality Weekly Report, CDC, Washington DC, 2008).

45. Mah, Cheri, *Effects of Sleep Deprivation on Performance* (Associated Sleep Societies, Minneapolis MN, 2007) and Allen, Richard, *Sleep and Neurocognitive Functioning* (Johns Hopkins University, Baltimore MD, 2003).

46. Montgomery, Kate ND, *Stress and Diet*, (Sports Touch, Elkhart IN, 2003) and Health 24, *Stress & Diet*, (Naspers Group, Cape Town ZA, 2008).

47. National Center for Education Statistics, *Trends in Adult Literacy* (U.S. Department of Education, Washington DC, 2002) and Vendemia, Mark, *Consumer Spending Survey Anthology*, 2005 (Bureau of Labor Statistics, Washington DC, 2005).

48. Shea, Kathy, *Learning Over the Lifespan* (University of Minnesota, Minneapolis MN, 2007).

49. This example refers to a privately owned company and reflects personal experiences or observations by the author.

Acknowledgments

With more than 30 years of leadership and management experience, as well as a love for the sea and its lore, the author has drawn upon his personal experiences and a wide variety of resources to provide the guidelines in this book. It is impossible to recall or cite every source from which a leadership lesson originated, but the following deserve special acknowledgment.

Historical facts about pirates were verified with the help of these publications:

- *Way of the Pirate: A Biographical Directory of Pirates, Buccaneers and Privateers* by Robert Downie (Brick Tower Books, 2006);
- *The Complete Idiot's Guide to Pirates* by Gail Selinger, Jr. & W. Thomas Smith (Alpha, 2006);
- *The History of Pirates* by Angus Konstam, Virginia Mariners Museum, & David Cordingly (The Lyons Press, 2002);
- *The Republic of Pirates: Being the True and Surprising Story of the Caribbean Pirates...* by Colin Woodard (Harvest Books, 2008);
- *The Sea Rover's Practice: Pirate Tactics and Techniques, 1630-1730* by Benerson Little (Potomac Books, 2007);
- *Black Bart Roberts: The Greatest Pirate of Them All* by Terry Breverton (Pelican Publishing, 2004);
- *Admiral Sir Henry Morgan: King Of The Buccaneers* by Terry Breverton (Pelican Publishing, 2005).
- *The Pirate Hunter: The True Story of Captain Kidd* by Richard Zacks (Hyperion, 2002).

Throughout the book are leadership principles learned by the author while attending the U.S. Coast Guard Academy and serving as an officer aboard Coast Guard cutters and operational shore units. Not only does the Coast Guard fulfill essential defense, security, and public protection missions (often with limited resources) – it presents young men and women with some of the greatest opportunities available for personal and professional growth. This was certainly true for the author, who salutes the members and veterans of all the armed forces – and especially the men and women who were a part of his leadership development experience.

The chapter "Embrace Achievement" was developed from ideas originally presented in a magazine article by freelance writer Robert Sheaffer (who is also a prominent researcher of UFO phenomena, Christianity, and feminism).

The steps for "Formulating a Vision" evolved from techniques presented by Richard Bellingham, Ed.D., Chairman and CEO of iobility, LLC (and the author of more than 50 books, articles, manuals, and training guides on human resource development topics), and Stephen G. Haines, founder and CEO of Haines Centre International (and one of the world's foremost authorities on strategic management – also a U.S. Naval Academy graduate).

The skills, processes, and techniques outlined in Part V (Communication) reflect the author's adaptations of a variety of formal methodologies and highly-regarded training programs. Two sources were especially influential:

- *DDI (Development Dimensions International)* – DDI has been in the business of developing workplace talent since 1970. The company's **Interaction Management** program was one of the first commercially-offered leadership development programs the author attended. (He was later certified by DDI to teach the program.)
- *Video Arts* – Video Arts was founded in 1972 by a small group of British television professionals including actor John Cleese (of Monty Python fame). The company revolutionized the training film industry with its humorous, engaging, and unforgettable programs (most of which the author viewed and put into practice as a manager). The firm is now owned by Tinopolis Group.

If you found the verbal communication techniques in this book useful, the author suggests *How to Say It at Work* by Jack Griffin (Prentice Hall Press). If you prepare written correspondence on a frequent basis, the author recommends *How to Say It* by Rosalie Maggio (Prentice Hall Press).

The *Employee Development (Learning Curve)* model utilized in "Performance Management" was derived from the Situational Leadership concept presented in the book *Management of Organizational Behavior* by Paul Hersey, Kenneth H. Blanchard, and Dewey E. Johnson (Prentice Hall, 8th Ed., 2000).

For leaders who want to delve deeper into the research and science that support the performance management and organizational development principles in this book, *The Cultures of Management* by Robert H. Roy (Johns Hopkins University Press) provides an excellent starting point.

Other techniques for performance management and employee development were undoubtedly influenced by Peter Drucker, Auren Uris, Benjamin Tregoe, W. Edwards Deming, Jocelyn Kung & Marianne Minor, Sheila J. Costello, Jane S. Flaherty & Peter B. Stark, Sharon Fisher, Terry Fitzwater, Mark Eppler, Donald E. Wetmore, Dr. Rollin Glaser & Christine Glaser, Stephen R. Covey, and Richard Y. Chang.

If you ever worked with the author, it's a safe bet that you heard a tape or CD featuring Dr. Denis Waitley – one of the world's most respected authorities on human performance and achievement (and another U.S. Naval Academy grad). His books *Seeds of Greatness* (Pocket, 1988) and *Psychology of Winning* (Berkley, 1986) – and their related audio programs – are classics in self-development.

The author is an Associate Partner of the **HRD Press** Performance Technology Group, and is licensed to offer many of the same instruments that guided him early in his career. For more than 40 years, HRD Press has been providing books, assessments, and course materials for workforce development.

The Karate Kid was written by Robert Mark Kamen, directed by John G. Avildsen, and released by Columbia Pictures in 1984.

The Crocodile Hunter was created by Mark Henderson and originally aired in syndication (on Animal Planet, Discovery Channel, and Discovery Kids in the USA) from 1997 to 2004.

Home Improvement was created by Matt Williams, Carmen Finestra, and David MacFadzean, and originally aired on ABC from 1991 to 1999.

Seinfeld was created by Larry David and Jerry Seinfeld, and originally aired on NBC from 1989 to 1998.

Survivor was conceived by Bob Geldof's Planet 24, created by Charlie Parsons, and began airing on CBS in 2000.

Additional information may be found on the website for this book:
http://PirateCaptainsGuide.com

Index

292-293, 296, 301, 302-304, 310, 314
formulating a vision and, 65, 69, 74, 78-79, 93-95
(*see also* Probing)
Assertiveness, 34, 38, 116, 137-142
Associative stage (of development), 189, 190, 210, 211, 214, 216, 217-226, 227, 236, 244
Attitude, 2, 11, 43, 169, 194, 202, 250, 287 (*see also* Negativity, Possibility, *and* Spirit Factor)
Autonomous stage (of development), 189, 190, 208, 210, 218-220, 223, 228, 230, 232, 236, 237-242, 244, 336

Barnacles, 323
Behavior,
assertive, 137-142
DISC model of human, 101-108
objectionable, 249-251
pace and focus, 102-104
predicting, 101-108, 194-198
power and, 85, 102
workplace pirates and, 19, 28, 33, 35, 41-44, 46, 50
(*see also* Motivation *and* Spirit Factor)
Behavior standards, 7, 13, 107,108, 174, 203, 245, 262, 283, 298, 312 (*see also* Performance Standards)
Belligerence, 315-316
Benefits (*see* Compensation)
Beta-endorphins, 339
Big picture, 48, 102, 116, 276
Blackbeard, 285
Body language, 135, 148, 163, 167
Brainstorming, 146, 153
Budgeting, 175, 179, 182, 183, 302, 320, 346
Bulletproof, 311
Bureau of Labor Statistics, 286

"C" (Conscientious) Spirit, 98, 107-108, 116, 119-120
Celebrating success, 319-320
Challenges,
addressing, 37, 50, 54, 69, 73, 77, 105, 112, 132, 136, 218, 237, 240-241, 257, 276, 277-281, 300, 306, 311, 320, 335-336, 339, 341
hiring, 5, 196, 198
noting, 65-66
(*see also* Opportunities *and* Problems)
Change,
defined, 305-306
power and, 307, 309
Change management,
accepting change, 50, 306, 340-341
breaking from the past, 312
creating support, 310-311
communicating, 107, 116, 118, 127, 307-308
enrolling others, 308-309
focusing on successes, 311-312
influencing, 12, 18, 32, 38, 44, 65-67, 72, 93, 203, 210, 258, 295, 344
locking in the change, 312-313
modeling the change, 309-310
overcoming negativity, 313-314
sharing facts, 307
Character, power of, 35-36
Cheering on, 71, 264, 268, 282
Close (persuasive skill), 149-150
Closed-end questions, 134, 225, 234
Closing,
appraisal meetings, 233, 236
coaching discussions, 221, 223, 225-226
mediations, 284
Coaching, 19, 32, 40, 124, 164, 189, 190, 199, 213, 216, 217-229, 234, 236, 238, 239, 241-

Fish!, 60
Flexibility, 103, 108, 115-116, 184, 282
Focus (within DISC), 102-108, 113-120, 282
Follow-through, 18, 38, 106, 261-262
Follow-up, 38, 149, 157, 164, 166, 207, 209, 221, 226, 235, 240, 241, 248-250, 284, 289, 294, 298
Formulated celebrations, 320
Four M's, 5
Fun,
    Commiserating and, 45
    communication and, 115, 117
    employee development and, 188
    leadership and, 345-346
    motivation and, 106
    teamwork and, 281
    vision and, 80
    workplace pirates and, 345
Fun factor, 345

General Duty Clause, 285
Goals,
    alignment of, 175-176
    levels, 175-176, 203, 206-210, 275
    methodologies, 177
    purposes, 176-177, 180, 275, 305
    qualities of effective, 177-178
    setting, 175-178
    types, 176-177
    (*see also* Outcomes *and* Results)
Goal setting, 175-178
Golden Age of Piracy, 5, 8, 35, 46, 87, 111, 169, 345
Gossip,
    defined, 295-296
    impacts of, 258, 283, 295
    intervening, 296
Group facilitation (*see* Facilitating a Group)
Gripes, 45, 143, 295

Group think, 304
Guiding change (*see* Change Management)

Health, protecting,
    diet, 339-340
    exercise, 339
    stress, 337
    positive perspective, 340
    sleep, 338
Hearts, winning, 93-94, 219
High value tasks, 331-332, 335
Hiring,
    interviews, 193-198
    job descriptions and, 191-192
    recruiting and, 192-193
Home Improvement, 113
Homer, 239
Honesty, 24, 35, 38, 39, 94, 112, 116, 138-129, 168, 170, 244
Hoover Dam, 151
Human Resource Development (see Developing Employees)
Hygiene factors, 88-90

"I" (Involvement) Spirit, 98, 105-106, 115, 117-118
Image, 77, 152, 167-170
Individual strengths, 275-277
Initiative, employee, 30, 184, 204, 326, 329-330
Innovation, path of, 277
Integrity, 36, 38, 41-42, 76, 94, 184, 300
Interacting, 25, 69, 98, 106, 112-122, 127-129, 133-137, 141-142, 159, 163,184, 217, 284, 289, 300-304, 326-327, 329, 343 (see also Communication)
Interrupting (verbal), 127, 155, 157, 260-261, 283
Interruptions (of work tasks), 128, 180, 326, 327-328, 330, 332
Interviews,
    hiring, 191, 193-198

de facto, 298
establishing, 61, 174, 178, 180-
186
impacts on, 7, 13, 31
output standards, 183
process standards, 184
stakeholder perspectives, 184-185
utilizing, 190, 206, 221-222, 225,
229-230, 233, 238, 245, 262,
283, 298, 312
Performance targets, 20, 227-231,
233-236, 239, 246-248, 250-251,
270, 295, 312, 319
Personality, power of, 34-35
Persuasion,
communication and, 145-150
influencing through, 12, 20, 38,
57, 58, 86, 92, 102, 106, 113-
114, 122, 129, 144, 160, 162,
168, 213, 278, 313, 340
Pike Place Fish Market, 59, 97
Pirate captain,
leadership approach, 5-6
qualities of great captains, 13, 33,
35, 97, 125, 345
Pirate Code (*see* Code of Conduct)
Pirates of the Realm,
mission, 5
key elements, 5-6
truths about, 7-10
versus workplace pirates, 3-14,
35, 46, 87, 111, 169, 345
Planned celebrations, 320
Plus, plus, dash, 327
Position, power of, 33
Positive attitude, 43-46, 340, 346
Positive feedback (*see* Praise)
Positive future, previewing, 212
Positive reinforcement (*see* Praise)
Possibilities,
evaluating, 142, 250, 331
power and, 45
radiating, 43-46, 340, 346
Power,
achievement and, 29, 31

change and, 307, 309
collaboration and, 264
commitment, inspiring and, 213-
214
communication and, 133, 144,
145, 159, 167, 169-170
crisis situations and, 50-51, 53-54
historical attitudes toward, 8, 11
initiative and, 330
leadership role and, 27
mentoring and, 240-241
motivation/behavior and, 85, 102
networking and, 343-344
of character, 35-36
of competence, 34-34
of personality, 34-35
of position, 33
praise and, 125
purpose and, 17
radiating possibility and, 45
revealing hidden, 213-214
self-esteem and, 121
sources of, 33-36
transition and, 213-214
trust and, 38, 42
vision and, 59, 72
Practical needs, 87-88
Praise,
as positive feedback and
reinforcement, 19, 39, 125-126,
164, 209, 218-220, 226, 229,
232, 234, 244, 248-250, 261-
264, 296, 314
power and, 125
Predicting performance and
behavior, 98-102, 194-198
Predictive mentoring, 240
Prejudice, 130, 315-316
Preparation,
communication and, 119, 145-
147, 152, 159, 161
for change, 65, 67-68, 306, 313
for conflict resolution, 283-284
for hiring interviews, 195-197
for investigations, 293

Rational decisions, 297-298
Reacting, 48, 91, 102, 114, 120, 122, 126, 135, 138, 155, 222, 234, 263, 290, 297, 308, 337-339
Recurring goals, 176-177, 180-181, 207, 275
Recurring problems, 3, 243, 246, 248, 251, 252, 325-326, 328
Recognition, providing tangible, 30, 40, 77, 106, 107, 212, 213, 215-216, 236, 257, 278-279, 282, 320
Recognized hazards, 285
Recruiting and hiring, 191-198
Refiner (team role), 276-280
Reflective mentoring, 240
Reinforcement (*see* Praise)
Relating, 136
Relationship-focused (behavior), 103-104, 114
Relationships,
  building, 24, 102-107, 113-120, 129, 136, 166, 193, 219
  mapping team, 265-270
  networking and, 24, 34, 113, 344
  performance management and, 42, 92, 102-107, 202, 216
  teambuilding and, 37, 258, 265-270, 293, 345
  work-assigning, 265-267
  work-initiating, 267-270
Resentment,
  leadership success and, 324
  motivation and, 90, 92-93
  performance problems and, 243
  self-esteem and, 121
  overcoming, 29-32
  (*see also* Achievement)
Resolving conflict, 281-284 (*see also* Conflicts)
Resource identification, 180
Respect,
  communication and, 64-65, 108, 119, 121, 134, 137-138, 142, 154, 157
  diversity and, 318

performance and, 184, 213, 249
taking command and, 9, 10, 12, 24, 34, 37, 41,-42, 47, 345
teambuilding and, 259, 260, 281, 284, 290, 309
Responsibility, taking, 259-260
Results,
  defining, 52, 57, 63, 173-175, 179, 183, 275
  documenting, 288, 313, 340
  influencing, 26, 98, 103, 105, 113, 115, 117-118, 120, 121, 152, 206, 239, 245, 299, 313, 323-324, 341
  role of a leader and, 17-19
  trust and, 37-39, 150
  (*see also* Goals *and* Outcomes)
Reticent management, 49
Rewards,
  assessing (mission-related), 67-68, 303
  utilizing (compensation-related), 30, 192, 232, 238, 242, 245, 257, 264, 285
Risks,
  assessing, 67-68, 135, 235, 288-294, 302-303
  managing, 40-41, 59, 88, 91, 98, 107, 116, 119, 125, 143, 150, 184, 220, 279, 285, 289-294
Roles,
  leadership, 5, 17-18, 31, 34, 36-38, 90, 112, 121, 187, 200, 205, 236-237, 284, 300, 309, 325, 336-338, 346
  team member, 27, 82, 98-99, 127, 242, 258, 271-274, 275, 277-280, 283, 320
"Rosie the Riveter", 205
Rules (*see* Code of Conduct)
Rumors, 37, 51, 295, 307

"S" (Stability) Spirit, 98, 106-107, 116, 118-119
Salaries (*see* Compensation)